R. A. H. King

Aristotle and Plotinus on Memory

W
DE
G

Quellen und Studien zur Philosophie

Herausgegeben von
Jens Halfwassen, Dominik Perler,
Michael Quante

Band 94

Walter de Gruyter · Berlin · New York

Aristotle and Plotinus on Memory

by

R. A. H. King

Walter de Gruyter · Berlin · New York

♾ Printed on acid-free paper which falls within
the guidelines of the ANSI to ensure permanence and durability.

ISBN 978-3-11-048155-6
ISSN 0344-8142

Library of Congress Cataloging-in-Publication Data

King, R. A. H.
    Aristotle and Plotinus on memory / by Richard A. H. King.
        p. cm. − (Quellen und Studien zur Philosophie, ISSN 0344-8142 ;
    Bd. 94)
    Includes bibliographical references and index.
    ISBN 978-3-11-021462-8 (hardcover : alk. paper)
    1. Aristotle.   2. Memory (Philosophy).   3. Plotinus.   I. Title.
    B491.M37K56   2009
    128'.3−dc22

                                                            2009036203

Bibliographic information published by the Deutsche Nationalbibliothek

The Deutsche Nationalbibliothek lists this publication in the Deutsche
Nationalbibliografie; detailed bibliographic data are available in the Internet
at http://dnb.d-nb.de.

Cover design: Christopher Schneider, Laufen.
Printing and binding: Hubert & Co., Göttingen

To G. and Ellie, with love

Acknowledgements

The present study is a revised version of my Habilitationsschrift (Philosophy Department, Ludwig Maximilians University Munich, 2004). It owes much to the many people who have played a part in its coming to be. In seminars in which the texts were discussed, several students were especially tough and helpful: Andreas Schwab, Franz Knappick, and Thomas Brunotte. The referees for my habilitation, Thomas Buchheim, Rémi Brague, and Wilhelm Vossenkuhl provided detailed criticism of a version of the study. Audiences at the occasions where I have spoken about aspects of the project – in Munich, Kassel, Humboldt University Berlin, Free University Berlin, Hamburg, Trinity College Dublin – have been most instructive. A version of Section 4: 'General Conclusion, Aristotle and Plotinus on memory' was read at the Sorbonne, and is appearing in: *La fortune antique et médiévale des Parva Naturalia.* Christophe Grellard, P-M. Morel, ed. éditions Peeters, collection "Aristote. Traductions et Etudes", Leuven. 2009.

Colleagues have been most generous in reading the book and commenting on it: Myles Burnyeat, Klaus Corcilius, John Dillon, Lloyd Gerson, Thomas Johansen, Denis O'Brien, Pierre-Marie Morel, Bob Sharples, Andrew Smith, and Daniela Taormina. Sabine Vogt discussed many aspects of Aristotle with me. A seminar on the Posterior Analytics given with Johannes Hübner made many things clear to me. My sister, Geraldine King, read a complete version of the text and made many suggestions as to style and coherence. My wife, Martina King, also read a version and gave me detailed comments; discussions of the problems have been unavoidable, she has contributed most generously and profitably. My parents in law, Charlotte and Johann Christoph Ottow, gave congenial conditions to a difficult worker in Niederpöcking. Kathrin Lukaschek made the Index Locorum. Christina Podewils provided an attic refuge from the demands of my family at critical moments. The *index locororum* is the work of Kathrin Lukaschek.

While the book was going to press, my sister Geraldine died of cancer. It is dedicated to her and her daughter, Ellie.

Niederpöcking 2009   R. A. H. K.

Preface – Abbreviations and conventions

Abbreviations

Aristotle's works referred to

Cat.	Categoriae
Anal. Pr.	Analytica Priora
Anal. Post.	Analytica Posteriora
Top.	Topica
Phys.	Physica
De cael.	De Caelo
Gen. et Corr.	De Generatione et Corruptione
Meteor.	Meteorologica
De an.	De Anima
PN	Parva Naturalia
Sens.	De sensu et sensibilibus
De mem.	De memoria et reminiscentia
De somn.	De somno et vigilia
De insomn.	De insomniis
De divin.	De divinatione per somnium
De longaev.	De longitudine et brevitate vitae
De juv.	De juventute et senectute, vita et morte
HA	Historia animalium
PA	De partibus animalium
De mot. anim.	De motu animalium
De inc. anim.	De incessu animalium
De gen. anim.	De generatione animalium
Met.	Metaphysica
EN	Ethica Nicomachea
EE	Ethica Eudemia

Other Abbreviations

AHA   Armstrong, A.H. 1966–1987. *Plotinus. Enneads.* VII vols. Cambridge, Mass./ London.

Bonitz   Bonitz, H. 1870. *Index Aristotelicus.* Berlin.

Bréhier Bréhier, E. 1924–38. *Plotin. Les Ennéades I-VI. Texte établi et traduit par E. Bréhier.* Paris.

DK   Diels, H. and Kranz, W. 1951. *Die Fragmente der Vorsokratiker.* III vols. (6th ed.) Berlin.

HBT   Harder, R., Beutler, and R, Theiler, W. 1956–1971. *Plotins Schriften. Neubearbeitung mit griechischem Lesetext und Anmerkungen.* Hamburg. IV vols. Text (Ia-IVa), IV vols. Notes (Ib-IVb).

HS   Henry, P. Schwyzer, H.-R. 1964, 1977, 1983. *Plotini Opera.* Oxford. (Editio minor).

LS   Long, A. and Sedley, D. 1988. *The Hellenistic Philosophers.* Cambridge

LSJ   Liddell, H.G., Scott, R. and Jones, H.S. 1990. *A Greek English Lexicon*, Ninth Edition, Oxford 1940 (often reprinted), Suppl. 1968 and 1996.

MacK   MacKenna, S. 1956. *Plotinus. The Enneads. Second edition revised by B.S.Page.* London.

SP   Sleeman, J.H., Pollet, G. 1980. *Lexicon Plotinianum.* Leiden.

SVF   Arnim, H. von. 1903–1905. *Stoicorum Veterum Fragmenta.* IV vols. Leipzig.

Conventions

Aristotle's writings, notably *De memoria et reminiscentia* and *De anima*, are referred to by title (in the notes as De mem., De an.), without noting the author. Editions and translations of Aristotle's *De memoria et reminiscentia* are cited merely by the name of the editor or translator. "Ross" refers to Sir David Ross, G. Ross to G.R.T Ross (for exact references, see the Select Bibliography). As is customary, Aristotle's works are referred to using page, column (a,b) and line of Bekker's edition.

Plotinus' writings are referred to using Porphyry's arrangement of his work into Enneads, along with chapter and line from Henry and Schwyzer's *editio minor* (Oxford). Thus "IV 3 30 11" refers to the third treatise in the fourth Ennead, Chapter 30, line 11. "I 1" refers to the first treatise in the first Ennead, and "I 1 12" refers to the twelfth chapter of that treatise. "HS" refers to this edition.

Translations are the author's unless otherwise noted. Greek, even when quoted, is not placed in quotation marks.

Contents

1 Introduction

1.1 Six problems about memory

The two short treatises on memory by Aristotle and Plotinus which are the subject of this study raise interesting conceptual questions about memory. There is an intuitive view of memory which one could describe very briefly as follows. A living thing perceives something; residues of this perception are preserved and may serve an act of memory. Very roughly, this is Aristotle's view. Plotinus opposes it, above all because he thinks the subject of memory is simply the incorporeal soul, and this cannot be affected and so preserve residues in itself. The present study is an attempt to describe and contrast these two ancient theories of memory.

The following six problems will serve as a framework for our investigation:

(P1) The derivation problem:
Memory requires certain other cognitive faculties as no one could just have memory and no other form of grasping things. This may be called *the epistemological dependence* of memory. How can memory be derived from these other faculties? What is the nature of this dependence? This derivation can be taken to be an aspect of explaining memory. If memory is not primitive (inexplicable, an element in the system), we need explanatory resources. A central part of the answer to this question in both Plotinus and Aristotle lies in representation. For representation shows how memory is derived from and connected to thought and perception.

Another, related form of dependence is ontological: memories are not independent entities; they depend on the subjects they occur in. Nonetheless, memory is in one sense primitive. For its relation to the past belongs to it alone, and is not derived from anything else, although it may depend on the grasp of time.

(P2) The present-past problem:
I remember getting up this morning. How is my getting up present to me now, when it is past? While sceptical approaches use this problem to deny the reality of the past, neither Aristotle nor Plotinus has inclinations in

this direction. For both, part of the answer to this problem lies in the continued existence of the subject of memory. This is a necessary condition for memory. Furthermore, this continued existence must in some way provide a link – a chain of causes – between now and then. But clearly the actual existence of such a chain would be insufficient for memory to occur; the traces have to stand in explicit relation to that of which they are the traces.

(P3) The memory-representation problem:
A face appears before my mind's eye; as we might say, I am thinking of a face. How does this differ from a memory of Socrates' face? An answer to this question would also be a contribution to a solution of P2, since representations can contribute to providing an explicit connection with the past.

(P4) The memory-recollection problem:
At the moment, I remember having my breakfast this morning, without searching for this memory. So I have some things, past perceptions, in mind without any searching (memory). Other things require a search (recollection), for example having breakfast on Tuesday last week. So can this distinction between memory and recollection be explained? It might look merely arbitrary. For does one really think of anything without wanting to, even if one is prompted by external influences? For example, I might think of Socrates' face, being prompted by the sight of Theaetetus.

   Explaining the relation between memory and recollection requires more than the concepts of capacity and activity: recollection is not simply the activity of the capacity to remember. Yet there must be one capacity with several realisations. And the way in which it is realised may differ. For example, one might think that while recollection is an intentional action, memory is something that happens to one. However, both are clearly end-directed.

(P5) The self-memory problem:
I can only remember things I have undergone myself. This seems to be part of what *memory* means. But what exactly is the relation between my self and my memory? This question is connected to the present-past problem in that a necessary condition for solving that problem is the continued existence of the subject of memory.

(P6) The universal-memory problem:
I have capacities (e. g. counting) which can be realised without any reference to (mention of) my perceptions. Is the exercise of such a capacity
memory? In modern discussions, "semantic memory" is an expression
used for stored information without any explicit relation to my perceptions. If memory can be split in two such radically different aspects,
this is an important fact about the concept.

A comprehensive discussion of these six problems would take us some
way towards a systematic account of memory; of course, that lies beyond
the scope of the present work. Nonetheless, a brief discussion of some relations between these points can serve as an introduction to the historical
work that follows.

The fundamental thing about memory is its derivation. Memory is
derivative from other ways of my interacting with things around me.
For memory has no way of its own to attach things I have in mind to
things outside my mind. This implies that perception is a useful lead
into memory, insofar as it is the fundamental way we and other living
things have cognition of the way things are.

Because memory relates to perceptions (P5), universals as such cannot
be in my memory (P6). The memory we are dealing with here is what is
called episodic, autobiographical or experiential; this requires that memory is closely connected to perception (P1); but on the other hand, perception also requires the use of concepts, if not always, and perhaps with
different degrees of clarity. For example, the perception can happen before I acquire the concept to describe it; I can see a red balloon before
I have the concept of a balloon. And still I can remember the perception
without the concept, for example something red, spherical and light,
when in fact it was a red balloon.

Suppose I have some representation in mind, how do I attach it to a
past perception, in an act of memory? Is that something that some things
just have as it were, simply a verb in the past tense which *eo ipso* means
that a connection is being made to the past? This problem touches both
the past-present problem (P2), and also the memory-representation problem (P3), and also the derivation problem (P1). To begin with the last
point, we need to move beyond a present perception to something that
lasts; and a first step in this direction lies in a representation of the perception. But even once I have the representation, it need not tell me itself
that it could serve to make a memory claim. Indeed, a *representation* does
not *say* anything; *I* do that, when I make a truth claim. And in order to

make a truth claim, at least in the case of memory, I need a representation, among other things. That is not to say that there is a process of deducing from the evidence of a present representation to a past perception. But the representation can form part of my capacity to have memories and play an essential role in my actually having them; and hence explain in part what memory is. So representation contributes to capacities to do things, without being a capacity in its own right. But representation can serve as a bridge between something I have in mind now, and something I wish to remember. To show how this is possible requires a solution to the memory-representation problem (P3).

Some things in my past are available without anymore ado; others require looking for (the memory recollection problem P4). Whether things have to be recalled or are there, available without a search, they seem to remain in some sense. This is the present-past problem (P2). Memory is not just the remaining of the thing to be remembered; some states do not need any activity to remain. My curtains do nothing but do stay green. The retention involved in memory is different, living things are continually active. So retention and retrieval may be related in a very different way from the way the butter is kept in the larder and may be fetched when needed. (This is the treasury or store house view of memory, a view we shall not be concerned with.)

1.2 Representational theories of memory in Aristotle and Plotinus

Two short works on memory have come down to us from pagan antiquity, Aristotle's *On memory and recollection*, and Plotinus' *On perception and memory*.[1] One very obvious connection between these two theories is that they use φαντασία. The claim that I will try to establish in this study is that the account of memory developed by Aristotle and adapted by Plotinus using φαντασία is not to be understood as an image theory of memory. Here I take an image theory in the following very simple sense. Socrates remembers Theaetetus, only if, when Socrates perceived Theae-

---

1   My interpretation of Aristotle's theory below in 2.1 and 2.2 is, in large part, a reworking in English of my commentary on De mem. in King 2004 (reviewed by Tsouni 2005 in English). The treatment of Plotinus in the present study is much closer to the text, since less work in general has been done on his treatises which touch on memory; see, however, Brisson 2006, Taormina 2010.

tetus, an image was fixed of Theaetetus in Socrates. The presence of this image is the presence of memory. This will act as our stalking horse, to set off two much more sophisticated theories.

First, some preliminary remarks. In a representational theory of memory, φαντασία, representation, provides part of the capacity to remember things. By this I mean something quite simple. We need to distinguish between actual remembering and the capacity to remember. Actually remembering things is not the presence of an image; rather it is saying that something is the case, or a perceptual analogue of such a propositional attitude. However, in order to say something about Theaetetus, Socrates must have a representation of him. So representation forms part of the capacity to remember and actually remembering things is a matter of saying or perceiving that things are the case. So φαντασία is part of a propositional and, thus conceptual, capacity.[2]

"Representation" is a translation of *φαντασία*. In both of the theories we are dealing with, in different ways, it is dependent on (sense-) perception: a φαντασία is what remains when perception is over, and requires a preceding perception to exist. So to start with, the approach we are following is epistemic, concerned with memory as connected to perception as a form of cognition. For, of course, the fact that we start from a concept of representation that is explained in terms of perception should not preclude a conceptual aspect to the theory. For we cannot simply assume that perception occurs without concepts; we can see a red balloon without the concept of a balloon, but we cannot see it as a balloon. For instance, someone who believes that concepts – those defined in an Aristotelian science, for example – are gained by experience should believe that in perception, conceptual elements are present in some way.[3] Another alternative is that innate ideas play a central role in perception. On either count, perception is a faculty that works with concepts. So if memory relies on perception, there will be conceptual aspects to this capacity. This

---

2   It is a difficult question as to whether φαντασία is itself conceptual; on the one hand perception is conceptual, at least in the sense that in humans concepts can be distilled out of perception using memory and experience (see below in main text). It seems an exaggeration to say that φαντασία *itself* is what allows humans at least to interpret perception (cf. Nussbaum 1978: Interpretive Essay 5); it is part of the perception *itself*, I think, for Aristotle, that we perceive things *as* something. De An. II 6 on incidental perception makes no mention of φαντασία. Klaus Corcilius has been insistent that I make this point.

3   Cf. Scott 1995: Chapter 5. Discovery and continuity in science.

in fact is quite obvious, if one accepts that actual remembering consists in making a propositional claim, at least in the case of humans.

The present approach might be thought open to the criticism that a novel translation of φαντασία – "representation" rather than "imagination"[4] – is being introduced in order to present a theory of memory that has nothing in common with modern representationalist theory except the name.[5] Let me try to banish this impression. For a start, at a colloquial level, *representation* and its cognates are closer to what is meant by φαντασία than *imagination* and its cognates.[6] And one should not exaggerate the similarity of "representations" in the present context with the entities in modern discussions of mental representation.[7] But there are things which are sufficiently similar to make it seem worthwhile to pursue this line, and reasons enough to claim that in so doing we are presenting a view of Aristotle and Plotinus that is novel. No serious attempt has been made to show how taking φαντασία as representation would work in the case of memory. The standard assumption is that φαντασία is to be understood as a faculty of images in Aristotle's theory of memory.

---

4   Burnyeat 2008a: 47 note 15 argues that *imagination* only fits III 3 427b17–24 in the treatment of φαντασία, and that *appearance* is the proper translation for the noun for the verb φαίνεσθαι, referring to Plato's usage at *Theaetetus* 152BC, *Sophist* 264AB. "Appearance" is, however, problematic, in that it is unclear what a potential appearance is, as it were, one that does not appear, now, but may do so later. Since Aristotle's theory of dreams requires that movements from perceptions remain in the living thing (see esp. Ins. 3460b28–461a8), to reappear in sleep, and these movements are certainly φαντασίαι, we have to allow for non-appearing φαντασίαι. Surely, for an appearance, apparere is esse. See also the discussion in Lefebvre 1997.

5   Another possible line of criticism is that in two main areas of cognition Aristotle is not a representationalist, since he thinks that thinking is identical with what is thought, and the perception with what is perceived. Firstly, this does not apply to memory. Secondly, it is not *prima facie* clear that the identity precludes representation. In the case of thought representations are certainly necessary (De anima III 8, De mem. 1 449b31).

6   See the definition in the *Concise Oxford Dictionary* s.v. represent: 1. call up by description or portrayal or imagination, figure, place likeness of before the mind or senses, serve or be meant as likeness of. S. v. Imagination: mental faculty forming images of external objects.

7   See e.g. the essays collected in Stich and Warfield 1994. Thomas Johansen has argued to me that in the modern sense perception and thought are representational, whereas these faculties do not involve φαντασία for Aristotle. Clearly, I agree that φαντασία is not involved in Aristotle's account of all phenomena which fall under the modern concept of mental representation (and the same applies to Plotinus).

The fundamental weakness of image theories of memory is that the presence of an image is neither sufficient nor necessary for remembering to take place. I can remember without an image. My memories of breakfast this morning (tea and toast) need be neither accompanied by nor constituted by gustatory, olfactory, visual, tactile or auditory images: no need to go through an experience as if having breakfast again. I can just say to myself or others: I had tea and toast for breakfast. And many images go through my mind, (for example when I am dreaming), without these being cases of memory.

Nonetheless, some residue of perception is required for us to be able to remember things. This residue is what I am calling a representation.

This study is an examination of representational theories of memory,[8] such as those developed by Aristotle and Plotinus. A representational theory of memory is one in which memory is a representational faculty, that in some sense "pictures", presents or represents the things to us. Versions of this theory are nowadays widely held to be untenable; usually such theories are held to operate with mental images, for the capacity to represent something may be held to be the imagination. Four difficulties with a representational theory may be mentioned:[9]

– How are we meant to have a picture gallery in our heads, which one inspects in memory acts?
– How is a present occurrence connected with the past?
– How is it possible to remember without images occurring in one's mind?
– How does one distinguish memory representation from other representations, e. g. imaginary ones?

These four problems in fact derive from a view of representation which borders on a parody, since, of course, for one thing there is no picture gallery in one's head which is inspected in acts of memory.[10] However, consideration of these problems, or ones like them, while using a more serious view of representation, will guide our discussion. Much depends on the way we understand representation. The most important questions are:

Does it only involve images?
Does it involve concepts?

---

8 Sutton 1998 is a large scale defence of the idea of memory traces.
9 See Audi 1998: 60–2.
10 See e.g. Mackie 1976: 41–47.

Can it be true and false?
From what has been said already, it should be clear that of these three questions, only the first is to be answered in the negative. But these epistemological aspects of representation do not exhaust its capacity to explain memory. A further aspect concerns the ontology of things that remember. For what we need is some form of bridge to the past. The representation is part of what has to be preserved from the past to the present for memory to be possible. So, remembering things persist through time. And they produce (under the right conditions) changes which serve the reconstruction of the past.

We need an example of memory to articulate the conditions under which someone can be said to remember:

Example (E) Socrates remembers (at t2) that he saw Theaetetus two days ago (at t1).

Three times are necessary for memory – t1 and t2, and the time span in between. Thus cognition of time is necessary, whether determined (this *amount* of time) or not. A theory which concentrates on t2, what we do when we actually remember may be called *a constructivist theory*: at its most extreme, such a theory might claim that all that is required is that one do something special at t2, namely, construct one's memory.

Some theorists tend to emphasise the activity at t2, as it were, the reconstruction of what happened. Socrates must do something when he remembers at t2, otherwise at all times of t1+n he would be remembering. Others concentrate on the nature of what happened at t1: something at t1 affected Socrates. And a third area is what happens between t1 and t2. That is to say, it is possible to insist on a certain configuration of the persisting causes.

We have said that part of the virtue of representation is that it can explain one of the things that have to exist, if there is to be memory. But of course representations do not occur independently in the world; they always belong to a subject. The approach we will follow essentially involves things capable of cognition. In other words, it is both epistemology and ontology. Furthermore, living things have an interest in the past, and the way they are affected by the past. Memory is in some ways unique, as it were, a bridge between past events and present behaviour: there are some things which, if we do not remember them, can no longer affect our actions. So memory provides at least in some cases a causal chain.

But in the reverse direction memory requires causal conditions to hold in the past: Socrates remembers seeing Theaetetus (in part) *because* he saw him. This is a necessary condition, but not sufficient. For we do not remember many things we see. But the force of demanding that there is a connection in Socrates between t1 and t2 is to insist that there can be no gaps in a causal chain. Causes must be continuously connected with their effects. They do not act at a temporal distance.[11] Thus our interest in representation lies at least partly in this aspect of the causal role it fulfils, that is the continuity it may provide. Not of course that one image persists from t1 to t2, but that there is a continuous chain which can preserve something of the original perception and constitute in part the capacity to remember it. Part of the causal story of how we can now at t2 remember what happened at t1 is a story involving representation.

The kinds of explanation in Plotinus and Aristotle are not restricted to causality in the modern sense. But the ideas of continuity, and passing on of information, and of the avoidance of acting at a temporal distance are present.

Thus this is primarily a study of the way these two thinkers tried to explain memory; in both cases one important part of this explanation lies in elucidating the connections between memory, and the conceptions of soul in each thinker. For memory is an obvious example of a cognitive capacity relating times in the lives of persisting beings. Indeed, memory may seem to be the only such capacity, but this is not the case. Thus an important theme is restricting memory to its proper sphere, and so of course, establishing just what this sphere is. In both Plotinus and Aristotle, we are dealing with *modest* theories of memory.[12] There are two kinds of modesty involved. Firstly, memory is only involved in some of our cognition. This is true even if it seems that we have cognitive capacities which exist over time. Thus a broad conception of memory is precluded which comprises all the information we possess.[13] Secondly, in these theories memory is modest in that it requires a subject to do the remembering. For living things and in particular humans exist through time and possess persisting capacities which can be exercised without the exercise

---

11   On causation and memory see Martin, Deutscher 1966.
12   In contrast e. g. to the "memorism", espoused by some ancient empiricists according to Frede 1990.
13   For such a broad conception, see e. g. Baddeley 1982: Ch. 1 What is your memory? The chapter begins (p. 11) with the words: "Memory is the capacity for storing and retrieving information. Without it we would be unable to see, hear or think."

of memory. Not all information that we have available is in our memory. Thus memory proper has to be distinguished, for example, from changes in our striving, in what we want, and from the acquired capacity to think certain things. So modesty, when applied to memory does not refer to the restrictions of memory to certain objects; in that sense, all capacities are modest, since they are capacities for some things, not others, and so relate to certain objects.

The philosophy of memory may be treated as a purely epistemological question, and some treatments of memory in ancient authors bring out this side to the concept.[14] Not so with Aristotle and Plotinus. The questions both authors are much more concerned with are ontological, namely what is memory and what are the subjects of memory. These are closely related questions. For memory, being what it is, makes certain demands of its subjects. They must be able to do certain things, as well as being persisting things. Thus souls or concrete living things in Plotinus and Aristotle respectively must, under the right circumstances, have a faculty for representing things and perceiving things. Characteristically, acts of memory are acts of saying that something is the case.[15] Furthermore the question of interest is also central: if one thinks that living things are guided by what is good for them, or what they take to be good, as both our authors do, then it is reasonable to think that when memory occurs, it does so because it fulfils a function or because it is, in the given circumstances, a good.[16]

These two thinkers can be contrasted and compared with one another in many ways, but a central contrast, in their theories of soul generally, and in their theory of memory in particular is the question whether body is needed for the soul in general to exist, and for there to be memory in particular. We shall see that the price that Plotinus pays for a non-embodied soul is a certain sparseness of explanatory resources: Memory can be explained in terms of the activity of an embodied soul in a perspicuous fashion, where the theorist of the bare soul reaches base rock in the bare capacities of soul. It is remarkable how far these thin resources take him. Aristotle in turn reaches his limits in not cashing out the material metaphors he offers in explanation of memory. This is disappointing in that the reader might like an explanation in terms of concepts, not metaphors.

---

14 Scott 1995, Frede 1990.

15 But note that the concept of belief (δόξα) plays no role in either of the theories under consideration here.

16 Philebus IIA7. On the *Philebus* see below p. 18.

But we shall see that Aristotle is nonetheless able to present a view on central philosophical questions raised by the phenomenon of memory.

The aim of Aristotle's work is to offer a definition of memory using the causes or explanatory factors that are involved. In IV 3–4, part of the large work *On problems of the soul,* Plotinus assumes a definition of memory, as something that does not need further discussion. We shall have to see whether he himself ever does give a definition, particularly in IV 6 3. This study will omit three important influences on Plotinus: his more immediate Platonic predecessors, the Stoics, and Alexander of Aphrodisias. These will be left out, partly because of the paucity of evidence and partly, because investigating them would go beyond the remit of this work.

The main questions we will be considering is how two thinkers with such widely differing views of the soul, in particular, whether the soul needs a body or not, can produce theories of memory with so many shared features. These works have in common that they both present theories of memory based on φαντασία, a view of memory that Aristotle developed and which became, in antiquity and beyond, something of a cliché. This similarity might strike one as surprising, above all because an important target of Plotinus' criticism are views of memory which use the model of a seal leaving an impression on wax; and Aristotle is one of the most famous friends of this model. But a model need not always be understood in the same way; the obvious polemic of Plotinus masks a deeper agreement with Aristotle. Both believe that in remembering, living things are active. Aristotle thinks that such activity is compatible with the passivity he sees in the imprint on wax, whereas Plotinus does not. Furthermore, both have theories of memory that are forms of *indirect realism via representation.*[17] Both think that we can remember the way things were, or be wrong when we remember.

Aristotle's account of memory is part of his physics: a theory of embodied existence with its vital and cognitive activities. In contrast, Plotinus is discussing the difficulties associated with the soul, including not only the problems of defining memory under corporeal conditions but also the question of memory in the underworld and in the disembodied contemplation of ideas. Actually, this broadening of scope does not mean a radical revision of the account of memory.

---

17 The most famous direct realist is Reid (*Essays* III 7, p. 357). Direct realism would entail that there is a realm of timed facts which can be the content of memory. It is hard to find a place for such a realm in the world of either thinker.

In Plotinus' approach to memory, many of his most characteristic views are present:

– The impassibility of the soul.
– The role of soul as mediator between intellect and perception.
– the immortality of soul, involving different phases of corporeality and incorporeality.

Souls go through various stages, characterised by different activities or forms of life. The cycle is in some sense natural: it lies in the nature of the soul to go through this cycle. But equally importantly, the way any individual soul goes is a matter of its own choice.

Plotinus and Aristotle are both successors of Plato's: what do they owe him? This is a large question, not least because Plato's own use of memory is a large and complicated topic in its own right,[18] but it is at least worth showing that Aristotle's approach represents a new start, above all in his use of φαντασία. In the case of both Plotinus and Aristotle the use of φαντασία shows their interest in what one may call the ontological side of memory: what must living things with memory be like?[19] A further similarity, which masks more differences, is the following. Like (the late) Plato, both Aristotle and Plotinus distinguish between μνήμη and ἀνάμνησις. But in both cases, their distinctions are very different from Plato's.

The Greek words we will be dealing with are μνήμη and ἀνάμνησις and the associated verbs μνημονεύειν and ἀναμιμνήσκεσθαι. Apparently there was to begin with no clear distinction between the pairs of concepts: the idea was simply to remember someone. The capacity to do this was μνήμη. The precise distinction between the terms is a philosophical achievement of the late Plato in the *Philebus*.[20] Long before that he had talked about ἀνάμνησις in the *Meno* and *Phaedo*;[21] μνήμη is first defined in the *Philebus*.[22]

---

18 See Scott 1995: Section 1, pp. 13–86 for an excellent treatment of some aspects.
19 A parallel point to this is important in the *Phaedo*, insofar as ἀνάμνησις is meant to prove that the soul is immortal, even if in the end it does not.
20 *Philebus* 34A-B, 39A. On Aristotle and Plato here cf. Ross p. 243–4, Sorabji p. 5, 38, 89, 99, Freudenthal 1869: 403, Lang 1980, Van Dorp 1992, Labarrière 2000: 276 with n. 12.
21 Freudenthal 1869: 402 remarks that Plato tried to mark the distinction between μνήμη and ἀνάμνησις, and he refers to *Phaedo* 73B7–9: Simmias has to be reminded (ἀναμνησθῆναι) of the doctrine of ἀνάμνησις; he almost remembers (σχεδόν γε…μέμνημαι), because of what Kebes is trying to say. ἀναμιμνήσκεσθαι,

Some distinctions that will play a major role are the following. We can distinguish between the capacity to remember something (μνήμη) and actually remembering it (μνημονεύειν). Aristotle's enquiry into memory starts from a claim, stated in non-theoretical terms, about what we do when we are active with memory. Basically, I will be using the term remember (μνημονεύειν) as the activity of memory (μνήμη); and recollection (ἀναμιμνήσκεσθαι) is a recollection that can end in memory, but starts from the unavailability of the content sought.[23]

1.3 Platonic preliminaries

1.3.1 The wax block model for false opinion in the *Theaetetus*

In the *Theaetetus*, Plato describes how in the heart of each of us there is a block of wax, which we use to remember things with.[24] Perceiving something and remembering things are two ways of grasping them, and the question is whether these two ways can account for misidentifying something remembered with something perceived. Depending on what the wax is like, (hard or soft, plentiful or meagre) our memory is good or bad. The description is literary and light hearted.

The discussion between Socrates and Theaetetus reaches the conclusion that the model does not allow us to describe how we can have false opinions about things.

ἀναμνησθῆναι can mean "to remember something" (72Cff., 75E). But, as Freudenthal himself sees, Plato was not concerned with the details. He knows a distinction between μνήμη and ἀνάμνησις, but it plays no role in his theory.

22 Cf. also *Phaedrus* 249B-C: recollection (ἀνάμνησις) has ideas as its objects and the soul of the philosopher is close through his memory (μνήμη) to that which makes the divine divine, and 274E: memory (μνήμη) is damaged by writing; but the latter does serve recall (ὑπόμνησις). On μνήμη cf. also *Theaetetus* 163D, 164D.

23 A note on the translation of μιμνήσκεσθαι, μεμνῆσθαι: μιμνήσκειν is a causative verb which means "to make someone think of something" (from the root *mna-). The passive may then have the meaning "remember" either in the sense of "to have in one's memory" or "to recall". The first is expressed in the perfect (e. g. Plato *Laws* 633D). And sometimes it is hard to tell which meaning is present (e. g. Plato *Philebus* 31A-B). Forms of μιμνήσκεσθαι are used by Aristotle for both having in one's memory (449b20, 452a7, 10, b27, 28, 29, 30 453a2, 3), and for recalling (451b26, 452a16, 18, 20, 22, 24).

24 *Theaetetus* 191A-195B.

In their explanations of memory, Aristotle adopts and adapts the wax block model, Plotinus criticises it severely.[25] Aristotle's use of it is closely connected to his use of the model of a sealing ring for the activity in perception.[26] This is not surprising, since the role the model has in the account of memory is to describe the initial perception. But, as we shall see, it would be premature to conclude that in the case of both Plotinus and Aristotle, the model is interpreted in the same way. Models need interpretation, and Plotinus' interpretation of the wax block model is very strict. He thinks that it precludes any talk of capacities of memory.

The reason, I suggest, that Aristotle can make positive use of it, whereas Plato and Plotinus cannot is that he is talking about the essentially embodied soul. Whilst for Aristotle as for Plotinus the soul cannot undergo change, this is obviously not the case for the concrete living thing made of the soul and the body. The concrete living thing, consisting of soul and body, undergoes a change. In other words, the wax block, if it is to make sense in the account of the embodied soul, must assume hylomorphism. The reason that the soul, as such, does not undergo change is that it is a form, in other words it is not material, and for Aristotle, matter is that which can be in two states.[27]

1.3.2 The five conditions of ἀνάμνησις in the *Phaedo*

Plato nowhere develops a thoroughgoing *theory* of memory. What is often known as "Plato's theory of recollection" is actually a theory of what recollection does or can be used to do, namely, learn ideas, that is, recover cognition of ideas that dates from before our birth. What is usually called *learning* is thus really recollection, and takes place largely through dialectic.[28] The theory is first presented in the *Meno* (without any mention of ideas), in the main as an incitement to the hard work of research. It is then used in the *Phaedo* as part of the attempt to prove the immortality of the soul.

---

25 Aristotle's use is polemical: in Plato the model fails when used for false belief; Aristotle uses it with assurance for perception. See Burnyeat 1990: 101. The model goes back to Democritus (DK 68A135 = Theophrastus *de Sens.* 51–2).

26 De an II 8 423b19–21, III 12 435a2–3.

27 Plotinus: III 6 1, Aristotle Met. VII 7 1032 a18–20. On Aristotle, see King 2001: 56–59. Menn (2002: 92–94) also emphasises this point about the soul. For other sources in translation see Sorabji 2004: 217–220.

28 See esp. *Phaedo* 75C10-D4.

The use of recollection assumes a certain view of recollection in general. Knowledge (ἐπιστήμη) is recollection, if it occurs under the following conditions (*Phaedo* 73C1−74A8):

1. One must have known (ἐπίστασθαι) the object X before (73C1−2).
2. If you cognise (γνῶσαι) Y by perception, then you become aware of (ἐννοεῖν) X (C7−9).
3. The knowledge (ἐπιστή´μη) of X and Y is not the same (C9).
4. This form of cognition happens above all with things that have been forgotten through the passage of time and a lack of attention (E1−3).[29]
5. X, the object of recollection, and Y, by which we recollect X, can be similar or dissimilar to one another. If the first, then Y falls short of X (like a picture and its original) (74A2−8).[30]

How does Plato proceed here? He starts with a situation in which there is something which one knew in the past, but does not now have in mind: Simmias once knew what ἀνάμνησις is, but now needs reminding of it. Plato chooses this approach to recollection, because it can be connected to investigations: these are possible because one can recollect something that one already knows, but does not now have immediately available. The decisive point is that it is a question of recollection, not of memory, in other words. It is not a question of how the things are preserved, but of how I get at them. It is this latter aspect that is comparable to the objects of investigations.

The objects of recollection here are not past perceptions, but the objects of past perceptions, Kebes, not the sight of Kebes. Hence recollec-

---

29 For this condition cf. 76A1−4.
30 Scott (1995: 55) gives only four "general conditions" for recollection from 73C1−74A8. He leaves out forgetting (condition 4), perhaps because it is not universally necessary. It does however play a decisive role in the special use of recollection for the knowledge of ideas. This seems enough to earn it a place among the general conditions. I use the expression "condition" because Plato expresses them using a series of conditional sentences. It is for our present purposes unimportant, whether these conditions are necessary or sufficient. Cf. Gosling 1965: 155, Gallop 1975: 115−116. Frede (1997: 48) thinks that Plato distinguishes "terminologically" between continuous memory and the "recovery of what is absent or forgotten (ἀνάμνησις)". She does allow that forgetting is not necessary for ἀνάμνησις: it can also be remembering things which one does not at present have in mind ('in Erinnerung bringen von Dingen, die einem nicht gerade gegenwärtig sind'). This is, however, an admission that the "terminological" distinction is not actually upheld by Plato.

tion here is not restricted, as far as the object is concerned, to the past, but there must have been cognition of the object.[31]

The second condition mentions perception. This seems an unnecessary restriction; it is not after all impossible to be reminded of something by a thought or an image. Plato's language here is determined by the fact that the *Phaedo* is his first attempt at psychology. He is operating with a very rudimentary distinction between perception and thought: thought is restricted to thought of ideas.[32] Hence it cannot serve any role in the general conditions for recollection. And imagination, or representation, (φαντασία), plays no role whatever in the dialogue.

Forgetting enjoys a special status among the conditions (in 4). To start with, it does not seem necessary: recollection happens

> *above all* (μάλιστα), if someone undergoes this about things which he has now forgotten through the passage of time or lack of attention.[33]

This sentence is ambiguous: Is recollection restricted to cases in which forgetting occurs or not?[34] The implication of "above all" could be that one need not have forgotten in order to recollect something. One sees Simmias, and thinks of Kebes, but had not forgotten Kebes. One could easily have the impression that Plato does not attach much importance to the question of whether one has forgotten or not. The status of forgetting is, however, much clearer, when we move on from the general conditions of recollection to the special ones associated with recollection of ideas. There knowledge is distinguished from forgetting as follows:

> If we did not always forget this knowledge, once we have acquired it, we would come to know (εἰδότας) it always and know (εἰδέναι) it throughout our life. For this is knowledge (εἰδέναι), to possess acquired knowledge (ἐπιστήμην ἔχειν) without having lost it. Or is that not forgetting (λήθη), Simmias, the loss of knowledge?[35]

---

31 Lang (1980: 387): Aristotle restricts memory to the past unlike Plato; cf. De mem. 1 449b9–10; and Plotinus IV 3 25 11, IV 4 6 2–3.

32 Perception: αἴσθησις, thought: λογισμός, διάνοια and the cognate verbs, cf. 65E-66B, 79A-C, 83A-C.

33 *Phaedo* 73E1–3.

34 Rowe (1993: 166 ad loc.) thinks that recollection after forgetting is the primary sense of recollection.

35 *Phaedo* 75D7–11. Ryle (1949: 272–3) calls this use of remembering the most important, and the least discussed; he notes one can replace it with "know".

Socrates goes on to claim that one loses this prenatal knowledge at birth,[36] that is, forgets it,[37] and then acquires it again through learning, i. e. dialectic: learning is the re-acquisition of this knowledge, and that is recollection.[38] There is no mention of memory.[39] Instead, one possesses knowledge: that is how knowledge is defined.[40] If Plato does not distinguish between memory and knowledge, then he cannot distinguish between the recovery of knowledge and the recovery of memory. Aristotle attaches great importance to this distinction. And as we will see Plotinus follows Aristotle here: a central aspect of his treatment of memory lies in the fact that we can grasp ideas without memory.

Plato begins with a situation in which the relevant knowledge is not there and has to be recovered. His main interest is in the epistemological use of recollection to activate our knowledge of forms. Aristotle in contrast has a broader interest in memory concepts, and is able to point to the phenomenon of having something which one has learnt or perceived in mind, without a process of recovery being necessary. This explains their different attitudes towards forgetting; we have seen that for Plato, at least in the case of ideas, forgetting plays a central role, as it does with Plotinus too. For Aristotle it has no importance whatever, at least on the surface of his text. He also adopts from Plato's account the idea that the thing recollected and the way to it must be related in a certain way (condition 5 above); these relations regulate the chain of association in his explanation of recollection. But even when discussing the recovery of perceptions along chains of association, Aristotle does not talk of forgetting; he does say that one recovers the cognition that one had earlier and the implication is that something has happened in the meantime. Just what happens in the meantime, Aristotle does not say. Perhaps the reason that he

---

36 *Phaedo* 76D1–4.

37 Plato defines forgetting (λήθη) *Philebus* 33E3 as the disappearance (ἔξοδος) of memory; cf. *Symposium* 208A5, where it is the disappearance of (ἔξοδος) knowledge (ἐπιστήμη). This supports the view that Plato is not concerned to distinguish between memory and knowledge. For another definition of forgetting, see *Theaetetus* 191D10-E1. Aristotle gives a school definition of forgetting as the loss (ἀποβολή) of knowledge (Top. VII 3 153b27).

38 75E2–7. See also *Meno* 85D3–7. In the birdcage likeness for knowing in *Theaetetus* 198D6 this expression is used of capturing the knowledge that one already has in the bird cage, but not in one's hand; see Brown 1991: 615–6.

39 For the connection between ἀνάμνησις and knowledge (ἐπίστασθαι) without memory, see also 76A9-B2, *Meno* 86B2–4.

40 The person with knowledge is then further determined as someone able to give an account (λόγον δοῦναι) (76B5); cf. e.g. *Republic* VII 534B4–5.

does not mention forgetting here is that if you have forgotten something, then you do not remember it, and you have to learn it again.[41]

1.3.3 The two definitions of ἀνάμνησις in the *Philebus*

In the *Philebus* Plato distinguishes between memory and recollection. Memory is defined as the "preservation of perception" (34A10 f);[42] perception in turn is said to consist in a common motion of body and soul, which occurs through their common affection (πάθος) (*Philebus* 34A3–5). Memory itself is purely psychic. In the context of the theory of pleasure in the *Philebus*, it has the function of preserving some past perception. Pleasure is defined as a replenishment, which restores the natural state of the living thing. Memory is necessary for this so that the natural state is present at a time when one has bodily deficiencies, such that one may have a desire for replenishment, that is, for pleasure.[43] This implies that memory can fulfil its function completely without body, once the perception which occasioned it, that is to say the common affection of body and soul, is given.

Recollection (ἀνάμνησις) is defined in two ways:

a) *Philebus* 34B6–8 'If the soul, on its own, brings back (ἀναλαμβάνῃ) that which soul and body underwent together, as far as possible without the body, then we say it recollects (ἀναμιμνῄσκεσθαι).'

41　See 451a31-b6. Sorabji (p. 92 ad 451b2–5) notes this difference between Aristotle and Plato: ἀνάμνησις in Plato entails that something has been lost (he cites *Meno* 85C-D, 86A-C, *Phaedo* 73E, 74B-C, *Philebus* 34B-C). On the *Phaedo*, where this condition is only "mostly" the case, see above p. 6. Aristotle, as Sorabji notes, insists that the capacity remains, even when one is not thinking of the thing in question (452a10). But Plato also allows for a capacity, especially if he thinks that the slave in the *Meno* recollects in conversation with Socrates. *Meno* 85C6–7: The man who does not know has true opinions (δόξαι) about that which he does not know which are wakened by questions (86A7). As long as he has this knowledge he knows (85D12). Brown (1991: 618) suggests that in the *Meno* we are dealing with virtual knowledge and that is the reason that there is no talk of forgetting, unlike in the *Phaedo*.

42　See also Alcinous, Didaskalikos 154.36–40.

43　*Philebus* 35A-B. It is important that the painter who plays a role in the account of memory in 39A-B is not imagination; it is anyway only an addition to the accounts of the scribes, and not, apparently, necessary for memory. Hence Plato is not a precedent for a φαντασία-based theory of memory.

b) 34B10-C2 'After memory (μνήμη), whether of a perception or of
   something learnt (μάθημα), has been lost, [the soul] recovers
   (ἀναπολήσῃ) [the memory] in turn in itself.'

Both are secular uses in that the objects of recollection here are things that
we have learnt or experienced. There is no hint here of the grand use of
recollection from the middle period (*Meno, Phaedo, Phaedrus*).

a) differs from b) as in the latter memory is recovered, that is to say,
the preservation of the perception (affection) or thing learnt is re-activat-
ed. It involves loss (forgetting), and relates not directly to the first order
perception or learning but to the memory of these, and so is not on the
same level as the memory, as it is in a). b) is in effect a reactivation of
memory.

Armed with these preliminaries we are equipped to approach Aristotle's theory.

2 Aristotle

2.1 Memory

2.1.1 The modesty of memory: The context of the enquiry into memory

In order to understand Aristotle's approach to memory we have to see how it fits into his enquiry into living things, and relate it to the body on the one hand, and to more basic forms of cognition, on the other. We shall see that memory depends on a persisting living thing, and on perception. These are two aspects of the modesty of memory: understanding memory in Aristotle requires understanding its systematic relations to more fundamental concepts.

Aristotle's investigation into memory forms part of the account of living behaviour begun in *De anima* and continued in the so-called *Parva Naturalia*.

Clearly, one question that we have to ask is the way in which body is present in the account of memory. I think that individuality is necessary to the account of memory, even if it plays on the surface no great role, simply because of the question of what the subject of memory is. This does not mean that Aristotle has any interest in defining as it were the small scale bodily changes coincident on memory.

As is well known, Aristotle explains psychic phenomena using body and soul; the example that he himself offers at the start of *De anima* is anger, which he defines as a certain kind of change of such and such a body. An affection (πάθος) is generally speaking anything that a thing can undergo (πάσχειν), and requires a substrate, of which it is a quality (ποιότης), in respect of which alteration (ἀλλοιοῦσθαι) is possible, e.g. pale, dark, sweet, or bitter.[44] In the case of living things, "passions", "emotions", or, as I will say: affections, are included.[45] Corresponding to the

---

44 On πάθος in general see Met. V 21 1022b15, Met. IX 7 1049a29–30, Met. XII 5 1071a1–2, Phys. V 2 226a29, VIII 7 260a27, De gen. et corr. I 3 319b33, Cat. 8 9b6. On activity and passivity in perception in Aristotle, cf. Johansen 2002.

45 I render πάθος "affection" (so too Sorabji, and Revised Oxford Translation at e. g. 450a26, Met. 1022b15).

formal account of anger: a desire for revenge for harm received is a material one: the boiling of blood around the heart.[46] Such "affections" as anger are "enmattered formulae" (λόγοι ἔνυλοι). This naturalist approach to the soul is closely connected with his hylomorphic view, namely that the soul is the form of the living thing. This relation between soul and body is one that is expressed most clearly in the definition of the soul as "the primary actuality of a natural body which possesses life potentially".[47] In the case of such affections as anger he concludes:

> The formula is the form of the thing and it is necessary for this to be in a certain kind of matter if it is to exist.[48]

This is a particular case of Aristotle's view that matter is necessary for the existence of forms.[49] Matter is not only generally necessary; it must be of a certain kind if the phenomena are to exist. Such phenomena are, furthermore, natural since they involve change, and change is the subject of the natural philosopher: nature is the principle of change and rest in a thing as such. Such phenomena are formal, but enmattered, that is to say, parts or aspects of the form of the thing. An actuality of this kind is only reached by the development of the body[50] and so minimally requires a body for its existence.

Whether everything that occurs in the living thing is equally represented by a concurrent change is a completely different question. Broadly there are two classes of affection which Aristotle allows for: those like anger which have a concurrent material change, boiling blood around the heart, and those like perception which do not.[51] Perception is, as it

---

46 De an. I 1 403a25–28. On this passage see Rapp 2006.
47 On the soul as primary *activity* see Hübner 1999, King 2001: 40–9.
48 403b2–3. The whole passage 403a3-b3 is an important witness for the central importance of things common to body and soul (κοινά a4) to the project of De an. Since things common to body and soul are the subject of PN (see below p. 24), this implies that PN is central to De an. See also King 2009b. Other important texts for the relevance of the body for the investigation of the soul are De an. I 3 407b15–26, II 2 414a19–27.
49 E.g. Met. VII 11 103b35–1037a2: only essence is free of matter.
50 De an. II 5 417b16–18.
51 The proof that this formulation does not apply to functions (ἔργα), especially perception is due to Burnyeat (1995: 432–3 with fn. 38). In 403a3 πάθη are the attributes of soul but in 403a16 the πάθη are only passions; the distinction between functions and passions is made at 403a10–11. Perception and other functions are among the attributes that require body, but not to the passions like anger which require a parallel material process.

were, not a passion.[52] We will see that memory, while it has a moving cause, does not appear to require specific material explanation. This may seem surprising since, of course, body is required for using one's memory. In Aristotle's terms, this can be made clear by referring to the phenomenon of change. Memory is in part a change, and that requires matter that can be determined now in this way and now in that. But remembering things does not, for example, have the accompaniment of a leaping of the heart, as Aristotle thought was concomitant with hope.[53] This comparison is germane since just as memory is directed to the past, so hope, or more generally, expectation is directed to the future.[54] But of course, hope is emotive in a way which expectation, in the sense of forming a belief about what will occur, is not. And his treatment of memory in *De memoria et reminiscentia* is free of associations between memory and emotions. Thus memory is to be associated with perception, not passion, in terms of the kind of bodily explanation to be given.

Memory depends on body, and this dependency is one way in which memory is a modest phenomenon. Memory is modest, that is, because, firstly, the living thing is assumed, namely that of which the soul is primary actuality. The living thing preserves itself through time by its metabolic activity ("vegetative soul").[55] This is one major dependency of memory, and the other is on perception. This is in a sense a triviality in Aristotle's system. For perception is the basic equipment of Aristotelian animals; and we assume plants do not have memory. Animals perceive because for Aristotle that is what being an animal is.[56]

However, the dependency becomes more interesting when we turn to representation (φαντασία). For representation depends on perception; and memory depends on representation. A major task for the interpretation of Aristotle's views on memory is to show what the function and nature of representation is in this context. The most important epistemological questions concerning representation have already been mentioned. They are:

Is it simply imagistic?

Does it involve concepts?

---

52 It is of course something living things undergo (πάσχειν), De an. II 5.
53 De part. anim. III 6 669a18–23, and cf. De juv. 26 479b19–26 on palpitation in the heart caused by fear.
54 De mem. 1 449b10–15.
55 See esp. De an. II 4, King 2001: 49–58.
56 III 12 434a27-b8. On difficult, borderline cases see Lloyd 1996: Ch. 3 Fuzzy natures?

Can it be true and false?

There is the further question of what it is and how it is related to the concrete living thing it occurs in. This last question is answered by Aristotle in terms of representation being the remains of perception, more specifically, being a change remaining from actual perception.

Since φαντασία derives from perception, we will need to take a step back, and briefly consider perception to answer these questions.[57] Of course, we cannot give a complete account of Aristotle's view of perception, although we will consider some aspects of it when we turn to representation. However, one feature must be underlined here, since it does not often take centre stage in the debates about Aristotle's concept of perception, which tend to be more about the kind of process that it is: perception is a critical faculty, that is, one for making distinctions, as Aristotle puts it.[58] Thus it is a form of cognition, indeed the only one that lower animals have.[59] Living things are able to distinguish things using perception.

How does Aristotle see this capacity to make distinctions? Aristotle thinks that perception is conceptual. In the summary definition of perception he says that what is received by the perceiver is the form without the matter of the thing.[60] Quite what this means, is, of course, contentious.[61] The following remarks are intended to capture the uncontroversial aspects. When one is affected by something red then the cause of the affection is the redness of the thing, and not the individual as such. This text is very important for the theory of memory; for the description of the process of perception is one that is taken up in *De memoria et reminiscentia*, as is the comparison of this process with using a seal to leave an

---

57   We discuss representation at length below p. 40–62.
58   De an. II 11 424a5–10, III 9 432a16, Anal. Post. II 19 99b35. On concepts in Aristotle's view of perception see Everson 1997: Ch. 5 Perceptual content, Welsch 1987: 32–59.
59   Anal. Post II 19 99b37–9, Scott 1995: 119, who sees Aristotle's conception of perception as involving "an unarticulated concept of the essence." (p. 135); Everson 1997: 222–5.
60   De an. II 12 424a18–21 – whatever quite "form" means here. He also says that it is difficult to decide whether it is something with a logos or a logos (III 9 432a30–1, cf. 426b20, 427a1, 9). Cf. Frede 1992: 283. On problems with the generality of the definition see Lloyd 1996: Ch. 6 The varieties of perception.
61   For the most comprehensive account of the alternatives, with a plea for a third way, see Caston 2005.

impression on wax, which immediately follows the summary account of perception in *De anima* II 12.

So far we have mentioned the dependency of memory on both a living body and on perception. These are the two features that make memory modest. Let us now turn to the treatment of memory itself.

Memory is common to body and soul.[62] This qualifies it as a subject of the *Parva Naturalia*,[63] which is expressly a continuation of *De anima*.[64] Perception serves as the criterion of what is common to body and soul, a role that it is able to perform since it is the principle of the unity between body and soul in animals.[65] He says the following about the subjects of *Parva Naturalia*:

> All occur with perception, some through perception, some are actually affections of perception, others are possession of perception, and others are the preservation and keeping of perception, and yet others the destruction and privation of perception.[66]

For our purposes it is worth asking which of these headings would best fit memory. Apparently, we are embarrassed for choice, as almost any of the descriptions might fit memory: memory might be an affection of perception, its possession or preservation. One may think that Aristotle may have had nothing very specific in mind; the effect is generally compelling that these phenomena are connected to perception. Perhaps he is not trying here to give a complete classification of things common to body and soul. Indeed, with the exception of memory it would seem not to be a real question at all whether the phenomena dealt with in *Parva Naturalia* are common to body and soul or not; waking and sleeping, youth and age, breathing in and out, life and death. None is really a candidate for existence apart from bodies. But let us consider the question of what memory is more closely. Three possibilities are

(1) An affection of perception
(2) The possession of perception
(3) The preservation of perception

---

62 Cf. also De an. I 4 408b25–29 on memory belonging to what is common to body and soul.
63 Memory is mentioned explicitly in the list at 436a7–10. On the subject of PN see Morel 2000:10–24.
64 De sens. 1 436a1–6.
65 See Morel 2006a.
66 De sens. 1 436b3–6.

Both of the first two, here used apparently for different phenomena, are alternative formulations for memory in *De memoria et reminiscentia*.[67] On the first blush one can make sense of both: Either memory is an affection of perception after time has passed or it is the continued possession of perception. The third possibility is that memory is the preservation of perception.[68] This could be taken as follows: In some cases at least, perception does not just fade, it remains and is preserved.[69] But it is certainly not the whole of Aristotle's theory; he thinks that the mere remaining of a perception does not suffice for me to say that I remember it. And the concept of preservation does not occur in *De memoria et reminiscentia*. To return to the problem of finding a suitable formula for memory at the start of the *Parva Naturalia:* On balance, it seems that either of the first two formulae would fit memory. Thus the start of *Parva Naturalia* introduces memory as something common to body and soul, and as common to body and soul because it is an affection or a possession of perception.

Memory is treated in the context of a naturalist psychology by Aristotle. Its connection to perception and body are guarantees of its modesty, binding it to an individual and the individual's perceptions.

So much for the modesty of memory.

2.1.2 The objects of memory

De memoria et reminiscentia begins by stating the subject of the enquiry, the capacity for memory (μνήμη) and actual remembering (μνημονεύειν).[70] The distinction is important, and we will have to establish how ca-

---

67 On memory as an affection of perception or conception (449b24–25 cf. also 451a30–31, 451b2) see below p. 35. In the case of memory of knowledge i.e. scientific knowledge (ἐπιστήμη) Aristotle is hesitant to call the possession or the affection (ἕξις, πάθος) the knowledge (Ch. 2 451a27–28), presumably because the possession or the affection is not the knowledge, rather it is possession of the knowledge or an affection which in some way represents the knowledge.

68 Alexander In de sens. 8.3.

69 This is the definition of memory in the *Philebus* 34A10–11, quoted in the *Introduction* p. 18.

70 This is how Michael (6.8–9) understands the distinction between μνήμη and μνημονεύειν, followed by Siwek, Sorabji and see also e.g. Ryle 1949: 272). The same pair μνήμη and μνημονεύειν occur 449b15–16, in setting the puzzle at 450b12 and also in the summary of the first chapter (451a14–15, cf. Ch. 2 451b5, 453b8–9). Bloch (2007: esp. 79–83, 98) denies that memory is

pacity and actuality relate to one another, and indeed to recollection,
which is also mentioned at this point and briefly distinguished from
memory. Aristotle assumes here that we can distinguish them, and indeed
that we are able to agree that different people excel in each of them, to wit
that slow people have a better memory and the quick, who learn easily,
are better at recollecting. We turn first to memory; later we will take
up recollection. Aristotle uses three questions to structure his enquiry
into memory:

(1) what is memory?
(2) what is its cause?
(3) what part of the soul is involved?

These questions are also applied to recollection (ἀνάμνησις). As Chapter 1 discusses memory, we shall begin with it too.

The aim of the enquiry is to give a definition of memory.[71] This is the
obvious point of the first question. The second question is ambiguous: it
is not clear which cause is meant, and some of the interpreter's options
may be mentioned at this point. One might take the question, in a
broad sense, to refer to all the Aristotelian causes, i.e. form, matter,
end and moving cause.[72] Or one might restrict it to some of these and
relate it to the definition insofar as the definition explains memory. It
says *why* memory is what it is. The explanations for something, in
other words, its causes, are in the final analysis contained in its definition.
A standard Aristotelian enquiry asks the question: what is X, and the enquiry is finished when the question has been answered.[73] A further option
of dealing with the cause here is to restrict it to the moving cause, in the

---

active on the grounds that it is a state (ἕξις). But one may distinguish between an
active state and a capacity to be in that state (Metaph. V 20, cited by Bloch p. 75
but not used in his discussion of memory). Of course, ἕξις may be distinguished
from an activity as the disposition for an activity; but that is, as Bloch sees, not
the relevant sense of ἕξις. His view is connected to his understanding of μεμνῆσθαι on which see below fn. 432. μεμνῆσθαι is the presence of the (relevant) moving power (Ch. 2 452a10). This is to be understood as the capacity for memory.

71 449b4. Except in Sens. und De longaev. all of the PN define their subjects using
    causes; see above all those at the end of De juv. Ch. 23 (King 2001: 130–139).
    Sens. and De longaev. are not really exceptions; on the latter see King 2001: 94;
    perception has already been defined in De an. II 12 (and cf. II 5).
72 See Phys. II 3. On the theory of causes, see Sorabji 1980: 26–44.
73 Anal. Post. II 2 esp. 90a9–11. See Bolton 1987. It is controversial just how much
    of the theory of science or enquiries present in Anal. Post. agrees with what Ar-
    istotle himself actually does in his own investigations; cf. Lloyd 1990, Kullmann
    1974, 1998: 97–115, Barnes 1993: XIX-XX.

sense that we want to know what makes memory actually occur.[74] We can put this option on one side for the moment, and turn briefly to the last question.

The third and last question is answered quickly by Aristotle,[75] to the effect that only those beings remember that perceive time, and they do it with that capacity with which they perceive. This answer is reached through consideration of the objects of memory, past experiences in the life of the thing concerned. Because these are *past*, memory requires cognition of time, and this is a function of perception, and perception is, of course, one function of the soul. The soul, and its parts or capacities, are, I suggest, formal causes of memory; they are not matter but what determines matter. And we should note that matter is not mentioned at all, at least at this stage of the enquiry, as part of the explanation of memory.

The first question is also answered quickly, in a provisional fashion:

Provisional definition (PD): Therefore memory is neither perception nor conception but the possession or affection of one of these, when time has passed. 449b24–25

We will have to unpack this dense definition in detail. First, some preliminary remarks. The provisional definition is used to decide which "part" of the soul memory belongs to, that is to say what faculty are we using when we remember. Thus we also have in **PD** the answer to the third question concerning the part of the soul involved in memory. The path to this goal uses the objects of memory. Aristotle distinguishes here between three forms of cognition, all directed at objects characterised by their own modus of time: perception is of the present, expectation of the future and memory of the past.[76] Each is distinguished from the oth-

---

74 Cf. the formulation at 449b4: διὰ τίν᾽ αἰτίαν γίγνεται, "through which cause it comes about".

75 449b29–30.

76 A word about the way the objects of the three forms of cognition are specified: "The future", τὸ μέλλον, refers to what is going to happen, above all what one is going to do (Rhet. II 19 1393a1–5), thus it does not have to happen, in contrast to that which will be (in De gen. et corr. II 11 337b5–7: τὸ ἔσται, τὸ μέλλει, De divin. 2 463b28–31: τὸ ἐσόμενον, τὸ μέλλον); divination deals with the future (De somn. 1 453b22–23). For Aristotle's own, sceptical view of divination see De divin., esp. 1 462b12–26, 2 464a19–24, and van der Eijk 1994: 60 on Aristotle's results. See also EE VII 14 1248a34-b3. "The past" (τὸ γενόμενον), "the present" (τὸ παρόν); the latter expression is also used in contrast to what is absent e.g. what is past and so the object of memory (450a25–7, b12–15), cf. Rhet. I

ers by the temporal status of its objects. Here we have the real starting point of Aristotle's enquiry: What is the object of memory? As is usually pointed out, he is using a standard feature of his enquiries into the capacities of things:[77] we learn about capacities by investigating their activities, and these are related in turn to the objects concerned. The object is thus the first thing to be examined. Aristotle answers the question of the object of memory by appealing to the temporal aspect of memory: it relates to the past. Hence we remember that we perceived or learnt something.

The appeal to the past at this point has one great advantage. If a capacity is defined by its object, it might appear that memory is a confusing case, for many different kinds of things can be in one's memory, e.g. perceptions and conceptions are named in the **PD**. And conceptions (ὑπόληψις)[78] include opinions, scientific theorems, and propositions of prudence (i.e. practical wisdom).[79] So there is quite a variety of objects, which might be enough to vitiate the approach to a capacity *via* its objects. Aristotle's strategy aims at reducing this complexity by finding a common denominator for all the objects of memory, namely their rela-

---

11 1370a32−35, where three *modi* are listed and related as here to their forms of cognition.

77 De an. II 4 415a18−22, cf. 6 418a7−8, Wiesner 1985: 170.

78 ἐπιστήμη, δόξα, φρόνησις De an. III 3 427b24−26; I translate "conception" with Sorabji, Beare not "supposal" (Hamlyn in De an. III 3) or "judgement" Revised Oxford Translation in De an. III 3; the former suggests a supposition that one makes in the absence of information (cf. Rhet. III 16 1417b9−10); but that is not what is meant here. Rather it is a form of cognition, a conception of the way things *are* (cf. Wedin 1988: 103−106). Thus conception, in my use, includes an assertoric element. "Judgement" is a better translation insofar as it reveals the propositional structure. Conceptions can be true or false, and can be contrasted with science (Cat. 7 8b10−12) and as closely allied to opinion (EN VI 3 1139b17). Here, conception is parallel to perception as a way of grasping something, presumably in an articulate proposition (cf. Met. I 1 981a7−9). See Wedin 1988: 103−106 for the meaning of this term; Wedin translates "supposition", which is one meaning the term can bear, but is not suited to capturing the meaning it has as the generic term covering opinion, science and prudence.

The *Topics* (IV 5 125b17−19) quote the following definition of memory: 'Similarly if someone calls memory a disposition that preserves a conception (ἕξις καθεκτικὴ ὑπολήψεως); for memory is not a disposition but an activity.' In the context, the point is that someone puts something mistakenly in the genus *disposition* and not the genus *activity*. On κατοχή in Plotinus see below fn. 742.

79 De an. III 3 427b25−26.

tion to time. Without the temporal marker, nothing is an object of memory.

However, one might doubt whether there are particular objects of memory. In what way does it make sense to speak of the objects of memory (τὰ μνημονευτά)[80]? Obviously, they are not a special class of things taken independently of cognition. Rather, we are concerned with the objects (ἀντικείμενα) of the activity.[81] They are relative to the activity of remembering. A good comparison is with objects of deliberation. These are things in the power of the deliberator, about which one is in doubt how they will turn out. Thus they are relative to the deliberator and, naturally, in the future.[82] Parallel to this the object of memory is relative to the living thing whose memory it is. If I remember Theaetetus, then Theaetetus does not have to be "past" (whatever that might mean – dead?). Rather it is my perception of him that is past.[83]

We may distinguish between past perceptions[84] and perceptions earlier than now, in other words between a relational property and a quality[85] of a particular perception.[86] Insofar as I only remember things that are in *my* past, my perceptions, the perceptions need only have the relational property. That we can only remember things we have undergone ourselves[87] is assumed from the beginning of his theory. Such things occur earlier than now, and are perceived to be earlier than now.

The restriction of the objects of memory is one of the roots of the epistemological modesty of Aristotle's conception of memory. But Aristo-

---

80 Cf. 450a24, Rhet. I 11 1370b1.

81 De an. II 4 415a20.

82 EN III 3 1112a30–31, b2–7. De an. III 10 433b3–7 mentions the connection between deliberation and the perception of time; the latter is of course also present in memory.

83 Sorabji p. 13–14 criticises Aristotle's view which he thinks is mistaken in taking the thing to be past, whereas he allows that the "past cognition view", as he call it, is correct. However, Aristotle clearly shares the "past cognition view". See the Canonical Formula, below p. 32.

84 It would be more natural for us to speak of "experiences", but I stick with the translation of the Aristotelian term αἴσθησις, and reserve "experience" for his term ἐμπειρία.

85 Cf. ποῖα 449b9.

86 This alternative arises from the two different ways to conceive of temporal relations: namely in the A series (past, present, future) and the B series (before, after and simultaneous), as they have been known since MacTaggart (1927: II 33). Hence the thing remembered may be earlier than now (450a21), or past (449b15).

87 The self-memory problem, above, *Introduction* p. 2.

tle has reasons for this view that show that this definition is not a mere stipulation. The modesty of memory is rooted in the way we talk. We claim, he says, only to perceive things that are present, and when one is actually contemplating a mathematical object one would claim to know it, not remember it.[88] Clearly, these claims are to be seen within the general context of Aristotle's method which relies on the way we talk about things, "we" being either the many or the wise or both.[89]

I wish to attribute to Aristotle a version of what I will call "the argument from activity". The conclusion of this argument concerns the capacity involved in an activity. The premises are obtained from the person performing the activity. Ask Socrates what he is doing when he is doing geometry and he will tell you: doing geometry, not: I am remembering these geometrical figures. The argument from activity is designed to allocate activities to capacities. There is no explicit relation to a past perception in the content under consideration, when actually doing geometry. Hence there is no need for memory here. For theorems are always true, and have no relation to time.[90]

This is not to deny that doing geometry implies having learnt it; far from it. Aristotle developed his *triple scheme* to describe psychic faculties of this kind:

(1) changing from being able to learn geometry, to
(2) having learnt it but not actually using it and
(3) actually doing geometry.[91]

The argument from activity has far-reaching consequences. The broad conception of memory which includes all the information which we have acquired is excluded.[92] Rather, remembering only occurs when we have the object of perception or science in mind but without actually perceiving or contemplating ("without the activities").[93] I remember Theae-

---

88 449b15–18.
89 EN VII 1 1145b2–7, EE I 6 1216b26–36, on which see Scott 1995: 133–140.
90 Met. IX 10 1051b15–17. Theorems can be accidentally in our memory since we can remember learning them; see 450a13–14 and below p. 42.
91 See De an. II 5 417a21–417b2, III 4 429b5–10, cf. II 1 412a21–27, and Wedin 1988: 14–18. On De an. II 5, and the triple scheme see Burnyeat 2002: 48–57.
92 See *Introduction* p. 9.
93 449b19 reading ἄνευ τῶν ἐνεργειῶν. If one reads ἔργων then it would have to mean "function". This is clear from the fact that ἔργον does not mean "thing" for Aristotle (cf. Bonitz s.v. 2: it can mean work sc. of art or nature (e.g. EN I 1 1094a4, Part. An. I 1 639b20) – Bonitz translates with *opus*. And of course

tetus, but I am not perceiving him now; I remember that the sum of the angles of a triangle equals two right angles, but I am not doing geometry now.

This argument might, however, seem to confound two things that are profoundly different. Are not perception and knowing to be distinguished here? For they are surely related to memory in different ways. When Socrates remembers perceiving Theaetetus, then he does not perceive Theaetetus; but when he remembers that he knows something, then surely he knows it as well? Yes, but not actively; when he is remembering, then he is remembering, and not actively "contemplating" the object of knowledge.[94] If you ask him what he is doing, then the answer will be: remembering, not doing geometry. That is one point.

Another is that, in a sense, perception is also involved in actual remembering. For one also perceives the representation that is part of what is required in an act of memory.[95] Another argument for the same end would be that one has to perceive the time involved in memory. But this perception is neither the same perception e. g. of Theaetetus yesterday, nor indeed is it the same kind of perception, that is not the same actualisation of the capacity to perceive. Representation may be a function of perception, in that representations are perceived, as well as originating in perception, but it should not be confounded with the perception of external things.

How does Aristotle reach the **PD** of memory? Through the **Canonical Formula (CF)** for memory. I call this formula canonical, since it is

---

the point about perception is that there is no ἔργον beyond the ἐνέργεια (Met. IX 8 1050a25); and in De an. he uses ἔργα for ἐνέργειαι (compare ἔργα I 1 402b9–14, with ἐνέργειαι II 4 415a19) when discussing whether one should investigate capacities or activities first. On the identity between function and activity see Met. IX 8 1050a21–22: τὸ ἔργον τέλος, ἡ δὲ ἐνέργεια τὸ ἔργον. (Wiesner (1985: 173) follows Ross und Michael (7.12–13) in reading ἔργων, which he understand as "thing"; the idea that memory is of an absent thing (πρᾶγμα) gains support from 450a25–27).

94 449b17–18.
95 Representations are perceived: "when its change is actualised, if it is in its own right, then I perceive it thus and so, and it appears to occur like a thought or a representation" (450b27–30). Gregoric (2007: 107) suggests that active perception is a constituent of memory in that we can remember someone we see; this is his reason for denying that memory belongs to representation alone. Cf. below fn. 138.

the standard or canon guiding the investigation.[96] It is given immediately before the provisional definition, and provides evidence for the temporal character of memory:

Canonical Formula (CF) For always whenever someone is active with respect to remembering, then he says in this way in the soul that he heard this or perceived it or thought it before. 449b22–23

To begin at the beginning: "For" shows that the **CF** is derived from 449b18–21. Saying something in the soul is to be opposed to saying it out loud, and means that one entertains a thought, which has the form of an assertion.[97] This formula is non-technical, not (yet) formulated in Aristotelian terminology. It is an assertion about what we do in active remembering.

Aristotle thinks that animals other than man have memory, namely those that perceive time.[98] Time is mentioned here in the cognition that happened "before", and, as Aristotle remarks, the before and after are in time.[99] The formulation of the **CF** seems, however, to exclude animals other than man, since it would appear that they do not say (λέγειν) anything,[100] whether in the soul or not.[101] Obviously, Aristotle is thinking primarily of humans since only they learn (e.g. maths) and think.[102] So how can we generalise **CF** to include all animals with memory? What is needed is some way to bring together, in the act of memory, the content of a perception with a time. This can most clearly occur in an articulate utterance. But if animals are to perceive time (whatever quite this means)[103], then time has to be distinct from what is perceived at this time. A dog will have to know that the bone is not there now, and distinguish the present perception from the past one. In the later version

---

96 Labarrière (2000: 269, 275) calls the final definition "canonique", but of course in a different sense: it is naturally Aristotle's own, official view.

97 "Saying something in the soul" is a Platonic account of thinking (διανοεῖσθαι), that can lead to an opinion (δόξα); see *Theaetetus* 189E-190A, *Sophist* 263D-264A, and on δόξα *Philebus* 38E. Thus even this formulation, involving the soul is not simply put in purely Aristotelian terms.

98 449b28–30.

99 450a21–22.

100 On Aristotle's theory of language and animals see Wedin 1988: 152–156, and Ax 1978, Sorabji 1993: 7–16.

101 Sorabji pp. 10, 71 ad 449b30–450a25.

102 449b19–22.

103 See below p. 62–69.

generality is preserved, at least on the surface, by the formulation that "one in addition perceives (προσαισθάνεται) that one saw or heard something earlier";[104] the "saying in the soul" of the **CF** is replaced by "perceiving in addition".

Explaining **CF** is the business of *De memoria et reminiscentia:* when we have explained under what conditions the state of affairs described in **CF** occurs, then we have a definition of memory. This may sound as though there is a confusion between what memory is and its existence. But it has to be shown how memory as defined in the provisional definition can occur, by referring to the living thing, composed of body and soul. The final definition will combine the requirements of the **PD** with the basic elements of Aristotelian psychology.

The aim of the enquiry is therefore to determine what these conditions are, and so explain what active memory is. These are the conditions, which are sufficient for such a state of affairs, which we call being active with one's memory, to obtain.[105] We can expect this explanation to use Aristotle's causes.

---

104 450a19–21. Gregoric (2007: 99) sees these lines as "an elucidation of what the perception of time amounts to", and takes this to be not the "awareness of the passage of time" but the "awareness of the temporal relation in which things experienced in the past stand to the subject in the present." While I agree that perception of time has this restricted meaning in De mem., I do not think the purpose of these lines is to elucidate this concept, but rather that of memory itself. It may be, however, that Gregoric sees this perception of time as identical with memory (p. 100: "The perception of time is constitutive of memory because we remember something only when we are aware that the thing currently present to our mind has been experienced before", cf. e.g. p. 105 when discussing the grasp of time at 450a9–14, he identifies this with the perception of time discussed at 450a19, and says that this is "constitutive of memory"; also p. 109 referring to these lines and 449a28–30; but of course, as he knows (see p. 106 on 452b23–9), awareness of time does not exhaust memory even if it is one constituent of it; the lines 450a19–21 are not restricted to the perception of time but also specify the content of memory.) Furthermore, Aristotle's argument (449b28–30) that only those animals can remember that can perceive time would be severely hampered if these two activities were identical. Finally, I can perceive time without remembering anything (see below p. 62 ff). While Gregoric (2007: 99) does wish to distinguish between perception of time in De mem. and the cognition of time generally speaking, it is not clear how he picks out just that grasp of time he wishes to identify with memory in a non-question begging way.

105 If we are looking for the necessary conditions of memory, we can contrast them with the five conditions of memory given in the *Phaedo*, above *Introduction* p. 15.

But what about the definition of memory? This is the question with which the treatise opens. The definition may be explanatory; but as we have seen, we have also already had a provisional definition. So we are aiming at a final definition having started from a provisional one. Let us now look at **PD** again:

PD Therefore memory is neither perception nor conception but the possession or modification of one of these, when time has passed. 449b24–25

This provisional definition uses Aristotelian terminology to express what he takes to be implied in the **CF**, which does not use technical terms. The provisional definition is argued for ("therefore") from the **CF**.

How can we understand the progress of the enquiry as a whole? The explanation will be concerned with showing how the content of the definition can exist in a living thing. The **PD** says what memory is; but this can only be valid if Aristotle can show that memory, understood in such a way, can actually occur. That is to say, he must give us an account showing that the conditions necessary for its existence are present in living things. We may compare here the enmattered formulae:[106] anger takes place in such and such matter, and must do so if it is to exist. Once that has been shown, the definition has been justified. There is thus a close connection between what something is and the requirements for its existence.

The **PD** is not simple to grasp, firstly, in that alternatives are offered, and secondly, in that the terms used to express them are ambiguous. In the provisional definition, there are four possibilities for what memory is, depending on how we combine each of the two alternatives in the **PD**, possession,[107] affection,[108] perception, conception:

---

106 Above p. 21.
107 449b25. These alternatives are mentioned also 451a23–24, 27–28. "Possession" translates ἕξις (Met. V 20 1022b4–10); an alternative translation would be "state" (cf. 1022b10): memory is the state a perception or a conception is in after time has passed. This possibility is very close to the idea that memory is an affection (or modification) of perception, in other words the other possibility that Aristotle mentions here. Taking memory as a state of perception reminds one of the decaying sense view of representation, which Aristotle mentions in the *Rhetoric* (representation is a weak perception; see below in main text) is to be rejected because he does not think that a memory is simply a perception or conception that has changed its state, as it were, grown weaker in time; rather

PDa1 the possession of perception when time has passed

PDa2 the affection of perception when time has passed

PDb1 the possession of conception when time has passed

PDb2 the affection of conception when time has passed

At first sight, the formulations in terms of possession, PDa1 and PDb1, seem straightforward: you have a perception or a conception and you keep it.[109] That is, you remember it. This reminds one of the Platonic formulation that memory is the preservation of perception.[110] One might reformulate this view by saying that Socrates remembers seeing Theaetetus when he has, or "possesses" this perception, stored as it were. But clearly we do not know what is required "to possess a perception", let alone "to possess a conception".

The situation is even less clear with the formulations in terms of affection (πάθος). In some sense, what this might mean is that perception undergoes (πάσχειν) a modification; it is affected in some way. But this only helps us some of the way. For if memory is the modification of perception or conception, and this is taken to mean that something happens to the perception or conception, then we must ask just what happens to it. One might try to answer the question using a celebrated formulation from the *Rhetoric*.[111] Representation is a weak perception, that is to say,

---

it has to be related by the activity of the remembering agent to the original experience. This is reflected in the **Final Definition**, which uses the word ἕξις also, but clearly in the sense of "possession". **Provisional** and **Final Definitions** must use the term in the same sense. All of the passages which use the term can be interpreted in this sense (Ch. 2 451a23–24, 27–28, 451b3).

108 See above p. 20.

109 Cf. also the distinction made in Ch. 2 451a29–30 between science or affection and memory: the latter is only present when time has passed.

110 Cf. on the *Philebus*, *Introduction* p. 18, and cf. p. 24.

111 I 11 1370a28–29. For the decay through time as a change cf. Hobbes (Hobbes translated the *Rhetoric* into English, of course, so the origin of his doctrine can hardly be doubted) Leviathan Part I Ch. 2 (Tuck Cambridge 1996 ed. p. 16): "As at a great distance of place, that which we look at appears dimme, and without distinction of the smaller parts; and as Voyces grow weak, and inarticulate: so also after great distance of time, our imagination of the past is weak…This decaying sense, when wee would express the thing it selfe, (I mean *fancy* it self,) wee call imagination, as I said before: But when we would express the decay, and sig-

time affects my perception in such a way that it becomes weaker, and then I have representation. But obviously a weak representation does not give us memory for a number of reasons. For, as we have seen, using our example, something has to be done at the time of actually remembering (t2), for the activity to count as memory. And a further, decisive, problem is that this account does not fit the case of a conception. Theaetetus' opinion that Socrates is good does not become weaker when he has it in his memory.[112] And of course, as with remembering a perception, Theaetetus has to do something, when remembering this opinion.

When considering the many possibilities offered by the provisional definition, we must, I think, keep in mind the fact that at this stage we are dealing with a provisional definition. The **Final Definition** will have to be less ambiguous; will have to come down in favour of one formulation. This implies that, in the rest of the enquiry into memory, we will get an explanation of what is required for this definition to be instantiated. This points to the direction the enquiry will take: the functions of living things, their capacities and the realisations of these capacities form the body of the investigation. In the course of the enquiry we will see how a perception has to be modified, and how it has to be "possessed" for it to count as a memory; and so too for a conception. This is a plea for saying that in the formulation on offer here "possession or affection" are alternative ways of saying the same thing.[113] Perceptions and conceptions are possessed, and they are altered in the course of being used to remember with. That is to say, they are not affected merely by the passage of time; they are affected by being made part of an act of memory. And if we want to know more about what it means for them to be possessed and affected, well, we just need to read on. As already indicated, the **Provisional Definition** looks forward to a **Final Definition**. And in fact, the **Final Definition** (451a15 – 16) is phrased in terms of possession, not affection[114]; one way of reading *affection* in the **PD** might be to say that it is the affection that lies in the act of remembering: one has to regard the representation that remains from the perception or that bears the opinion in a certain way and so modify it.

---

nifie that the sense is fading, old and past, it is called *Memory*. So that Imagination and Memory are but one thing, which for divers considerations hath divers names."

112 An answer to this objection might be that the conception does not become weaker, but the representation does, on which entertaining the belief depends.

113 Cf. Bloch 2007: 81, n. 126.

114 Below p. 81.

So much for the ambiguities of affection and possession. It is not clear how perception and conception are to be cashed out here. Both are ambiguous. The following are some possibilities for perception,[115] with sight as the example:

seeing pale
seeing that the pale is Socrates
seeing pale Socrates
seeing that Socrates moves

Obviously, the conceptual richness of perception varies greatly between these possibilities. But still we are dealing with conceptual cognition all along; this is the reason one is justified *in all cases* in translating Aristotle's notion of αἴθησις *perception*. It is to be expected that the memory will vary in its conceptual richness depending on the perception concerned. A further problem arises from this list, namely that whilst it is clear that all conceptions (opinion, knowledge and prudence)[116] are propositional in structure, only some perceptions[117] are. As we have seen from the **PD**, memory is propositional in character, and we have to see which perceptions can be remembered. For example does it make sense to say: 'I remember pale'? Clearly, those animals that cannot speak but can remember will do something else than speak when actively remembering. Clearly, if their only form of cognition is perception, then what they do when remembering is perception; more precisely, as we have seen, they perceive in addition that the perception is past[118] using their perceptive capacity to represent things to themselves. And what they do in the final analysis, as we will see in the **Final Definition**,[119] is to perceive representations as being images of what they represent.

Perception has a variety of possible objects for Aristotle,[120] and paleness belongs to the simplest form, the special objects of the senses, e. g. colour for vision. Hence we started with such an attribute, paleness, in our consideration of what the possession of a perception might mean. But obviously, there are other forms of perception besides the special ob-

---

115 Taken from De an. II 6, III 1, III 3.
116 Above p. 28.
117 Thomas Johansen suggests to me that in fact most perceptions can be regarded as propositional, with references to De an. 418a15, 428b21. This is of course a very weak claim.
118 450a19–21, above p. 93.
119 Below p. 81.
120 De an. II 6, III 1.

jects of perception, especially the common objects of perception, that is, those that belong to more than one form of perception, such as unity, number, movement, extension and figure.[121] This form of perception is related in two ways to memory. On the one hand, of course, the perceptions of such things can be remembered, as it were incidentally, if they are made to play a role in a proposition (I remember that there were three trees by the house); on the other hand, they relate to time insofar as time is perceived and is connected to magnitude and motion.[122] For it would seem that just as one can hear or see something move, so one can hear or see some regular motion serving to measure time. And, as we have seen from the start of *De memoria et reminiscentia*,[123] the perception of time is a prerequisite for memory. We will have to discuss the relation between common perception and memory in more detail when we come to the perception of time.

The third and final form of perception is what Aristotle calls incidental perception.[124] Perception of the particular objects and perception of the common objects of perception are both direct (*per se*); as such, these things are objects of perception. In contrast, individuals can be perceived accidentally, insofar as the attributes that belong to them are perceived. Indeed, perception is particularly connected with individuals, as opposed to scientific knowledge, which is linked to universals.[125] But the individual is not perceived as such, merely accidentally, namely insofar as it is qualified in a certain way.[126] The important thing is that the object of perception, and hence of the memory of this perception, is an object localised in space, and perceived at a certain time. Mention of Coriscus as an object of memory[127] shows that it is the individual *via* the perception of him that is remembered, and not simply the representation, as it were, taken on its own, as a simple psychological datum. It is of course a crucial question how this transition is possible, and this is

---

121 De an. II 6 418a17–20, III 1 425a14–21; see for example Welsch 1987: 307–380, Brunschwig 1996.
122 Phys. IV 11 219a12–13, 12 220b24–26.
123 Above p. 27.
124 The classic treatment is Cashdollar 1973.
125 De an. II 5 417b22–23, Anal. Post. I 31 87b28–39, Met. XII 10 1087a15–21. See Wedin 1988: 202–8, Scott 1995: 152–6.
126 De an. II 12 424a21–24.
127 450b31; notice also the formulation at 450b12–15.

part of what I called "the present-past problem" (**P2**) in the *Introduction*.[128]

So much for perception and memory. The **PD** says that memory is the possession or affection of a perception or a conception. What we have now done is to review the variety of objects which can be perceived, and hence serve as objects of memory. We shall return to the subject when we come to consider representation and memory. For representations are derived from actual perceptions. We may thus hope that discussion of representation will show more clearly what it means for a perception to be modified or possessed.

Memory of a conception here may refer to any or all of the three kinds of conception that Aristotle recognises, namely, opinion, science and prudence.[129] Thus we might remember, for example, that we had an opinion, had entertained such and such a theorem, or that such and such an act was brave. The connection with time, which lies at the heart of this passage, is one of the questions that arise here. For clearly opinions and judgements of prudence may be connected to time by their content; they concern particular things that change.[130] This is not the case with science, which is concerned with universals.

Our sixth problem concerned the exclusion of universals from memory.[131] It would appear in the **CF** that the understanding of memory here is one according to which I can remember having thought something.[132] Obviously, it remains possible that it is not the content that is linked with time but rather the act of thinking it, and this through aspects incidental to this act, on this reading. It is primarily the thinking, rather than the thought as such that is remembered. Nothing prevents one from remembering concepts, in Aristotle's view, but one only remembers them accidentally. For as such they are not temporally marked. One might instead remember (the circumstances surrounding) learning a concept, or perceiving an instance falling under a concept.[133] Possession of a concept is not, as we have seen, a matter of remembering it; but of having learnt it. This was one point of the triple scheme.[134]

---

128 Above p. 1–2.
129 On "conception" see above p. 28.
130 EN VI 6 1141b9–18.
131 See *Introduction* p. 3.
132 449b23.
133 Ch. 1 449b17–18 450a13–14, 450a23–25, 450b20–22, 2 451a28–29; cf. Wiesner 1998: 126, Michael 22.17–19.
134 Above p. 30.

What have we achieved in this section? The aim of Aristotle's enquiry is the definition of memory. This is to be accomplished using the causal factors responsible for memory occurring. These factors relate to living things, persisting through time and endowed with perception. These are two aspects of the modesty of memory, its dependence on persisting things and on their perception. Memory is distinguished from other kinds of cognition by its object, namely something past: it is related to past perception or past conceptions. He finds this view of memory in our way of attributing memory to people, when they actually remember. He encapsulates the view in the **Canonical Formula**, which in turn he translates into his own technical terms in the **Provisional Definition**: memory is possession or affection of a conception or perception after time has passed.

What remains to be done is to show how time is grasped, and how, after time has passed, the original perception can still be available (our P2). In order to answer the question of how memory requires time we have first to ask how representation is part of the explanation of memory. Aristotle uses the objects of memory to establish the part of the soul responsible for memory, namely the perceptive part. This in turn is responsible for representations.

2.1.3 Memory and representation

Representation, φαντασία, enters *De memoria et reminiscentia* to begin with through Aristotle's approach to the question of what part of the soul is responsible for memory. His answer to this question is based, in part, on consideration of the subjects of memory: animals other than humans have memory, namely those that perceive time, and these animals only perceive, and do not think, therefore their memory must also be (a function of) perception.[135] The following section gives reasons for thinking that memory, even that of thoughts is a function of the percep-

---

135 449b28–30. This line of thought provides support for Wedin's contention that φαντασία is not a faculty for Aristotle. Wedin (1988: 45–57) takes this claim to mean, inter alia, that there are no specific objects of φαντασία: he shows that the investigation of φαντασία does not follow the lines laid down in *De an.* II 4 for the investigation of faculties. The fact that φαντασία is not a faculty in its own right means I take it that any cognitive capacities that it confers are inherited from perception, above all conceptual content.

tive system in the form of representation.[136] This very difficult section is of great general interest for the insights which it offers into the way in which Aristotle conceives of thought and representation. We will be asking primarily what its consequences are for our understanding of representation in the context of memory.

Representation serves many functions for Aristotle: it is a kind of hinge between perception and thought, something that remains from perception, and, in perceiving things, is able and necessary to support the thought of abstractions. It is to the discussion of this function in *De anima* that Aristotle refers, in *De memoria et reminiscentia*, when he has discussed the object of memory.[137] In order to understand the fundamental role that representation plays in the investigation of memory, we will have to go beyond this function of representation, and consider what Aristotle thinks representation is quite generally. As we shall see, representation forms a central part of the **Final Definition** of memory. Two fundamental aspects of memory will be illuminated by this dependence on representation. Firstly, the question of the relation between memory and change, and hence the relation of memory to the body. Secondly, the question of the extent to which images and concepts are responsible for memory.

Let us now turn to the passage in which representation is introduced into *De memoria et reminiscentia*.[138]

---

136 449b30–450a14. On this passage, see the excellent treatment by Wiesner 1985.

137 Ch. 1 449b30 referring to De an. III 7 431a16–7, 431b2 and 8 432a10 (cf. Wiesner 1985: 181).

138 My interpretation follows Wiesner 1985: esp. 186–7, in the account of the three steps in the passage. Gregoric (2007: 101–107), who does not mention Wiesner 1985 in the discussion of this passage, presents a version of the argument preserving the order of the text at 450a10–13: he thinks time is grasped, i. e. perceived not by imagination, but by the more general capacity comprising both imagination (i. e. φαντασία), which according to his interpretation is referred to by the phrase "common sense" both at 450a10 and at PA IV. He thinks this because perception of time, i. e. in his view memory, may be not only of things imagined, but also of things perceived: "I can see a person on the street and realize that I've met that person before; or I can imagine a certain person and know that I have met that person before." (p.107) But the grasp of time here is one thing, and the perception of the person another. The former is a matter of imagination, the latter of perception. I see Socrates and remember him; my seeing him is not part of my remembering him. On the perception of time, see also Veloso-Rey 2005.

The first step[139] is to show how all thoughts require representation, to offer a basis for abstraction. Aristotle uses a comparison with the process of drawing a geometrical diagram, where one abstracts from the exact magnitude. So too in thinking of magnitudes. And even the thought of things with no magnitude requires magnitudes, Aristotle thinks. However, they are not thought of *as* magnitudes. Thus the latter, magnitudes serving as the basis for thinking of things without magnitudes, are also abstracted from.[140]

The second step[141] is to show how magnitudes and changes are grasped by the same thing[142] as time. They are grasped using representations. Since representation is a function of common perception, the cognition of these three things (time, change, magnitude) is a function of the primary perceptive capacity.[143]

The third step[144] applies this argument to memory, both that of thoughts and that of perceptions. Both are functions of perception, although the memory of thoughts is accidentally a function of the capacity to think.[145] In this way, Aristotle can allow that animals other than humans, which have no capacity to think, may have memory.

What does this argument allow us to conclude about representations? One line of thought which may exercise a certain attraction is the follow-

---

139 449b30–450a9.

140 Aristotle does not talk of "abstraction", restricting himself to νοῦς and its cognates. On the separation of νοῦς from magnitude, cf. De an. III 4 429b10–22.

141 450a9–12; the question why time is necessary to think things is posed and postponed here (a7–9) by Aristotle, but not answered anywhere in the *Corpus*.

142 ᾧ line 450a10. Wiesner (1985: 185) sees that as being the φάντασμα also mentioned in that line. But I see no reason not to think that it is the capacity, i.e. the primary sense faculty in lines 11–12; obviously it will not (always) be the numerically same φαντάσματα with which time, change and magnitude are grasped. Cf. Gregoric (2007: 105) says that the passage not say strictly that time, magnitude and change are all grasped by the same thing, but it assumes that time is grasped by one thing, and then says change and magnitude must be grasped by the same thing. This is a stronger claim than the usual reading of these lines, and implies that reading.

143 Sorabji p. 74–5 finds a second argument in 450a9–14 for attributing memory to the representative faculty, namely that memory relies on an image of the thing remembered and this is a function of the imagination, i.e. the representative capacity. In fact, this argument is not used in the present passage. It plays an important role in the **Final Definition** (below p. 81). Gregoric 2007: 99–111 argues that the order of the *textus receptus* should be kept in lines 450a10–13.

144 450a12–14.

145 Reading 450a13 τοῦ νοητικοῦ with ms. P.

ing. One could think that by *representation* Aristotle means pictures of the thing concerned because he starts from a diagram, and says that what happens in thought is the same affection (πάθος) as in drawing a diagram.[146] Thus, on this reading, when he talks of thinking things without magnitude, he is saying that to think the concept 'lion' we need a picture of a lion,[147] from which we abstract to gain the necessary generality. A line of thought like this would offer support for the view that what is meant here by φαντάσματα are images. I think this reading is much too restrictive. Representations may be images, but need not be, for example that kind relevant to dreams; but Aristotle's net is cast much more widely. He nowhere equates φαντάσματα with images; this simple textual fact places the burden of proof on those who think that he does in fact subscribe to this equation.[148]

The main thing to be found in this passage is the thought that representations are magnitudes, in which the objects of thought are present to the thinker. As we shall see, representations are changes in perceiving things. This is Aristotle's answer to what representations are. Thus these changes may occur in the perceiving things and serve a variety of functions, and take a variety of forms. They may serve memory without being a picture of what was perceived and is now being remembered. The fact that representation is a function of perception should not lead us to make the mistake of thinking that what we are doing is engaging in a form of inner perception, like external perception, but inside us. Indeed, Aristotle does talk of perceiving φαντάσματα,[149] but one need not think that every function of perception is on the same level; one need not confuse perceptions of my own states and affections with that of those external to me. For one thing, imagination is in my power – I can activate it or not; and that is not true in the case of perception.

With regards to any pictorial presentation of concepts, although one certainly does need the presentation of the way in which the concept can be applied to an individual, an image is ill-suited to perform this task. For a start, images, on their own, are not propositional in character, and

---

146 See above p. 20.
147 See esp. the language of "placing a magnitude before one's eyes" (450a5), and cf. De an. III 3 427b18–20. Wiesner (1985: 181–2) follows Michael's account (9.3–15) of how the φαντασία serves as a πίναξ for νοῦς: the latter understands the φαντάσματα as impressions; the generality of νοῦς arises from the τύποι of perception.
148 For example, Bloch 2007: 64 simply asserts this.
149 E.g. Ch. 1 450b16–18.

therefore do not include the instructions of how to apply concepts needed to make assertions. Such an instruction might be, for example: "use the concept of a lion only if the animal is such and such." Aristotle does say, in an important text from *De anima*,[150] that φαντασία is different from assertion and denial; since truth and falsity consist in the combination of thoughts (νοήματα).

So if representations are magnitudes necessary for thoughts, just what are representations? The passage in *De memoria et reminiscentia* under discussion does not tell us. As already mentioned, Aristotle refers us to the treatment of representation in *De anima*. Despite the fact that this reference may be to later parts of the treatment,[151] let us turn to the main discussion in III 3.[152] For it would seem that only there will we get an explanation of the nature of representation. Only then will we be able to explain its role in memory.

As any reader of Aristotle's treatment of φαντασία, representation, will realise, there are many different mental phenomena which he is trying to account for.[153] Representation is, in its terminological use, the capacity, and what this capacity produces are φαντάσματα.[154] What are

---

150 III 7 432a7–14.

151 See above note 137. In fact, the dependency of thought on representation is noted at 427b14–16, part of the introduction to the main treatment in III 3. The dependency of representation on perception is further emphasised by the order of exposition (perception: II 5-III2, representation III 3), and is directly relevant to the explanation of memory insofar as memory recurs to a perception by means of the remains of that perception.

152 In later chapters of Book III the connection between φαντασία and the motion of living things is discussed. See esp. 7 431b2–10, 10–19, 10 433a10–14. Practical aspects of memory are only touched on in De mem.; hence the practical role of representation is also peripheral to our concerns.

153 I follow Wedin's suggestion (1988:24–30) that there is a central theory in the third part of De an. III 3 esp. in the lines 428b10–17 which is meant to explain the phenomena, especially those noted in the second part (427b16–428b10).

154 De an III 3 428a1–5, Wedin 1988: 46–49, Morel p. 39, and see 449b30–31, 450b10 and cf. 450a31–32. φαντάσματα are sometimes called φαντασίαι e. g. 425b25, 428a12, 433a11, 27. On φαντασία in Aristotle see Freudenthal 1863, Nussbaum 1978: Essay 2, Welsch 1987: 381–8, Modrak 1987: 81–110, Wedin 1988, Schofield 1992, Frede 1992, Caston 1996, 1998: 269–86, Rapp 2001. The translation "representation" is preferable to "imagination", for a number of reasons. Firstly, in standard English "imagination" means a creative ability; and this is of course not meant (cf. Schofield 1992: 251). One might use the word to mean the power to produce mental images. But again this is unsatisfactory, since there is no reason to think that all φαντασία is concerned with

φαντάσματα? One possible translation is: "images", another might be "appearances" or "apparitions". Because Aristotle wishes to exclude a metaphorical use of φαντασία without saying what this is, commentators have wished to exclude either images or appearances from his treatment.[155] It must, I think, be admitted that he is concerned with both mental images and the way in which things may appear to me. The famous example of the sun appearing a foot across shows his interest in the latter;[156] and the fact that dreams are to be explained by reference to φαντασία demonstrates his concern for the former. Both of these aspects are captured, at least to some degree, by the idea of representations. For we can say that things present themselves to me in such and such a way, and dreams may be taken to represent things. Hence the translation used here for both the capacity and its products.[157] It is of course another question whether these aspects can be explained satisfactorily by Aristotle's treatment; there is no need for us to answer this question here in all its generality. All we need to do is to take the resources from *De anima* that Aristotle appeals to for the account of memory.

A large part of the treatment there is purely negative, and has the purpose of showing that representation is distinct from those capacities by which we are right and wrong about the way things are (opinion, science, and prudence).[158] The positive part of the treatment aims to show that

---

mental images. See Lycos 1964, Nussbaum 1978: 241–55, Caston 1996: esp. 50–2, Schofield 1992: esp. 264–71, Frede 1992: 279 f., 285, Rapp 2001: 79, Lefebvre 1997, Labarrière 2000: 269, fn. 1, plumps for 'representation' but Morel p. 38–39 chooses 'imagination', on the grounds that this is more of an activity. I do not see that this argument is enough to exclude representation; for representing things requires doing something.

155 Schofield (1992: 252–253) remarks that images are not the focus of attention in the sections of III 3 in which the connection with perception is established (428b10–429a10), so too Burnyeat 2008a: n. 15, Hicks 1907: 460 ad 428a1 comes to the opposite conclusion; Wedin 1988: 64–71 argues against Schofield; Nussbaum 1978: 252–4 follows Freudenthal 1863: 30 in allowing both senses and excluding "show" or "pomp" as the metaphorical use. I follow Nussbaum and Freudenthal.

156 De an. III 3 428b2–4, De ins 1 458b29, 2 460b18.

157 Thomas Johansen has insisted to me that the fit between representation and φαντασία is less than perfect: for of course in modern parlance perception and thought may be counted kinds of representation, and they are not φαντάσματα, although they may require it. I stick to my view that *representation* is a good term to capture crucial functions of φαντασία.

158 427b27–428b9.

representation can arise from perception.[159] The following argument provides the starting point:

one thing that undergoes change changes another thing;[160]
representation is a change or change of a kind;[161]
therefore representation can be a change remaining from actual perception.[162]

The argument is reflected in the concluding definition of representation:

[Representation] is a change which arises from actual perception.[163]

The kind of change is not specified, that is, whether it is alteration, locomotion or change in quantity.[164] This leaves the interpreter with a variety of possibilities. For, in the last analysis, saying that we are dealing with changes cannot be enough, as changes that are just changes and not also changes of a specific kind presumably do not exist. Such an answer would be provisional, at best. There are two options one might consider, and they are not mutually exclusive.

Firstly, we might conclude that we are dealing with changes of a kind,[165] and interpret this change in terms of *De anima* II 5.[166] There

---

159 428b10–429a9.
160 Thus even when the mover, the perception has finished, its effect may continue. The commentators standardly refer to Phys. VIII 5 256a4, but see Ins. 2 459a28-b23, where he postulates a similar process for the transport of perceptions, as a kind of alteration, to that which happens when locomotion is passed between bodies. Cf. the theory of throwing Ph. VIII 10 266b28, Cael. III 2 301b23–30 used in the theory of recollection (Mem. 2 453a19–28) and dreams (Ins. 459a23–459b7, cf. also Div. 464a6).
161 428b11. He says that representation is taken to be (δοκεῖ) "a change or a kind of change". Aristotle does not say: by whom. The remark is mysterious since the only person, as far as we know, who had even the rudiments of a theory of representation was Plato, and he does not say that representation is a kind of change (but cf. Laws X 896E on the kinds of psychic change; memories (μνῆμαί) feature among them at 896D).
162 III 3 428b10–11.
163 III 3 429a1–2.
164 The four kinds of change are specified in Phys. III 1 and V 1; in the context of the psychology, see also De an. I 3 406a12–13, and the soul as cause of the various forms of change II 4 415b21–28.
165 τις alienans. (See e. g. Goodwin 1894: §1016, p. 217–8: "τις sometimes implies that the word to which it is joined is not to be taken in its strict meaning"; he gives as an example *Republic* 334A10.) A major weakness of this alternative is

the triple scheme is used[167] to distinguish two ways of changing. The first way consists in changing from a privation (not-smooth) to the acquisition of a new property (smooth). The second way consists in exercising a capacity that has already been acquired through changing in the first way. The first way refers primarily to the biological development of the subject.[168] Now, we might want to fit representations into this scheme by saying that they exemplify the second way of changing.

An alternative move would be to see Aristotle leaving the terms of reference of his *Physics* and adopting a concept of mental change. The formulation "representative changes" in *De insomniis*[169] might suggest such a move. The first move, interpreting representation as change of a kind, in the sense of the exercise of an acquired capacity, is only as helpful as it is in the case of perception;[170] and as the ongoing debate shows[171] it has not been possible to reach a real consensus about Aristotle's view of the role of matter and change in perception. It is very difficult to say if there is some particular material change underlying perception, or if perception is only a change of a different kind. The lack of consensus is perhaps not surprising. For saying that something belongs to a class such as change *only in a way* is only informative, when we say in what way it is a change.[172]

Even in the absence of clarity about the way we are to understand representation as a change, something is gained by taking it as a change. We can explain what happens in representation, at least in the sense of pointing at the events that go to make it up. The changes in question only occur in living things which perceive, and in fact are restricted in their causes to those things which are perceived, because not all the changes happening in a perceiver have to do with its being a perceiver. This is perhaps a modest restriction, as we do not really know what the changes are. But some general things can be said about change. Change is a reality (ac-

---

that the τις occurs only in the introductory passage (428b11), and not in the final definition 429a1–2; on the difficulties with the final definition see esp. Wedin 1988: 28–30.

166 Cf. Wedin's (1988: 14–18) use of II 5 as a "Framework passage" for psychology in general; on this chapter see Burnyeat 2002.

167 See above p. 30.

168 De an. II 5 417b16–18.

169 462a8–9.

170 Cf. II 5 esp. 417b14–19.

171 See esp. Burnyeat 1992, 1995, 2002, Johansen 1997, Sorabji 1974, 1992, Nussbaum Putnam 1992, Everson 1997: esp. 10–11, 58–60, Caston 2005.

172 For a plea that it is relative change that is meant, see Burnyeat 1995.

tuality)[173] with causal efficacy. The efficacy of change means that it can propagate itself under the right conditions and pass change on. Change is incomplete *reality*, so that even before it is bound into a function or an action, realising an end, it is something that exists. Furthermore, since it exists, but has not yet attained the end of the action but can do, it explains the possibility of failure; and change requires matter that can change from being such and such to being thus and so.[174] This last point is not really new; in fact it amounts to the following tautology: since soul is the actuality of a body, then anything that occurs in the body insofar as it has a soul will also require body. But we can ask precisely how the general dependency on body is to be understood in this particular case. Actual perception requires organs, so representation requires body, because it arises from actual perception. But one cannot without further ado draw conclusions from this about the existence or nature of the changes in the living thing that might then be identical to or correlated with the representative change.

The fact that changes are incomplete reality needs a little explaining. As long as the change is occurring it has not reached its end. Being for change is, in Aristotle's view, essentially connected to its end. Yet the change is only as long as it has not reached its end: on reaching the end it is no longer. Hence change is, as such, incomplete. So much for incomplete reality. What about function and change? If a change serves a function, this function will only then be performed when the change is complete, as, for example, the building is complete, when the changes leading to its completion have been finished.[175] And while every change, except the eternal motion of the heavens, comes to an end, at some time, in some way, it need not end in the way requisite for a given function to be fulfilled.

These are all useful things for a theory of representation to explain; let us recapitulate briefly, using an example. Socrates sees pale Theaetetus,

---

173 Mentioned both in II 5 417a16: "actuality of a kind, but incomplete", with a reference to the *Physics*, and in III 7 431a6. See the definition of change Phys. III 1 201b4–5. For change as something that exists, see also Met IX 3 1047a32-b1. On this aspect of Aristotle treatment, the rescue of change from the status of non-being, see Brague 1990: esp. 8–12.

174 See below p. 125 on Plotinus' use of first and second potentiality from De an. II 5. The main point is that of course Plotinus wants to ensure that the soul does not change and he thinks that by using alteration of a kind, he can have mental activity without physical realisation.

175 EN X 4 1174a23–29.

and a change, arising from the actual perception, remains in him. Thus something remains after the time of the original perception. The point of talking about representation is that there is some representation in the perceiver of that which he perceived. And such remains of perception might serve to explain a dream, for example, or the ability to recognise Theaetetus. There are, however, limits to Aristotle's explanation, in terms of physiology, for example, where his explanation is perfunctory in the extreme. Not only that, but the way in which a change can be a representation is not even considered problematic.[176] Perhaps one should take this to mean that for Aristotle it is simply a fact of nature that certain changes in certain living things, ones that perceive, and do so in a fairly sophisticated way[177] are just representations.

Representations are changes and provide at least part of the explanation of memory. They explain in part why it occurs. Before going on to discuss further aspects of the theory of representation, it is worth asking what kind of explanation they provide for memory. We have seen that there are three questions that Aristotle asks at the start of the treatise and one of them is about the cause of memory.[178] And if memory involves a change then this cause might be the moving cause of memory. Admittedly, representation does not seem to fit the usual way of understanding a moving cause, the way a father causes a child by setting a process in motion, or suchlike.[179] Rather, a representation explains memory in the way a moving cause does, in the sense that it is a cause that itself moves or changes (intransitively). We need to specify more closely the way that this moving cause explains. Part of the story is clearly that change can be transmitted; in other words, the change that is representation is preserved by transmission, as it were passing on change to other matter. An example for the failure of transmission is the way in which changes in the living thing can destroy the potential for memory.[180] But transmission of change, even in a thing that perceives and in relation

---

176 For some modern speculations on this and related subjects see Shields 1995, Caston 1998: 262–3.

177 Some animals appear not to have representations (428a10–11). Caston 1996: 44 argues against taking this text to mean that Aristotle endorses this view.

178 See above p. 26.

179 See *Physics* II 3 195a21; the examples are seed, doctor, adviser and, in general, the agent.

180 See below p. 73 on flux.

to some thing that it has perceived,[181] is clearly not a sufficient condition
for memory – otherwise memory and representation would be the same.
It is not the case that memory comes about simply because one is moved
by a representation, because several other factors have to come together.
This is true too of other cases of moving causes, such as the father causing
the child as formal cause. In that case, there is a final cause and a material
cause as well:[182] Aristotelian explanation is always multicausal, even if, of
course, not all causes need be involved in all cases. So it would seem at
least plausible to see representations as one cause of memory, and to identify this cause as the moving cause. However, one still has to leave room
for the other causes. So the precise reference of the second introductory
question cannot be just to the moving cause alone.

The material cause is not mentioned here explicitly, but one should
bear in mind that both change and the soul imply that we are also dealing
with bodies:[183] change requires a body as something which can change
between the termini of change and soul is the primary activity of an organic body.[184] And all of the phenomena discussed in *Parva Naturalia* require body and soul.[185] For the modern eye, something may seem to be
missing: Why does Aristotle not ask about the relevant part of the
body?[186] The part of the body in which the part of the soul responsible
for memory is situated is merely mentioned, and it is the central organ.
This is to be identified with the primary perceptive part (πρῶτον
αἰσθητικόν), involved in the production of representations.[187] Memory
is described using perceptions, which happen "in the soul and in the
part of the body which contains the soul"[188]. Recollection is described
as being bodily, without any mention of a specific bodily change which
it involves. All in all, it is characteristic for *De memoria et reminiscentia*
not to go into details about the body.

---

181 Furthermore, representations have to correspond to the previous perception
    (451a4: κατὰ τὸ ἠσθῆσθαι). Presumably this is meant to exclude certain kinds
    of distortions and disruptions; which kinds is not clear.
182 E.g. Met. IX 8 1050a4–10, XII 5 1071a13–17.
183 On material explanation in the PN see Morel 2000: 21–23.
184 For this concept of matter see Met. VII 7 1032a20–22, Gen et Corr. I 4
    320a2–5.
185 Sens. 1 436a7–10, b1–8, see above p. 24.
186 As he does e.g. De somn. 1 453b11–14.
187 450a28–29. In Ch. 2 453a14–26. Note also that the causes of the occurrence
    (γίγνεσθαι) of recollection are mentioned at the end (453b10–11).
188 450a28–29.

While we are on the subject of causes, the final cause should also be mentioned, for, apparently, Aristotle does not consider here either our interest in our memories,[189] nor indeed the various functions, epistemological and biological, that memory fulfils. But it is clear that he thinks we are guided by interest in what we remember, that memory plays a central role in higher level cognition,[190] and that many other living things also use memory. Of course, at the simplest level, the way Aristotle defines memory, its relation to the past, underlines its uniqueness; there are some things we know and can only know via memory, namely our past perceptions.[191] That is the basic good we gain from memory.

But more generally, it is clear that memory is necessarily related to the good, that is, the ends or aims of the living thing.[192]

For both memory and recollection are actions, according to their definitions they are things we do,[193] and that means that they are related to an end: remembering is characterised by the end we pursue in remembering. This is important for a variety of reasons. Firstly, that no criterion is needed to decide of any given act, whether it is memory or not: in performing it, it is evident that it is memory. There can be no mistake about that, since the memory-claim is enough to perform an act of remembering. Furthermore, memory acts are ones in which we can have success or not.[194] As often in the *Parva Naturalia*, it is a question of how matter and its motions achieve ends.[195]

Let us now return to our discussion of representation. So far we have discussed the definition of representation, some of its implications, and the way it relates to Aristotle's causes. We can now approach one of the crucial problems of a theory of memory: the distinction between representations and memory, mentioned at the outset (P3).[196] We are now in

---

189 An example is EN IX 4 1166a24–27.
190 See below p. 88 on Anal. Post. II 19.
191 See Wiggins 1992: 347–50.
192 Plato's Socrates classes memory (unlike perception) among the goods along with other forms of cognition in the *Philebus* 11A7.
193 Ch. 1 450a19–21, 451a2–5.
194 Ch. 2 451b24–8. Ryle (1949: 278) thinks that "remember" is a "success verb", that is, to say of someone that he remembers implies that he remembers correctly. Intuitively, this is perhaps plausible; but there still must be semantic room for the notion of mistaken or deceptive memory, whether or not it is "grammatical" to speak of remembering wrongly. Imagining something is a different activity from being deceived by one's memory.
195 Morel 2000: 44.
196 See above p. 2.

a position to give an Aristotelian account. Broadly, the distinction can be stated from Aristotle's point of view as follows. On the one hand, representations can simply remain, through the regulated changes in the body.[197] On the other, representations have to be used for something; otherwise they are simply psychic data, doing nothing. But they are capable of fulfilling a function, and one such function is memory.[198] This ability is closely linked to the status of representations as changes. For changes can fulfil functions (the beating of the heart, the motions of a saw), and they exist before the function is actually fulfilled, and are independent of whether this function is actually fulfilled.

Aristotle is concerned to limit representations on the one hand to those things that perceive, and on the other, to those things that are perceived. They are, as has been said, changes which arise from actual perceptions, and are similar to these.[199] We will discuss the nature of this similarity later.[200] Furthermore, representations are responsible for "living things doing and undergoing many things"[201]. And finally, he is concerned with the truth and falsity of representations. Thus although representations do account for (some kinds of) error[202], they are primarily in this theory not bound to error, but to truth-or-falsity. Appearances may deceive, indeed, may mostly deceive, but they do not need to.[203] If representations are to help living things live, then, things will have to be as they are represented at least sometimes.

The way representation is being used here is includes imagination, but is broader. Representation includes furthermore more than non-standard appearances[204]: for the "brutes" capable of representation cannot *normally* guided by "non-standard appearances". So: representation – a way of a perceptual content to be present to me, "*to appear to me*",

---

197 See below p. 73 on the relation between the remaining of a representation, as a condition of memory, and metabolism.

198 Another is, of course, action (De an. III 7); see Canto Sperber 1996, Buchheim 2002: 401–6.

199 428b11–17.

200 Below, p. 59.

201 De an. III 3 429a5–6.

202 Caston 1996: 44–52 sees the explanation of error as the most important motive in Aristotle's account of representation.

203 Cf. III 3 428a12–13: perceptions are always true, whereas most representations are false or deceptive. This implies that some are true. Things are sometimes the way they appear.

204 Schofield's (1992) formulation for φαντασία.

which may be deceptive or not. It can be true or false.[205] While Aristotle might appear to restrict truth-and-falsity to perception, opinion, knowledge, intellect,[206] this line of thought would indicate that representations can deceive, that is be false, or not be deceptive, that is be a good guide to the way things are; in other words, they can be true. Truth and falsity in representation derive from perception.[207]

Consideration of the different relations between representation and truth and falsity will underline the fact that representation must be conceptually rich enough to be true or false, misleading or informative. This is the case although representation is neither a form of conception, nor an achievement of the critical faculty, and distinct from affirmation and denial.[208] This does not preclude it from being realised as forms of images, and yet does not restrict it to the actual occurrence of images. Representation includes a broad range of phenomena, from images taken on their own, to images which, when bound into a context may be true or false, and finally changes presenting conceptual content for articulation in propositions. The point about these changes is that there is at least something in the subject occurring which serves as the ground of the capacity to articulate propositions.

Aristotle explains the various relations between truth and falsity in representations by recourse to the different *modi* of perception.[209] But he denies representation in the guise of "appearance" a role in all perception. This emerges not only from the disposition of *De anima:* perception is treated and defined before getting on to φαντασία; but also, because actual perception brings about representation, one has good reason to think that perception explains representation, and not the other way round. There is a further pointer in the same direction in the account of representation itself:

> Then we do not say, when we clearly perceive, [of] the perceptible thing that this appears to us [to be] a human, but when we do not perceive clearly whether this is true or false.[210]

---

205 428b10–17.
206 428a4–5.
207 That is the point of 428a25–30.
208 De an. III 3 427b27–428b9, III 8 432a10–14, De ins. 2 460b16–20, 3 461b5–7.
209 428b17–30.
210 De an. III 3 428a12–15.

There are two lessons I wish to draw from this passage. Firstly, it is denied, on the basis of the way we talk about perception, that representation has a role to play in a clear actual perception at all. When we perceive things clearly, we do not say they appear to be such and such. Representation is concerned not with straightforward cases of perception, but with its aftermath or side effects.[211] Here we have the close connection between φαντασία and the way things appear, with a strong suggestion that that is not the way things are.

Secondly, this quotation provides an argument against positing a role for representation in all perception.[212] It does not of course mean that when one describes what happens in perception there are no changes in the body which arise from the process and which are representations; for this is precisely Aristotle's claim. There have to be changes arising from perception for there to be representation in the first place. Representation is not a part of the explanation of perception. Rather, it is the other way round: perception explains representation. Another argument for the same thesis lies in the fact that representation is subsidiary to perception, and therefore not necessary for perception e. g. in applying concepts to perceptions.[213]

A useful metaphor for Aristotle's view of representation is an echo:[214] representation is an echo of perception. If one takes the metaphor seriously, then it makes sense to say that representation does not play a role in explaining perception. Echoes do not explain sound. This is true even if every sound produces an echo, to some degree. It is plausible to think that perception in Aristotle's view always produces change in the living thing, as a bye-product. But bye-products do not explain the process by which they are produced.

One response to this line of thought is to point out that there are different kinds of perception, and the simple perception of the special objects of the senses may occur without a complicated combination of perceptions and hence representations, but this is generally not thought to be true for incidental perception and the perception of the common or

---

211 See Schofield 1992: 252.
212 For the importance of this aspect, see Schofield 1992: 260.
213 See Strawson 1970. For a Kantian reading of Aristotle see Frede 1992, 2003; and cf. Nussbaum 1978: 255–261 Essay 5 *phantasia and asithêsis*.
214 See e. g. Caston 1996: 47–49.

shared objects.[215] We shall see below that the perception of time can plausibly be held to involve a concatenation of representations.[216]

I posed above[217] three questions about the relation of representation to images, concepts and propositions. Let us now turn to consideration of these questions. Representations are capable of being true and false, although they are distinct from conceptions.[218] For they need not be either true or false.[219] This suggests that they at least have this property in common with images: In itself, an image is neither true nor false. A portrait on a wall only acquires a connection with its subject for a viewer through the presence of a title, with its implicit assertion of a relation to the sitter. (Put slightly differently, the picture neither tells you anything nor does it deceive you; for either to happen there must be some form of assertion involved. It has to be taken as something.) Hence we retain a degree of freedom *vis à vis* representations and portraits which we do not have in the case of opinions, science and prudence. There are two aspects to this liberty. Firstly, we can conjure representations up at will;[220] and secondly they are not bound by having to be true or false, as opinions are. But the status of representations remains evasive: Are they propositions? Are they images? One thing in *De anima* III 3 suggests that they are images in any straightforward sense, namely the illustration of the freedom just mentioned: at wish we can "put things before our eyes" as in mnemonics. This shows that φαντασία is in our power as opinion is not (428a18–20). Later, representation will explain dreams in *De insomniis*, so that representation will have to be able to take the form of images.[221]

What about propositions? If opinions, prudence and science exhaust the kinds of propositions that Aristotle recognises, then he denies representations are propositions. In fact, however, it would appear that because representations can be true or false, we do have to admit that in the way things appear, or in the ways things represent themselves to me, something at least analogous to one thing being said of another is being done. This is true despite the fact that he explicitly distinguishes a repre-

---

215 See e.g. Caston 1996: 42.
216 See p. 62.
217 p. 22–23.
218 On this term see above p. 28.
219 De an. III 3 427b17–21.
220 See III 3 427b17–21.
221 The description of dreams as images is not unproblematic, of course. When the Greeks talk of εἴδωλα in dreams, they are referring to figures that appear to one (Ins. 1 461a15, 3 462a11, 17, cf. Div. Somn. 464b9 of reflections in water).

sentation from assertion and denial, and says that representation is not up to the critical faculty.[222] A way of approaching this problem is through the connection between representation (φαντασία) and appearances (φαινόμενα, φαίνεται),[223] which has already been mentioned several times, last in the quotation we have just given from *De anima*.[224] It seems to me that it is reasonable to think that appearances are intimately connected with the way we represent things to ourselves, not of course primarily by way of intentional actions, but rather because of the nature of our cognitive apparatus.

Appearances have a close connection with truth and falsity. Consider a famous example of an appearance, or if you prefer, a perceptual representation:[225]

(1) The sun appears a foot across.

We have here an assertion of the way something appears. We can ask if this appearance deceives us. The relevant proposition, which is to be judged true or false, is not (1), but:

(2) The sun is a foot across.

or else:

(3) The sun is as big as the world.

Whether the representation is deceptive or not depends on which of (2) and (3) is true. Clearly, the representation itself will not decide which is the case, but it still has certain structural similarities with saying that such and such is the case, while of course not involving an assertion. Aristotle's explanation for this phenomenon is that the faculty of distinguishing (κρίνειν) and that by which φαντάσματα come about are distinct. Again, it would be a great mistake to translate κρίνειν by "judge" or such like and conclude that representation is hence not a judgement, and hence not propositional in character. It is merely that, on its own, representation does not distinguish between true and false. Nonetheless, appearances (may) have a dyadic structure:

Something appears [as] something.

---

222 See the texts cited above fn. 208.
223 Cf. Everson 1997: Ch. 5.
224 De an. III 3 428a12–15.
225 428b3–4.

Clearly, such a structure has something in common with saying (predicating) one thing of another, and may be true or false.[226] There is a fact of the matter as to whether such appearances are deceptive or not. Such a structure also appears in the more complicated forms of perception, when I see the pale as the son of Creon; or when I see the son of Creon move. In such cases, one is convinced by the perceptions, as long as they are sufficiently clear. If not, then one might want to say, X appears to be Y. In the case of a representation, the dyadic structure does not need to be true or false since one does not necessarily believe the representation, just as in the case of the sun appearing small. The point of this example for Aristotle is that one can have the right (scientific) conception of the sun, while the sun still appears the same as it does to others. All people are subject to the same appearance or representation of the sun. The contrast with conception (in this case, science) in fact underlines the *quasi* predicative structure of appearances: X appears to be Y, X is represented as Y; while also showing that the two, conception and representation, do not compete. No conviction need accompany the representations; though, of course if one's critical faculties (cf. κρίνειν) are numbed, then one may well follow the appearance.[227]

I have claimed that Aristotle nowhere says that representations are images, but in several places he *compares* them with pictures or images.[228] These comparisons have often seemed sufficient ground for taking representations to be images. I think we should be more careful, even if we do not take the severe step of saying that φαντασίαι cannot be pictures if they are compared with them. Let us take a look at these different comparisons. We shall see that they make distinct points. I begin with the one that makes the point that we do not believe pictures.[229] The comparison with a picture is combined with the contrast with an opinion: representation is like a picture, and unlike an opinion. How? Above, I have suggested one similarity between representation and pictures, following Aristotle: One does not make a belief claim with it *eo ipso*. When confronted by a picture, we do not believe anything. To do that we must take the picture in some way; we shall say more about this presently, when we dis-

---

226 Nussbaum (1978: esp. 255–261) sees this structure as peculiar to representation in Aristotle. It plays a crucial role in the final definition of memory, below p. 81, but as a way of regarding representations, not as a function of the representative faculty.

227 III 3 429a6–8.

228 This point is emphasised by Nussbaum 1978: 250.

229 III 3 427a21–24.

cuss the comparison of representations with pictures from *De memoria et reminiscentia*. Here, Aristotle gives the example of something appearing frightening: in that case one is not afraid, unlike the case when one *believes* that something is frightening. Obviously, the point of this comparison is not that representations are pictorial, but rather that our epistemic attitude to pictures and representations is the same. Just as when confronted with a picture, we can entertain a representation of something without having the attitude towards the representation which the relevant thing or state of affairs would normally demand of us. This is not true of conceptions. An opinion that such and such is the case requires that we adopt a definite attitude to it. And so too with science and practical judgements.

The second and most important comparison with a picture comes from *De memoria et reminiscentia*. It is used to solve the present–past problem (P2), namely how is it possible to remember something that is not present:[230]

> For *as* the picture painted on a panel is both a picture (ζῷον) and an image (εἰκών) and one and the same thing is both, although their being is not the same, and it is possible to regard it both as a picture (ζῷον) and as an image (εἰκών), *so* we must conceive the representation in us both to be something in itself and to be the representation of something else.[231]

The words *as...so*[232] mark the comparison. We are being presented with two ways in which the subject of a representation can use it. These two uses are parallel to two things one can do with a picture. You can see it either as a collection of lines, or as an image of something.[233] In a way, the position is reversed: instead of claiming that representations are related to things by being images of them, Aristotle is saying that even images only act as images in the sense of being *images of something* when we take them as such: and this point applies equally to representations. Thus it is clearly not the case that representations are, simply and

---

230 *Introduction* p. 1–2.
231 450b20–25. See Labarrière 2000: esp. 275–81 on this comparison.
232 lines 20 οἷον, 24 οὕτω.
233 This reading has been doubted on the grounds that a φάντασμα has some content and thus is related to something; hence the point of comparison cannot be a collection of lines. See Wedin 1988: 138–9, Caston 1998: 282 with n. 80, Everson 1997: 196–200. But the point is not that there are some φαντάσματα without content, but it is possible to regard all of them merely as data, entities in their own right. This is of course not to deny their dependence on their subject; merely that they can be entertained with no intentional content.

straightforwardly, images.[234] At most one might say that pictures and representations belong to a common genus of which the members may be
regarded as related to something absent. We will discuss the nature of
the *regarding as* relation when we come to discuss the present—past problem below.

Of course, one important reason one may be inclined to view representations as images is that they are *like* perceptions.[235] And images are
like the things of which they are the images. So one might think that representations are pictorial copies of perceptions. In order to counter this
argument, all we have to do is to show that the similarity of representation to perception does not entail that representations are pictorial copies
of perceptions. So let us now turn briefly to the concept of similarity or
likeness. Likeness is for Aristotle a three place predicate: X is similar to Y
in A. A may be any one of a variety of attributes, or a cluster of attributes.[236] Thus A may be e.g. a form or an attribute that X and Y share.
Prima facie, there seems to be no reason to restrict the likeness of representations to perceptions to any one or more of the kinds of likeness. The
real question is rather whether, in the case of representations, A can be
something other than a pictorial quality. The problem with such a quality
is quite how one would establish of a perception P and a representation R
that they are similar to one another. Similarity might then always be relative to the one observer. Then it would not be so much representations
and perceptions that are like one another, taken on their own, but rather
having such and such a representation might be like having such and such
a perception for some individual perceiver.[237] Having the perception and
having the representation might appear to their subject as being like one
another, namely in certain pictorial qualities. But that is unsatisfactory,
not merely in epistemological terms, also in terms of what representations
have to do in the economy of living things for Aristotle. For they have the
function of causing action or rather enabling living things to act. So if the
similarity is not pictorial how are we to understand it? In *De motu animalium* he says that these effects of representations are like those of perceptions. This would lead one to think that the similarity in question is

---

234 A further occurrence of the concept of an image occurs in the **Final Definition**
of memory, below p. 81.
235 De an. III 3 429a4–8.
236 Aristotle discusses the likeness relation at Met. X 3 1054b3–13; cf. Everson
1997: 201–3.
237 This is suggested in part by the way in which representations function in recollection; see below p. 90 ff.

causal and that perception and representation move the animal in a similar fashion.[238] A dog can chase the hare it sees, or follow the hare it no
longer sees, but of which it has a representation. This reading fits in well
with the remark that Aristotle makes in this context, namely that living
things undergo and do many things in virtue of representations.[239]

Besides causing movement, we have already met another function of
representations, namely that they are necessary for thinking.[240] But such
representations need not involve any pictorial likeness. Indeed, Aristotle
says that the representation is like the perception, not that it is like the
concept, which would anyway hardly be comprehensible. The relation
between thinking and representations is rather that the one is the necessary condition for the other, not that they resemble one another.

So far we have shown that representation is the remains of perception,
and we have seen that the similarity with perception lies in the nature of
the representation as a change: Because they are changes, perception and
representation can move the living thing similarly. But perception is a
many-facetted capacity, and we need to isolate those aspects relevant to
representation. A good point of orientation, as often with Aristotle, is
the order of his exposition. The first two chapters of *De anima* III are
concerned with unitary, centralising aspects of perception, those things
which are not perceived by any single sense organ, but may belong to several; and with the perception that we perceive which is an aspect of perception, since otherwise it would not be possible for living things only to
have perception. These are the most important functions of the perceptual system taken as a unity. This unity is provided for by a central organ,

---

238 Here I follow Caston 1996: 48–51, 1998: 276–9. He refers to De mot. anim. 7
     701b17–22, 11 703b18–20, De insomn. 3 460b18–27. Note that this does
     not mean that the mere representation of something can affect the animal in
     the way a perception does *and deceive it*; the point is that a representation can
     guide action, and given that some animals depend on this form of guidance, it
     must be reliable to some extent. Thus representations by no means always de-
     ceive. Thomas Johansen has argued to me that the image theorist, that is, some-
     one who thinks that *phantasiai* are always images in acts of memory, and as such
     similar to perceptions, has an answer to the question why these mental states
     should count as similar to the perceptions, even though others may have the
     same outcome. I think that there is no textual evidence for the image theorist,
     and that positing the imaging relation as a primitive explanans would not do Ar-
     istotle any favours.
239 De an. III 3 428b16–17, 429a4–8.
240 De mem. 1 449b30.

the primary sense organ, in which all of the senses run together.[241] So too with representations: they are a function of the primary sense organ. This connection is also asserted in *De memoria et reminiscentia* in some lines from the passage in which representation is introduced into the work:[242]

> It is necessary that magnitude and change are cognized with that with which (ᾧ) time also is cognized. And a representation is an affection of common perception. Thus it is clear that the cognition of these things is through the primary perceptive capacity.[243]

This is an argument for ascribing the perception of time, magnitude and change to the primary perceptive capacity. This follows for Aristotle from the fact that all three are perceived by the same means, to wit a representation, and representations are an affection of "common perception". How time is perceived using a representation is the subject of the next section: there we shall show that it really is a representation with which time is perceived.

To return to the present passage. "Common perception" does not refer to a supernumerary sense, responsible for cognising size etc, but is an aspect of the unitary system of perception.[244] Representations are not affections of any single organ of sense, but they are, as changes, derived from such actual perceptions, and so are affections, the states resulting from changes, of the common perceptual system.[245] Common perceptibles are those that are perceived by more than one sense; their cognition is not ascribable to any one kind of perception, it is an aspect of the system as a whole.

Let us sum up the results of this section.

Representations are changes remaining from perceptions, affecting the central organ of perception. Because they are changes they can serve as causes of motion. In representations things are presented as something, and this presentation can be misleading or not. Thus there is a

---

241 De juv., King 2001: 64–73. See also the point analogy in De an. III 2 427a9–11.
242 Cf. above p. 41.
243 450a9–12. On the preservation of the original text here, as against Freudenthal's suggestion, followed by Ross, see Wiesner 1985: 179–80. Gregoric 2007: 101–107 also wishes to preserve the original reading.
244 For a discussion of the texts, see Gregoric 2007.
245 For the idea that unity is the central idea in common perception see esp. Welsch 1987: 307–380 VI Aristoteles' Gedanke der Sinneseinheit. On percepts see below, p. 71.

close connection between representation and truth and falsity, although it is not the office of representation to distinguish the two.[246]

Representations are necessary to the perception of common perceptibles such as change and magnitude, and also for the cognition of time. Because representations are a function of perception, this means that time is perceived. The importance of the fact that time is perceived lies in the consequence that memory is perceptual, that is also a function of the primary sense organ.[247] This leads us to our next topic, the perception of time.

2.1.4 The perception of time

Aristotle's definition of memory makes it dependent on the cognition of time;[248] memory relates to what is past. It is Aristotle's doctrine that this cognition can be performed by perception. As we have seen, because memory is performed by perception, non-rational animals can also remember.[249] In this section we shall examine how it is possible to perceive time. We wish to show that memory depends on the perception of time and not vice versa.[250] Only if this is possible can Aristotle's definition of memory be defended. He says that it is necessary for change and magnitude to be perceived with the same thing ($\overset{\hat{}}{\omega}$) that time is perceived.[251] Our account will have to explain what this "thing" is, and why all three are perceived using it.

There are two questions we will ask:

How does he think that time is perceived?

What aspect of perception is responsible for the perception of time?

The second question has already been answered: representation is responsible for the perception of time. But it has not been spelt out how this works. That is the job of the answer to the first question. Clearly, an account of the way time is perceived shows how the perceptual system

---

246 For the contrast between representational faculty and the ability to distinguish things, see Ins. 2 460b16–20.
247 Cf. 450a13–4.
248 For the expression 449b29, 450a19, 451a17; see also 450a9–12. On the importance of the perception of time for De mem. see Taormina 2002.
249 See above p. 43; cf. 449b28–29, 450a16–19.
250 *Pace* Irwin 1988: 316; cf. Taormina 2002: 38. There is no mention of memory *at all* in the discussion of time in *Physics* IV 10–14.
251 Ch. 1 450a9–12. See above p. 41.

performs this task. We will see that the answer to the first question in fact leads to the answer to the second one. The reason is that perception of change requires representations, i.e. which remain from perception; and representation is an affection of the common sense.[252] Hence the perception of time belongs to common sense.[253]

It is important to distinguish the question of the measurement of time from that of perceiving time. Aristotle thinks that memory can take place either accompanied by a measured perception of time or without it: we can remember that something happened at a certain time in the past, or simply that it happened.[254] Shortly, we will go on to consider briefly some of the things Aristotle says about grasping "longer and shorter times". But first, we have to understand what perceiving time is. When we say that time is perceived, there are a variety of things we might take as the object of the perception:

1) relations of before and after, and simultaneity
2) tense
3) a (certain) duration
4) change

As we shall see, Aristotle thinks that all of these elements are perceived.[255] This is clear from some arguments in the discussion of time in the *Physics*. Time is defined there as "the number of change with respect to the before and after"; "number" is here not an abstract ruler, as it were, it is rather that which is counted.[256] We say that time has passed when we grasp earlier and later in a change.[257] The change is marked by our saying *now* and *now*; that is how we mark off the before and after in time. Saying *now* has to be thought of as occupying no time, like an instant. "The now", Aristotle's expression for an instant, is the temporal analogue of a point, that

---

252 450a10–11, see above p. 42.
253 This is the claim of Verbeke 1985, (and cf. Goldschmidt 1982: 27–8) which Taormina 2002 argues against, (followed by Gregoric 2007: 107). It is puzzling why she does so, since she thinks representations ("images") are needed for the perception of time, and she also (p. 53–8) discusses the text 450a9–12 where these are said to be affections of the common sense.
254 452b29–453a4.
255 We have also noted that he does not distinguish strictly between relations of before and after and tense; see above p. 29.
256 On the connection between the definition at 219b1–2 and the preceding lines 219a22-b1; see Hussey 1983: 150–2: he thinks the definition at b1–2 was inserted here later from 220a25.
257 Phys. IV 11 219a23–25.

is, a boundary or limit (πέρας).[258] Because of the presence of the moving thing, in one sense the now is always different, and so serves to count the change.[259] The basic units are nows[260] which are used to divide up the change, so enabling one to measure time using the change.[261]

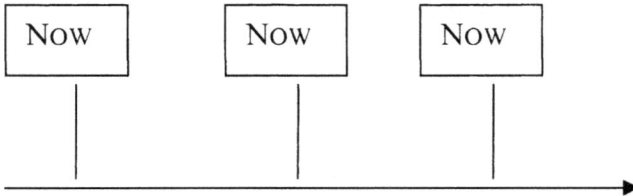

The arrow marks the direction of change.

Aristotle derives central arguments for his view of time from phenomenology, in particular from the perception of change: if we perceive no change, then we do not think that time has passed.[262] We perceive the change,[263] which has to be present so that one can distinguish the instants.[264] Perception of time includes the perception of the order (before, after, simultaneous), namely that in the change.[265] We mark off change by taking the nows, i.e. the instants, to be different. Some other thing is in between and this is the time, that is, a duration. So we perceive time only on the basis of perceiving change.[266] This perception of durations between nows arranged according to what is before and after suffices for the perception of time insofar as this is simply duration. This does not provide the measurement of time, which is necessary insofar as time is the number of change. A further step in this direction is the ability to per-

---

258 Phys. IV 11 220a4–24, esp. 8–11, 18–20.
259 220a13–14. Two passages on the sameness and difference of times: 220b5–14, 223a29-b12 (Hussey 1983: 160–3). See also Coope 2005: Ch 5 on time as a number and ch. 7 on the now.
260 219a25–30, 219b25, 220a3–4. Strictly, a now is not a unit, but a way of dividing time into units, provided by some regular motion.
261 IV 12 220b14.
262 IV 11 218b21–219a10.
263 De an. III 1 425a13–20.
264 See Phys. IV 11 218b21–219a1. Cf. also De mem. 1 449b25–26: there is no memory of the now now, i.e. of the concrete content occurring in my mind now; and cf. Ch. 2 451b19.
265 219a22-b1.
266 219a3–4; Sorabji p. 66.

ceive periods; this requires the perception of regular change which provides the measurement for other changes.[267]

These considerations make it clear why change and time have to be perceived by the same thing.

One might object to this theory on the basis of the following intuition: only an instant is now present, and so only an instant is available to perception.[268] Aristotle does not discuss this possibility, presumably because, firstly, his theory of change does not allow for change or rest at an instant,[269] and also because his theory of time requires the cognition of change, rather than being itself a presupposition for the cognition of change.[270]

A plausible way of accounting for the way in which change is perceived consists in pointing to the fact that a series of perceptions of something changing can be taken together, since, as we have seen,[271] the representations caused by the perceptions remain.[272] Hence we can solve the problem that a length of time can after all be perceived without using memory.[273] Memory requires the perception of time, and not the other way round in Aristotle's view. The decisive point is that representations, merely by remaining from actual perception, are not thereby memory

---

267 See Phys. IV 11 219a14–21 on the before and after in place, change and time. We will return later to the need for what is nowadays called an oscillator for the measurement of time.

268 Taormina (2002: 54, and cf. p. 52) suggests that there are two forms of cognition of time, the one ("sensation") grasps it insofar as it is present, and another grasps it as far as it is coming to be and hence in its relations of before and after. It is hard to see how these two aspects can be separated. How would one tell that the first sensation is a cognition of time?

269 Phys. VI 3 234a31-b9; Owen 1957, Sorabji 1979, Lear 1988: 85–9.

270 Aristotle does have a concept of the now which is extended (Phys. IV 13 222a20–24, Sorabji p. 21, 70): someone is coming now, we say, because he is coming this afternoon. The time in question is near now, hence this manner of speaking. This should not be confused with the technical notion of the specious present (Russell 1921: Lecture IX): a period of less than a minute leading up to now; and which is also not an object of memory.

271 See above p. 40–62, below p. 84.

272 See Taormina 2002: 50–56 for a convincing presentation of this case. She also points to the fact that the change which makes one aware of the passage of time in the absence of external perception is a representation (Phys. IV 11 219a5).

273 This is Sorabji's problem p. 70 ad 449b29.

content.[274] Here, remaining representations make it possible to perceive time, which is one of the preconditions for memory.

Since representations are an affection of the common sense, this reading would imply that time is grasped by the common sense.[275] That this is the case is suggested by two texts in *De memoria et reminiscentia*. The first one, which we have already discussed, is concerned with the attribution of the cognition of time to perception.[276] The second deals with the cognition of longer and shorter times.

We will now turn briefly to this latter text. In a difficult section in Ch. 2[277] Aristotle discusses the cognition (γνωρίζειν) of time, which he says is "the most important thing", whether done "with a measure or indeterminately". Here, he is here concerned with establishing the way in which different lengths of time are represented in the mind using movements or changes. As is generally realised, the passage is of great interest for his theory of mind as a whole. For my purposes it is of crucial importance because it commits Aristotle to representing at least a wide range of things in the mind; magnitudes, times but also forms are said to be represented. Since I am pleading for a representationalist theory of memory, and time is essential for memory, the fact that time is represented is of the greatest importance. However, the words I translate by "representation", φαντασία and φαντάσματα do not occur in the passage. What does occur, is "change" (κίνησις).[278] We have seen that representations are changes,[279] albeit ones left behind by actual perception, and it is an allowable extension of the meaning of the term to apply it to a mental dia-

---

274 De an. III 3 429a4, 2 425b24–25, I 4 408b17–18. Representations seem to have certain similarities with what is nowadays known as short term memory, used for example in remembering a telephone number as one is dialling it. Cf. his mention of after-images in perception De ins. 2 459b7–18; this passage is closely connected to the idea that representation are what remains from perception, see above p. 24, 26, below p. 84.

275 Taormina (2002: 46–49) drives a wedge between the common sense, (on which she follows Brunschwig esp. his 1996) and the primary sense faculty, although these appear to be joined in the crucial argument at 450a9–12. She allows for overlap between the two, but offers no argument for saying that time is not perceived by the common sense.

276 450a9–14, see above p. 42.

277 452b7–22.

278 452b12, 13, 17, 20

279 Above p. 49.

gram: the changes are those one has in mind while drawing a mental diagram.[280] In this way, the changes are representations.

It is wise to talk here of cognition of time, rather than perception. For not only the language indicates the presence of νοῦς.[281] The operations involved, relying as they do on a geometrical model, encourage one to think that the mental processes involved here are more complicated than those attributed to animals other than humans.[282]

Aristotle posits some way of distinguishing the longer and shorter times,[283] and he thinks it reasonable to illustrate what this way is by considering how we perform an analogous task in the case of magnitudes. He develops a model for doing this, but does not then say how it is to be applied to time. Aristotle denies here[284] that we cognise magnitudes "by stretching out" our thought, as some people claim we do in the case of sight. The reason he gives is that we would then think of things which do not exist[285] in the same way. The implication is that we cannot stretch thought out to something which does not exist, when we think of something which does not exist: hence it is not plausible that we stretch thought out to things that do exist. If we do not cognise magnitudes by stretching our thought to them, how does Aristotle think we do it? He suggests that we do it by means of changes in us that are proportional to the things thought of. Everything in us, he says, is smaller, that is, than the objects represented, but in proportion. This thing in us that is in proportion to the thing outside is a change. He says that in this pro-

---

280 Cf. Frede 1992: 290.
281 452b10 διάνοια, b11 νόησις, b13 bis, 21 bis, 22 νοεῖν.
282 One should, however, not hurry on to conclude that this process is restricted to recollection on the grounds that it is a form of calculation and furthermore treated in Ch. 2 which is ostensibly at least devoted to recollection. For it is clear that recollection too is an activity of the capacity to remember: its result is memory. Hence presumably, when one has worked out when something occurred, one remembers when it occurred. The restriction of the cognition of time to recollection would also make it hard to understand why the cognition of time is "the most important thing" (452b7).
283 What is here postulated (ἔστω 452b8) is not common sense or the primary perceptual organ, since Aristotle has no reason to postulate these, but rather some such means of representing time as that which he then goes on to present, analogous to the cognition of other magnitudes.
284 452b9–12.
285 It is an interesting question whether *being* here is veridical or existential; but it does not make any difference to the present argument. On this passage see also Caston 1998: 260–1, who takes it existentially.

portional change the figures and changes are similar (ὅμοια): so we see a
tree, and the representation of the tree is like the tree. So Aristotle thinks
that when we cognise magnitudes, we undergo changes in proportion to
the thing represented. If the thing can also undergo changes, then our
representations of it will may track the change also, change with it and
remain at rest when it is at rest. In this way we could track also the
shape and the changes in the thing.[286] The changes in us are in proportion to those in the thing cognised.

In this passage, Aristotle does not actually say how time is measured.[287] This problem is perhaps not so serious, as far as interpreting
De memoria et reminiscentia goes in that he says, twice,[288] that we can cognise time either "indefinitely or with a measure". Simply, we must grasp
that something is past, or we may grasp how long ago it happened. So the
simplest case of memory involves merely the grasp that the perception
concerned is past; and even animals are capable of that. What abut measuring time? As far as representing a certain amount of time goes, of
course we want to know how long ago something took place, and for
that we need a measure.[289] This requires a regular motion, what is
known now as an oscillator. But it is questionable whether Aristotle
postulated oscillators in living things, not merely for his theory of memory.

Modern accounts of the temporal regulation of living things involve
regular processes, oscillators, which serve as biological clocks.[290] It is clear
that for Aristotle too living things are temporally regulated, but the only
clock, a regular change necessary for measuring time, that he allows is the
motion of the heavens. He has theoretical reasons for believing in the
necessary, and hence reliable, regularity of this motion.[291] However,
some interpreters of Aristotle's theory of memory have simply posited

---

286 For a discussion of the diagram which is meant to give an example of the cog-
    nition of larger and smaller magnitudes see my note King 2004: 136–138.
    The reconstruction of the diagram is a matter of great scholarly debate. In gen-
    eral, the suggestions for doing this made independently by John Beare and David
    Ross have been accepted. I too accept their diagram, and my contribution to the
    debate consists purely in a reading of the diagram, and how it is to be applied to
    memory.

287 Hussey 1983: 151; for Aristotle's general theory of measurement see Met. X 1.

288 452b7–8, 452b29–453a4

289 Such an oscillator is not mentioned in the passage on the cognition of time; that
    there is a standard measurement of time is, however, assumed.

290 See, for example, McCormack 2001: 290–3.

291 De cael. II 6.

such a clock at this point in his theory.[292] Or is it possible to account for temporal regularity in living things with no oscillator in them? Two obvious examples of temporal regularity from Aristotle's biology are sleep, and life spans;[293] in both cases he uses the idea of temporally limited capacities, belonging to living things essentially, as a matter of their nature, closely related to the regular processes by which they are maintained, in particular nutrition and breathing. In both cases there is no kind of internal, biological clock.[294] This leaves it obscure quite how a temporally limited capacity is to be understood, that is, just how the temporal limitation is inscribed in the capacity. There does seem to be a relation to the regular change of the seasons in the case of life-spans.[295] It seems to me that Aristotle's difficulties in describing how we measure time are closely connected to his lack of the idea of an internal clock.

2.1.5 The acquisition of memory: the comparison with using a seal to make an imprint

The last two sections offered a sketch of what representations are and discussed at least some aspects of them which are important for memory. Namely, they remain from perception and they make the perception of time possible. Before we get to the **Final Definition** we need to consider several aspects of perception more closely and what exactly happens in a perceptual act. This will deepen our understanding of what a representation is, and how it remains from actual perception.

---

292 Sorabji p. 20 makes the tentative suggestion that one looks at the diagram dynamically, and at a pace determined by human nature.

293 See De somn. 1 454a26–32, and De juv. 24 esp. 479a29-b3, and cf. De gen. an. IV 10; and De long. on the explanation of longevity. See King 2001: Ch. 4.3, and Ch. 5.

294 See e.g. Campbell 1994: 53–7 for an account of circadian clocks and how living things measure time using an oscillator, related to the length of a day, which can be entrained to certain times of day.

295 For the use of the heavenly clock in providing a unit and so measuring time Phys. IV 12 223b12–20; Phys. VIII has the aim of proving that the circular motion of the sphere carrying the fixed stars is the only uniform and everlastingly continuous motion. The uniformity of its change can be known without reference to another measurement of time since there is no cause for any variation. For the effect of the regular change of seasons on living things and their life spans see esp. Gen. et Corr. II 10 336b10–15, and cf. King 2001: 83–84

The account of the original perception in *De memoria et reminiscentia* is centred around the comparison with the action of a seal on wax. This is meant as an illustration of what happens in the original perception. Recall that we need three times for memory, t1 which occurs before t2, and the time span between t1 and t2.[296] The original perception occurs at t1. The second time is that of remembering itself (t2). In the next section, on the present-past problem, we discuss what the person remembering at t2 does.

Let us now consider the original perception. The crucial point is that something remains from it. Only in this way can the act at t2 have access to the original perception. In order to describe the process of having a perception which we can later remember, Aristotle uses two images. Firstly, he says that "the affection, the possession of which we claim is memory, is like a painting."[297] We have already discussed the extent to which representations are images.[298] Secondly, he uses the model of a seal which is used to put an imprint on wax. The model is familiar from Aristotle's account of perception.[299] Since the occurrence of which we have a memory is a perception, this is hardly surprising. However, the emphases in the two uses of the model are different. In the former, the model is used to illustrate the point that the transference is purely formal. Only the form of the seal is received by the wax, and, in perception, only the form of the perceptible is taken up by the perceiver.[300]

In the case of memory, the emphasis is on the fact that a change occurs and leaves "something like"[301] a print or cast (τύπος) of the percept (αἴσθημα). This is expressed by using the term *affection*, which as we have seen, plays a crucial role in Aristotle's views on how to investigate the soul.[302] Obviously, *print* or *cast* (τύπος) is not a specifically mental

---

296 See *Introduction* p. 8.
297 451a29–30 (keeping the reading of the Mss. against Ross).
298 See above p. 57.
299 See above p. 23.
300 See *Introduction* p. 13.
301 Michael notices this and adds that it is something like a picture (ἀναζωγράφημα) in the primary perceptive organ (2.32, 14.8; cf. Alexander, *De Anima* 60.6); he is actually following Alexander's interpretation. Alexander thinks that τύπος is used because a proper term is missing (4.4–5 cf. Wendland's remark, p. xii, and Sophonias 5.11–12). Michael often uses τύπος without a qualifier (e.g. 5.13, 18, 7.15), but he sticks to the view that the comparison with a signet ring, wax and an impression (ἐκτύπωμα) only implies that "something like that" (τοιοῦτον τι) comes about in actual perception in the primary perceptive organ (14.3–9).
302 See above p. 20.

term; if it were, there would be no need to say that we are dealing with *something like* a print or cast. Aristotle is using a comparison to do his explaining and the interpreter must interpret the comparison. He is not inventing a conception of mental impression, for example. The fact that he is using a comparison does not hinder him from using technical terms, here αἴσθημα "percept". A percept is an effect of perception that preserves the perception after it has ceased and it occurs in the organ concerned.[303] Dreams are a kind of percept, that is, the remains of the realised percepts which remain in the living thing as a change.[304] Clearly, percepts have much in common with representations (φαντάσματα). The difference between percepts and representations consists in the fact that the latter are "without matter";[305] this cannot mean that they are simply form, that is, form occurring without any material substrate. Rather, they are without the matter that the percepts have, but have their own matter in that they are localised in the living body. For representations are affections of the primary perceptive faculty. Thus they are changes in the central organ, rather than in the peripheral sense organs.[306]

How are we to understand this "cast" of the percept? A first remark about translation is necessary: an easy translation would be "impression",[307] which one could then assimilate to the common Empiricist idiom of impressions arising through sensation. Yet that would be a mistake; for the word, τύπος as I have already noted, is used in a comparison with what happens in the cognitive process, and so cannot be itself a term for a mental phenomenon. I will argue that it corresponds to a representation in the process of perception, and that it is a change in the living

---

303 De insomn. 2 460b2–3. On percepts: they are perceptibles that remain when the external perceptible is gone (De insomn. 2 460b2–3). It is unclear if percepts play a role in all perception, in that they play no part in the account of perception in De an. II, and occur only in the context of the explanation of more complicated phenomena like memory which involve the perceptive capacity. Nonetheless, Wedin 1988: 36–9 sees them as an ingredient of all perception (see also Everson 1997: 174–7). Dreams are a kind of percept (De somn. 2 456a26), namely the remains of the actual percepts which remains in the living thing as a change (De insomn. 3 460b28–32, 461b22–26, 462a15–16). On percepts in De mem. see 450a31–2.

304 De insomn. 3 460b28–32, 461b22–26, 462a15–16, De somn. 2 456a26

305 De an. III 8 432a9–10

306 So too e.g. Freudenthal 1863: 25, Wedin 1988: 107, Caston 1996 48–9; and see De mem. 1 450a10–13, above p. 42.

307 Cf. LS 39 on the Stoic use of φαντασία which they translate *impression*.

thing, indeed: a change which remains.[308] Obviously, it is not merely a
fixed stamp, as on non-living matter like wax.[309] The reasons for identifying this change or affection with the representations are that it itself is a
change, and it is described as arising from a change.[310] This means that
the *quasi* cast or print is not just a mental item, but one essentially connected to the body of the subject. The change can only be received and
transmitted because we are dealing with an embodied soul. This is a point
not about the meaning of the term τύπος here, but about the nature of
the thing it is used by Aristotle to refer to.

We must now try to determine whether Aristotle needs or wishes to
specify the change that the seal causes. We have already met the parallel
question in the case of representation above, and came to the conclusion
that it is probably best to take it as a change of a kind, along the line suggested by *De anima* II 5. That chapter describes the change happening in
a perception as a change of a kind, using the triple scheme:[311] the only
change, specifically "alteration of a kind", that a perception is, is the realisation of a capacity which has arisen through changes in the strict sense.
We have already briefly discussed the problem of what "alteration of a
kind" may mean, and pointed out that it may refer to a form of mental
change, thus going beyond the doctrine of change developed in the *Physics*. Or else there may be some change in the strict sense involved which
Aristotle does not specify.[312] Since we are here, in the discussion of the
original perception, discussing precisely the same question, namely the
nature of the change which perception is to be identified with, we should
expect that there is no further specification of the change in terms of the
Physics doctrine, as either alteration, or change in quantity or locomotion.
If we analyse both the seal comparison and the process of perception, it
will become clear that the comparison does not in fact suggest that there
is a separate material level of change.

Here is a list of the factors in the process of imprinting a seal on wax:

(S1) the concrete ring

---

308 Cf. Wedin 1988: 35–42 on percepts.
309 Freudenthal 1863: 21–25 pointed this out. Whether conclusions about the na-
     ture of the change in perception itself can be drawn from this passage is a moot
     point; see Frede 2002: 98. See above n. 171 for literature about the nature of
     change in perception.
310 See the definition above p. 46.
311 P. 30.
312 Above p. 47.

(S2) the form of the ring – its imprint
(S3) the change, the process of imprinting
(S4) the form of the ring is transferred onto wax by the imprinting

In the process of acquiring a memory, that is, in perception, we then have the following:

(M1) a concrete perceptible
(M2) the concrete perceptible's form
(M3) the act of perception
(M4) the perceiver receives the form.

M4 says that the perceiver receives the form in perception. What it does not say is that there is a material impression on one level and a psychic event on another: quite simply, the perceiver receives the form. The way Aristotle describes what happens here lays great emphasis on change.[313] The perceiver is a living thing, and as we have seen explanation of living behaviour requires both body and soul, that's to say, something subject to change, and something not subject to change which regulates the change. It will become clearer what the significance of change in the context of memory is, if we look at the reasons Aristotle goes on to give[314] for the fact that some people, people, that is, at certain stages in the life cycle, do not remember well or indeed at all. This is an obvious phenomenon for a theory of memory to explain. For the old tend to re-member less well; and no one expects memory in babies. So what is the reason? Aristotle's explanation is that their bodily flux,[315] their metabo-lism, does not allow the change to remain either, in the case of infants, because they are so fluid that it disperses, and so the affection is lost, or because they are too hard for the "imprint" to be effective in the first place, in the case of the old.

Thus it is clear that at a general level psychic activity, which is neces-sarily corporeal, provides one of the necessary conditions for memory, namely a stable body. Aristotle's conception of soul requires its embodi-ment; this is reflected in the explanation for memory. His explanation of memory thus precludes memory in disembodied things. But when we ask more specifically, not at the level of living things generally, or perhaps hu-mans, moving through their life-cycle, but rather about what happens

313 450a30–31.
314 450a32-b11.
315 They flow ῥέουσι (450b6); another, crucial, text on flux in living things is De juv. 5 469b29–470a5, King 2001: 96–101.

when the memory is acquired, that is, when the original perception takes place, then we may well be disappointed. For Aristotle has recourse to comparisons, not merely the "sort of cast", or "impression" (τύπος) which we have been discussing, but rather less famous, not say obscure, images are appealed to, namely, that in the case of those who flow too much the seal or the change falls, "as it were into water", and so does not remain; and with the aged, they are too hard, like some kind of a wall which does not take the impression.[316] The general idea is clear, but there is a notable lack of specific detail, and one may well ask why. Does the lack of clarity mask an important gap in Aristotle's account, or are they merely harmless images which serve a superficial rhetorical purpose, and which can easily be translated into good Aristotelian concepts? I will argue that there is no gap here, and that we have already met the Aristotelian concepts which are relevant, and indeed sufficient.

The way we deal with this question is fundamental to our reading of *De memoria et reminiscentia*, and indeed of Aristotle's philosophy of mind generally. What role does corporeal explanation play within this theory? Memory is common to body and soul; but the contribution of body might exhaust itself at the level of a necessary condition. For among the affections of living things, there are some which require body as necessary condition. That is, they only happen in things with body, but they are not, like a second group of affections, defined by a change in the body. The first kind of affections are things like perceptions, and the second are things like passions.[317] The fact that Aristotle does not give an account of how φαντάσματα arise in terms of the physiology of living things would suggest that there is, in his view, no story to be told here. Memory is dealt with presupposing no more, and no less, about φαντάσματα than we have discussed from *De anima* in the last section.[318]

---

316 450a32-b5.

317 For this distinction, see above p. 20. It is quite conceivable that even a modern empiricist should discuss memory phenomena without discussing the neural processes involved – but there would be no doubt that there is some kind of a story to be told there; e. g. See Baddeley (1982: 7): physiology in its then state of development has very little to teach us about memory.

318 When Aristotle comes to dreams in De ins. he does discuss the physiology of φαντάσματα (esp. 1 459b1–23, 3 460b28–461b7) because he needs it to explain how current perception drowns out the residual changes in the sense organs. These texts are often used to pad out the account of memory or perception (see e. g. Wedin 1988: 36–9). But I think that if Aristotle needs something in his theory, he tends to make explicit use of it.

Representations are changes arising from perception, and they serve thought as a material basis. There is no more that need to be said for the purposes of Aristotle's theory. The point may be put by saying that organs are needed to perform the function, but the actual performance of the function is not identical with specific, bodily changes. The actual end is reached by way of changes, but is distinct from the changes.

More light is shed on these questions if we look at the way in which body is brought into the account in *De memoria et reminiscentia*. The first thing to mention is the fact that the material cause does not feature in the list of questions posed at the outset.[319] Nonetheless, there are points at which he appeals to specific parts of the body, for example, to the primary perceptual organ or capacity,[320] and also to "the part of the body which has the soul in it".[321] The part referred to is the heart in sanguineous animals and its analogue in others animals.[322] Now, even if there is some form of change in the central organ, we do not know what it is, and the central organ is one with various functions, so that pointing to it is by no means to make clear what occurs in the process of perception and hence memory.

One aspect of the involvement of the central organ in perception should be mentioned at this point. For the affection ($\pi\acute{\alpha}\theta o\varsigma$)[323] to be complete, the organ has to be involved; otherwise the perception just affects the peripheral organs. The idea is that there is a moment when the perception is complete, namely when it reaches the central organ.[324] But the important thing here is not so much the physiology, but the temporal structure of memory: only after the perception is over is memory of it

---

319 See above p. 26.
320 450a14. I speak of central "organ", since the heart is both homoiomerous and anhomoiomerous, being involved in both the causation of locomotion and perception.
321 450a28–29.
322 See esp. De juv. 3 469a5–12, King 2001; 70–1, 97, 125.
323 See above p. 20.
324 451a25–26. The expression is unclear; I follow Sophonias 7.19, and Ross, p. 244 on 451a25–31 who compares Sens. 7 449a16–18; see also De an. III 2 426b16–23, 7 431a19-b2; and De mem. 1 450a13; on this view of perception in Aristotle see Neuhäuser 1878: 83–84. One problem with this view is how a perception, which is indivisible, can be completed by reaching an extended organ; one would have to conceive of the organ as a whole in some sense. See G. Ross p. 17–18, Neuhäuser 1878: 85, 104–5.

possible. Perception has to be past for it to be remembered. This is what we expect from the **CF**.[325]

Is there any sign that Aristotle felt the need to be more explicit in the matter of the physiology of memory? He seems to be quite content to give a definition of memory without any specific matter being named. A change is named, namely a representation; but the discussion of representation does not really convince the reader that there is a detailed material theory in the offing, nor indeed that one is felt to be desirable. Rather, it is enough that perceptions can leave changes in the living thing.

This vagueness is also unmistakeable in the passage at the end of chapter 2 in which the bodily nature of recollection is being explicitly discussed (453a14-b7): in the best part of a Bekker column Aristotle does no more than associate recollection with various changes in the body and bodily afflictions and affections. This reticence has not prevented some interpreters from speculating about the kind of fluid, e. g. which is mentioned as making some people bad at recollection (blood or black bile). But even a definite answer to this question would not amount to the identification of a concomitant change.[326] Thus, for the status of memory, we are left with changes of a kind, made possible by the standard changes involved in growth and nutrition.

This view would fit with two aspects of the process described here, which are clear, up to a point, but cannot be pressed too far:

(1) the result of the action of the seal is a change in the wax.
(2) whether there is memory or not depends on the (rate of) flux in the living thing.

(2) is important insofar as Aristotle regards the living body as in an equilibrium constituted by the changes that make up its metabolic processes. If there is too much or too little process, this affects the ability of the living thing to remember. We have already touched on these points above. The comparisons that Aristotle uses here are clear enough even if one cannot quite see how they could be converted into physiological terms. The wall is too hard to be impressed, as it were, hence the old do not remember, and the fluid young are too impressionable so the impression does not remain in their fluid state, which resembles water.[327] The qualities of the living things appealed to are relative to the function under consid-

---

325 Above p. 32.
326 Althoff 1991: 134: blood; van der Eijk 1990: 36–8: black bile.
327 450a32-b11.

eration, rather than being independently ascertainable quantities. The living thing may be too hard or too fluid for memory to occur. Functional stability is necessary for memory, not the presence of independently identifiable impressions.

So Aristotle thinks he is able to define memory and recollection without much recourse to physiology. This does not alter the fact that physiology plays an important role in that memory and recollection only occur in animals i.e. living things that perceive. This is more than just a triviality.[328] Firstly, the persisting living thing is necessary for memory; secondly it must be able to perceive; and thirdly these perceptions remain in some sense. Furthermore, there are certain aspects of his physiology which he does mention *en passant*, without really drawing any explanatory power from their use. Above all, I am referring here to his idea of a central organ unifying the sensual system, and which is identical with the central organ responsible for metabolism. But he does not discuss the way in which any such living system has to be constructed if it is to be capable of memory. So it appears that memory in Aristotle's view places no specific constraints on what happens in the living system which is to have it, beyond the retention of perception, and the perception of time. The perceptions must remain, and the living thing must be able to tell them apart from present perceptions. It is merely necessary that there is some such system, and that it is able to preserve the representations in such a way that they can be used for memory. No particular process, apart from representation, is named as responsible for memory and recollection although the latter is said expressly to be something that happens in a bodily context.[329] The images used to describe both memory in general, the wax imprint, and the images for the bad memory of the old and the young, the hard wall and the water, can all be made

---

328 Cf. Ch. 1 450a27-b7. The important article by Solmsen 1961 on the discovery of the nerves is cited by Burnyeat 1995: 420 for the lack of interest on Aristotle's part in such physiological questions.

329 Van der Eijk (1997: 251) remarks that in De mem. only the cases of memory failure are mentioned in connection with the body. The physical factors of normal or successful memory are not explained. One can contrast the role of the liver in *Timaeus* 71A-B: because of its shiny surface, it serves as a sort of mirror for the images of thoughts (εἴδωλα καὶ φαντάσματα 71A5–6), which may consequently influence the mind in dreams and the day time. (Note that memory is not mentioned in the *Timaeus*; but cf. *Critias* 26B.) In Aristotle's account of memory there is no analogue to the liver's shiny surface.

comprehensible in terms of Aristotelian conceptions. The central point is
a stable body that is able to preserve representations from perception.

2.1.6 The Final Definition: a solution to the present-past problem

Something remains of the original perception; this is the representation:
how are we able to relate it back, in the act of remembering, to the original perception or conception? Aristotle's answer is beguilingly simple. In
actually remembering we are doing something, and what we are doing is
to use the representation in a certain way. The *use* of a representation
plays an important role in distinguishing memory from mere representation (the Memory-Representation problem P3)[330]. Representations are
not merely psychic data that remain from perception; they can be
made to serve a function.[331] Only on this basis can they contribute towards constituting memory. When we, and other animals, use the representations, we use a capacity to regard something as something. When we
understand how these factors co-operate, we will have solved the Present-
Past problem (P2)[332], and hence be in a position to define memory. The
present-past problem is, after all, the puzzle that Aristotle uses to structure his approach to defining memory in Chapter 1.[333]

Let us use our example of a perception again:

Example (E) Socrates remembers (at t2) that he saw Theaetetus two days
ago (at t1).[334]

The perception at t1 consists in the reception of a form; a certain time
must pass, and then at t2, the subject of the perception can remember
it. At t2, the subject of the perception is in a certain state: how is it possible for this state to represent a perception or conception that was in the
past at t1? Obviously, not merely by being the causal continuation of that

---

330 P. 2.
331 To what extent is memory intentional? It is at any rate end-directed; a decision to
recall something is rather different, and differently related to the end; this is of
course the Memory-Recollection problem (above, p. 2); for Aristotle's solution,
which does not use the difference between the functional use of representation
and an intentional act, see below, p. 95.
332 P. 1–2.
333 450a25–451a8.
334 Cf. above p. 8.

past state, since there are innumerable causal continuities between different times in the life of an individual. We need some representation of that past event: representation only occurs in things with perception, and presumably only insofar as they have perception, so not any event in the past in the living thing's body will be causally relevant to a memory. But nor will any event even if these are restricted to representations; for clearly there are representations that cannot count as memories, indeed, which no one wants to count as memories; representations serve as many things, and we need to isolate, if not which representations are memories, then what are we doing with our representations when we remember something.

What we are doing in remembering is taking something as something.[335] This solution to the Present-Past problem (P2) relies on our ability to see, grasp things in a certain way. Interestingly, Aristotle will have to ascribe this kind of capacity to animals without language if they are to be able to remember. Thus it is a function of perception.[336] This should not surprise in that perception is a form of cognition for Aristotle.

We have already met Aristotle's use of the notion of taking something as something when we discussed the question of whether in his theory representations are images.[337] The conclusion we came to was, no. We considered the comparison of the use of representations in memory with the use of pictures to refer to the thing of which they are the picture. Aristotle thinks that simply on its own, a picture is not a picture of something; it is only that when it is taken to be of something.[338] So too with a representation: a representation only refers to something when it is taken

---

335 If any argument is needed, the role of taking something as something in memory, interpreting a representation as an image, shows that it is not representation that does this (*pace* Nussbaum 1978: Interpretive Essay 5 esp. 255–261); for memory depends on how the representation is taken. Hence representation itself is not responsible for the way we take things (interpret them). Taking something as something would seem to be a function of perception in general; cf. the problem of incidental perception in De an. II 6.

336 On representations in animals see Labarrière 1984.

337 See above p. 57.

338 The same theory of memory appears in De mot. anim. 8 702a5–7: memory and expectation (cf. De mem. 1 449b10–13) of courage, fear and other emotions cause heatings and cooling, by using such affectations as images (εἴδωλα). Nussbaum (1978: 355–6) thinks that this theory is an improvement on De mem., since she sees the theory here as one in which not the object of the experience is remembered, merely the representation; lines 450b11–451a2 show that this is not the theory of De mem.; cf. above p. 39.

to be of that thing. When a representation simply occurs – floats through my mind, as it were – , it does not refer to anything beyond itself, it is merely a psychic datum. In contrast, in memory it is made to serve a purpose, and so to refer to something else. We take a representation to be the image of a past perception. In taking the representation to be the image of the past perception we remember that perception. This view of how to explain what we do in actually remembering provides him with his final definition of memory.

There are several reactions that one might have to this suggestion. A conventional image-based theory of memory might seem to offer the advantage that there are aspects to the image which make it a memory image. An image with the pictorial quality P might then be a memory image of a perception which involved P, and image without that quality would not be. In contrast to an image theory of memory, Aristotle's account might seem to be arbitrary in that there is apparently no principled way of deciding what kind of psychic events can be memories of what kind of perceptions. He does not offer us anything like an interpretation scheme.[339]

Against this view, one can plead the case of the constructivist view of memory: what is really important is what I do at t2. Furthermore, it would certainly appear that, just as many things can be taken as pictures, so many states of mind can serve one as memory for any given perception or conception one may remember. That is not to say that by using a representation as an image of that of which it is the representation one guarantees the correctness of the memory. That depends on what the facts of the matter are: I remember meeting Socrates, and this view is right or wrong depending on whether I actually did meet Socrates. Whether or not I am right in my claim, what I am doing is remembering.[340]

Let us recapitulate the course of the enquiry, now that we have all of the pieces necessary to define memory. It will be remembered that the three questions posed by Aristotle at the outset were:[341]

What is memory?

What is the cause of memory?

Which part of the soul is responsible for memory?

---

339 Cf. Wedin 1988: 138–41.

340 This is the message of the certainty and deception passage above p. 51, below p. 85. On the possibility of deceptive or mistaken memories cf. also above n. 194 on Ryle.

341 See above p. 26.

The **Final Definition** (**FD**) will offer an explanation of memory by list-ing the factors involved and showing how they co-operate to produce memory. Thus we will not merely have the moving cause of memory, a representation,[342] we will also have a formal cause, namely in the part of the soul involved,[343] which was the subject of the third question.

The question of the definition, that is, now, the final definition, is to be answered using the answers to the other two questions The point about the final definition is, finally, that it explains in theoretical terms the pre-theoretical understanding of memory which was articulated in the **Canonical Formula** (**CF**).[344] What Aristotle is doing is fitting the way we speak about memory into his theoretical framework. The defini-tion is hardly comprehensible unless one understands the way in which he is using his technical terms, and, more broadly, how his theory of the soul works.

Let us recall the **CF** and the **PD** which Aristotle distilled from it by application of his terminology:

CF For always whenever someone is active with respect to remembering, then he says in this way in the soul that he heard this or perceived it or thought it before.[345]

PD Therefore memory is neither perception nor conception but the pos-session or affection of one of these, when time has passed.[346]

PD does no more than extract the content of **CF** using Aristotle's tech-nical terms. That this is a true definition of memory is, I think proven in Aristotle's view by the fact that he can show how memory, when under-stood in this way, occurs. He is able to show how perceptions are pre-served ("possessed") and modified ("affected") in such a way as to provide memory. Now for the **Final Definition** (**FD**):

τί μὲν οὖν ἐστι μνήμη καὶ τὸ μνημονεύειν, εἴρηται, ὅτι φαντάσματος, ὡς εἰκόνος οὗ φάντασμα, ἕξις.

---

342 450a25–451a14 for memory and 451b10–452b7 for recollection.
343 Notice, however, that the soul can serve as any of the causes with the exception of the material one (De an. II 4 415b8–28).
344 See above, p. 32.
345 449b22–23.
346 449b24–25.

Final Definition What memory is, and remembering, has been said, namely, that [memory] is the possession of a representation as an image of that of which it is the representation.[347]

A representation is mentioned in this definition. This of course implies the part of the soul involved, namely the perceptive part. But the definition also mentions the way in which the representation is taken, namely as an image of the original perception or conception.[348] The point of the qualifier "as an image" lies in the fact that one might be in possession of a representation, but not use it to remember the thing in question. Without the qualifier, the connection with the original perception is not given. Of course there is *a* connection, since the representation remains from the perception.[349] But that is not sufficient for memory. Only if the representation is taken in a certain way do we have a way of solving the present-past problem.

It may look as though the temporal aspect is not contained in the final definition. This would be very surprising, given the space at the start of the treatise[350] devoted to the role of time and its perception in memory. So let us try to make clear where the temporal relation is, by using the simple example of a perceptual memory from the *Introduction:*

Example (E) Socrates remembers (at t2) that he saw Theaetetus two days ago (at t1).[351]

The act of memory in **E** has a certain proposition as its content: Socrates saw Theaetetus at t1. At t2 a representation is taken by Socrates as an image of this content. By being taken as an image the representation at t2 is related to the perception at t1. Taking the representation as an

---

347 451a15–16.
348 Morel p. 37. Contrast Wiesner (1985: 168) who speaks of "Gedächtnis als ununterbrochenes Behalten von Eindrücken aus früherer sinnlicher oder geistiger Tätigkeit"; this view of memory ignores the central role of taking the representation in a certain way. While Wiesner mentions (p. 170, 189) both the **Provsional Definition** and the **Final Definition**, he does not discuss their relation to one another
349 Can Aristotle exclude cases from falling under his definition in which we make a correct assertion about the past, using a representation which as a matter of fact has no connection with the original perception? I don't see how he could; he has in fact no way of guaranteeing the origin of representations.
350 See esp. 449b9–30, cf. also 450a25–7, 450b11–15.
351 See *Introduction* p. 8.

image of the perception at t1 relates it back to that perception. In this way it is clear that the temporal structure of memory is implicitly contained in taking a representation as an image of that of which it is the representation. Solving the Present Past problem (P2), as the final definition does, implies a role for the perception of time in the act of memory.

If one asks oneself how the representation is related to the original perception, then it is clear that in the way that the representation is considered as an image there is a relation to the past. To begin with, this is a question of perceiving that Theaetetus is not there now, but that *this* representation relates to an earlier perception.[352]

At first blush one may think that we are only concerned with a temporal order among representations. The representation can only be related to the past perception if this one perception is temporally determined among the series of representations: the perception is dated with reference to other perceptions. The dating would then have a kind of indexical or demonstrative function: it marks this one perception from the perspective of the person concerned. But we can go further than this in that, while actual representation is uncoupled from the external world, perception as a whole is not. For actual perception presupposes a relation to a concrete thing outside the soul.[353] It is not, of course, the individual as such that is the object of the perception, but rather the individual as qualified in a certain way.[354] But the individual that is perceived in this way is spatially and temporally fixed.[355] Hence perception relates to temporally ordered things. And of course, memory implies temporal order: perceptions that are remembered are past ones. This is the reason that the cognition of time is said to be "the main thing".[356] Hence memory is the possession of a perception after time has passed, because the possession of a representation is related to the original perception by being taken as an image of it.

Aristotle's definition of memory enables us to give answers to several of the problems raised in the *Introduction*[357]. We have now looked at the Present past problem (P2); the Derivation Problem (P1) has also been

---

352 Cf. Ins. 3 461b22–30.
353 De an. II 5 417b18–26.
354 See above on the definition of perception, p. 23.
355 See Anal. Post. I 31 87b29–30. For an interesting, if controversial, treatment of the connection between concrete things, time and autobiographical memory, see Campbell 1997.
356 Ch. 2 452b7; see above p. 66.
357 See *Introduction* p. 1–3.

solved. Another question concerned the way representations in memory are to be distinguished from other ones (the memory-representation problem, P3). The procedure is simple; just place the definitions of the two phenomena side by side, and you can read off how they are distinct. Here are the two definitions again:

Representation is a change arising from an actual perception.[358]

Memory is the possession of a representation as an image of that of which it is the representation.

That is, of course, simple enough for the Aristotelian scientist; one may complain that that does not help since what one needs is a guarantee that the user of a memory will be able to tell memories from other contents of their minds, specifically from other representations. If they cannot do this, then they will be in no position to use their memory. For the Aristotelian scientist, too, this state of affairs is unsatisfactory. For the **PD** is based on the way we talk about memory; and if we, people with memories, are in no position to distinguish memory from other psychic activities, then the Aristotelian scientist is deprived of a starting point for his enquiry.

So how are memory and representation to be distinguished quite generally? The representation is a change that arises from actual perception. Thus the representation may simply be a psychic datum, something floating through my mind like a day-dream. Another activity connected with representation is imagining things to oneself. This is part of what representation does for Aristotle. One can for example represent a scene to oneself in one's mind. Imagining things is a particular intentional activity.[359] But imagining something is doing something different from remembering. In the case of both of these end-directed activities, one knows what one is doing.[360] Both are different from a non-intentional

---

358 See above p. 46.
359 De an. III 3 427b18–20. Wedin (1988: 74–77) denies this, on the grounds that images here are in the service of mnemonics. This is right. Nonetheless, we should not deny that Aristotle here refers to the intentional activity of imagining something; and that is something we can do without putting it to any use.
360 Does this account make memory too active? Bloch (2007: 79–118) claims that for Aristotle memory is merely a state, indeed passive; see above for some remarks on this. Another point is some forms of pathological memory – of terrible experiences – persist or remain actual even though the subject does not want

representation. Aristotle thinks that on the one hand the act of remembering is self-evident, but, on the other hand, what one remembers may deceive one.[361] The first point concerns the activity of remembering: this activity is evident since it is distinguished by the end remembering has. This distinguishes remembering, for example, from imagining something; imagining something requires a particular intention to be adopted. Remembering meeting a dragon, even wrongly, is a different activity from imagining a dragon. Deceiving yourself into believing you remember meeting a dragon is different from imagining you met a dragon.

We have already discussed the way in which the two activities, imagining and remembering, are distinguished by the intention one has when performing them.[362] The **PD** of memory[363] tells us what we do, when remembering: this is the stating point of the enquiry, one familiar to us. So too with imagining something. The activity of imagining must be distinguished from a representation. For a representation is merely the remains of a perception. It may, however, as has been remarked before, be used to do something, such as intentionally imagining something. Thus the remains of perceptions of an iguana may be used to imagine a dragon. In contrast, memory is a form of cognition that uses what has been retained from the earlier cognition to refer to it. This is the way Aristotle escapes problems with a simplistic representational theory of memory. In so doing two things are needed: the representation has to be regarded in a certain way and the time passed has to be perceived. In fact, as we have seen, these two seem to be aspects of the same action: in regarding the representation as the copy of something, I am taking into account the fact that it is not a perception, something originating in a past perception. Because the distinction between memory and representation rests on what the living things does, it is a distinction that the living thing itself is in a position to draw. These are distinctions between representations and memory quite generally, and not that different distinction between correct and false or misleading memory.[364]

---

them; thus they would appear to be non-intentional. Still, some form of function is being performed.

361 The certainty and deception passage: Ch. 2 452b24–28, cf. Ch. 1 451a8–12, and cf. above n. 194.
362 Above p. 51.
363 Above p. 27.
364 See Ross 1924: 116 on Met. I 1 980b26; Sorabji p. 11–12, Fn. 1, discusses this distinction, but sees it as that between real memory and imagined memory. He is interested in the question how one knows whether the "image" is in one's mem-

The provisional definition is transformed into the final definition by displaying the cause for the occurrence of memory. This cause relates to the capacities of the animal, namely to perceive. Perception has a variety of functions which are relevant here. The capacity to perceive enables the living thing to perceive time on the one hand, secondly to have representations, and thirdly, to regard the representation in a certain way. Memory occurs when these uses of perception coincide.[365] Not only are representations a function of perception, perception is also responsible for the cognition of time; and perceiving something as something is perception.[366] The representation which remains from a perception is explicitly related to the perception of the thing by being put in a temporal relation to the perception. The representation is thus seen to be an image of *this* dated perception, and at the same time it is seen as an image of the individual perceived.

2.1.7 Some epistemological aspects of memory

Memory is unique from an epistemological point of view in that it, and it alone, gives us veridical access to perceptions that we have had and so to the things which we have perceived. That this aspect of memory is crucial to Aristotle emerges clearly from the way he distinguishes memory from other forms of cognition, namely those connected with the present (perception), and the future. Memory is epistemologically direct in the sense that we do not have to draw conclusions, for example, from a representation in order to have something in one's memory. We use representations but we do not draw conclusions from them. Thus memory is direct, in that we remember directly, without ratiocination. For of course ani-

---

ory or not. And he quite rightly points out that one cannot see this simply from the "images" themselves. As we have seen it is anything but obvious if Aristotle thinks of representations like this. On their truth and falsity, see above p. 55; we have seen this is due to the way in which the perceptions they arise from are put together, and has nothing to do with their character as images. Truth in memory is only possible when the representation is regarded as a *quasi* image of the experience – that is to say not just taken as a representation. Thus in the way we treat representations there is a distinction between representation taken simply and memory.

365 See De mem. 2 452b23–24: the movement of the thing and the movement of the time have to occur together for memory to be present.

366 See above p. 57, 79.

mals remember and in Aristotle's book they cannot reason. But this directness of memory does not mean that it is not susceptible to explanation. The fact that memory can be explained, in terms of the faculty of perception, and the remaining of representations which are then used in remembering, does not mean that memory is epistemologically indirect, merely that it is explicable.

It is clear from what has been said that these are aspects of memory which are accounted for in Aristotle's account. The crucial aspect of his account lies in seeing a representation as an image of a perception. For in this action we make a claim about the way the past was, using the way it appears to us now.

Whether we are right or not in so doing is another question. The relation to truth and falsity emerges very clearly because of a peculiar kind of memory failure that Aristotle mentions; perhaps he has a kind of madness in mind. People are mentioned[367] who are meant to have regarded all their representations as things that had happened. Whatever this failure of memory is, it makes clear that the cognitive responsiveness of memory lies in our flexibility to see some representations as images and others not. In this way bringing things together or separating them is the basis for memory being able to track the way things were. Here is a suggestion for a way to take this phrase. To separate the representation from the original perception is to say that *that* is not the way it was, in other words that I regard a representation as not being the image of the perception in question; to bring representation and perception together is to regard the representation as an image of the perception, and claim that is the way it was. There are two ways of regarding the representations in this context, namely as images or not. This is why we can be in doubt as to whether things were the way we say they were.[368]

For if we were like the unfortunates Aristotle mentions, then we would be stuck in a fictional world. This is so not so much because of the content of the representation; after all, it just might be the case that all the representations in question really do correspond to the way things were. But if they did so correspond, it would be a matter of chance, and thus not a justifiable memory. Memory has to be responsive if it is to be responsible. In their case, a lack of flexibility does not beto-

---

367 451a8 – 12.
368 451a2 – 8. Aristotle suggests that improving our memory is a related phenomenon. Memory can be exercised by remembering something repeatedly by using the representation of it as an image.

ken certainty, but a mad fixity. Flexibility hinges on the capacity to take a representation as an image, or not. There are two alternatives here.

So much for some basic epistemological aspects of memory according to Aristotle. We can now turn to rather more sophisticated uses. The object of *De memoria et reminiscentia* is to define memory and recollection. Nothing is said about the further reaching cognitive capacities which are based on these two, especially memory. For this is implicated in experience (ἐμπειρία), and so in the acquisition of arts and sciences; and in a certain respect it is also involved in ethical learning. The relation between memory and science and arts form the subject of two very celebrated chapters in the *Corpus: Metaphysics* I 1 und *Posterior Analytics* II 19. The subject of the chapter in the *Analytics* is how one comes to know the principles of science. The passage in the *Metaphysics* discusses wisdom (σοφία) as the apex of all forms of cognition, which one can only reach by way of memory.[369]

The question I wish to discuss is whether the concept of memory that is used in these passages is the same as that defined in *De memoria et reminiscentia*. I think it is. The main reason for thinking that it is not lies in the view that what is at stake in *De memoria et reminiscentia* is personal memory, and memory of one's own experiences would seem to import an extraneous element into the genesis of science. For the fact that memories in each case are had by someone, relative to their own past, is not really relevant to science. This view may seem to be supported by the fact that Aristotle goes out of his way to deny that memory relates to reason as such.[370] From this view, might try to argue that memory, at least conceived of as the memory of an individual relative to their own perceptions, is not relevant to reason, that is science. Of course, this question touches one of the problems we considered at the outset, the universal-memory problem (P6):[371] Actually doing science in the Aristotelian sense, entertaining the axioms of a completed science, seems to require no use of my memory.

But memory is relevant to the acquisition of universal concepts. After all, some individual has to acquire the concepts; learning is always someone's learning. But does this not import something extraneous? No, because all that is imported is the idea that they are one's own perceptions and they can be distinguished from the perceptions one is having now.

---

369 See Scott 1995: 107–117 for this interpretation.
370 νοητικόν De. mem. 1 450a12–18.
371 P. 3.

Thus they fulfil in a minimal way the criteria for being memory set up in *De memoria et reminiscentia*. On the path from perceptions to universal concepts, one will be moving from a series of perceptions, each of which is preserved as representation, but also considered as an image of the perception, that is: related to the original object of perception. This is work an individual does in the course of learning science.

The basis for the value of memory for science lies in the fact that percepts (αἰσθήματα) are preserved by some living things.[372] Clearly, the mere preservation is not enough: among some of these living things a λόγος comes about; this phrase presumably includes definitions.

The formation of concepts presupposes a sum of remaining percepts. If this implied that memory were the preservation of the percepts, this conception of memory would not be compatible with Aristotle's canonical formula (**CF**) as, then, one would not need "to say in the soul that one had learnt or perceived something, when one is active with one's memory".[373] Collecting percepts is not the same as saying that one has perceived something in the past. Aristotle's concept of memory is, in view of our common opinions, very restricted. He only describes personal memory which requires that one also has the relevant perception or learning in mind as well as their content.

It is not at all easy to reconstruct Aristotle's conception of the work of the scientist at this point. The account is too terse. But the work of collecting perceptions of some subject of science, say: a kind of animal A, by a scientist, requires clearly more than the remaining of percepts. For example, the explicit relating of the remainders of perception to the objects of perception may include a truth claim (a least: this appearance is not deceptive). For what we want to gather are claims about what A is. These claims are memory claims, and so go beyond the mere remaining of percepts. This agrees with our concept of memory from *De memoria et reminiscentia*. Percepts only then lead to experience (ἐμπειρία) when they are collected, i.e. those of a single thing, e.g. of a natural kind, through memory.[374] Contrary to what one might expect, the memory is not the storage of the percept – that is the prior step. Rather the memory relates a present percept to a past perception. This may lead to experience. And

---

372 Anal. Post. II 19 99b36–37, Met. I 1 980a27–29.
373 Ch. 1 449b18–22 see above p. 32.
374 See Gregoric and Grgíc 2006 for an account of experience in Aristotle.

such an experience may represent a step towards the scientific definition of our kind A.[375]

2.2 Recollection

It is perhaps appropriate to approach recollection through Plato, although in *De memoria et reminiscentia* Aristotle does not, contrary to his usual, but not invariable practice, say what his predecessors thought about memory, or indeed, recollection; instead, when turning to the latter topic at the start of Chapter 2, he refers to some form of dialectical exercises in which theses on memory were discussed, and says that everything true in these discussions should be assumed.[376] These exercises were perhaps also concerned with questions about the content of memory and recollection. At least the thesis that recollection is neither the acquisition nor the recovery of memory seems to be taken from these discussions, and argued for again.

Although Plato is not mentioned, at least one important part of Aristotle's views of memory and recollection is derived from him.[377] Memory and recollection are both directed at the same kind of content, namely, some perception or knowledge one has grasped in the past. It is crucial for Aristotle's conception of recollection that we are clear about what is recalled in recollection. However, he parts company from Plato with the idea of a *first perception*, which we have already discussed above.[378] Unlike Plato, Aristotle thinks that we can learn something new by perception rather than merely being reminded of something we already know.

There are further aspects which are profoundly un-Platonic in his account. For example the insistence that we pay attention to the way in

---

375 This process is sometimes divided by Aristotle into four and sometimes into three steps: perception, memory, science; and the fourth step, experience, may come between memory and science. Three steps: Anal. Post. II 19 99b34–100a3, four: 100a3–9, Met. I 1 980a27–981a3. The commentators disagree on how to explain this discrepancy. Barnes 1993: 262–6, Detel 1993: II 867–884. Strikingly, the place of representation is taken by percepts in this account. It is hard to see what point if any is intended by the substitution. Frede (1992: 292) notes the substitution, but treats the passage just as if representation were used.

376 Sorabji p. 88. Ch. 2 451a19. On the start of Chapter 2 see esp. Wiesner 1998.

377 We have already seen that Aristotle rejects (implicitly) the account from the *Philebus*. See above p. 24–25.

378 P. 69.

which the faculty for memory and representation exists, a physiological slant which is very characteristic of Aristotle's investigation into living behaviour in *De anima* and *Parva Naturalia* generally. In the account of recollection, the salient point lies in the use of the concept of change to account for the associative chains leading to recollection.[379]

The allusions to Plato are the first things we will discuss in relation to recollection. Our approach to recollection will be negative like the account given by Aristotle: he begins by saying what recollection is not,[380] namely that it is neither the recovery (ἀνάληψις) nor the acquisition (λῆψις) of memory. Now, Plato's writings do not contain the assertion that recollection is either of these two;[381] so the passage before us can hardly count as a refutation of Plato, as some interpreters have claimed.[382] Nonetheless, his influence is evident in the passage, the point of which is to move towards a distinction between memory and recollection. In fact, Aristotle is using part of Plato's account of recollection ἀνάμνησις), namely that it is a recovery of knowledge, or more generally cognition (ἐπιστήμην ἀναλαμβάνειν). For this is precisely what Aristotle in the end will want to say. Recollection relates to earlier cognition. Crucially, Plato does not use the relevance of time for his theory, although time is of course implicit in the idea of *recovery*. And furthermore the relationship of memory to science is rather a different one in Aristotle's view, as it is an indirect one, mediated by the representations that science depends on when we think its theorems.[383] In both the *Meno* and the *Phaedo* the soul recovers[384] something in itself of that which it had undergone when with the body. Hence it is not the recovery of memory, but rather of that which, when combined with a time, makes the content of memory.[385]

A central role is played in Aristotle's theory by the idea of a first perception, that is to say, there is a first time in which something, namely the

---

379 Cf. above p. 75 on the nature of the material explanation of memory and recollection offered in De mem.
380 Wiesner 1998: esp. 131on 451a18–451b10, the negative account is at a18–31.
381 Freudenthal 1869: 404.
382 Ross on 451a18-b10, p.243 expresses the view that Aristotle's claim that recollection is not the recovery or acquisition of memory (451a20–1) is a criticism of *Meno* 85D6–7, *Philebus* 34B6–8.
383 See above p. 42.
384 The only place Plato does talk about repetition (ἀναπολήσῃ) of memory is *Philebus* 34B10-C2.
385 *Phaedo* 75E5–6, *Meno* 85D3–7. These points are consistent with the reference to the dialectical exercises at 451a19 being to Platonic dialogues.

perception associated with an individual, enters the mind. Of course, the capacity does not enter the mind, and so this is compatible with theories of recollection such as Plato's in which innate capacities are realised by perception. These capacities have been acquired before birth.[386] We have already taken a closer look at the acquisition of memories, and seen that the original perception is not the acquisition of memory. This only happens when a certain time has passed after the perception. This thesis follows from the **PD**, which requires that, for memory to be present, we possess a conception or perception after time has passed.[387] The original perception is not the memory and only becomes a suitable object for it after time has passed.[388]

Let us turn to recollection. We begin by distinguishing it from memory.[389] It is crucial to understanding *De memoria et reminiscentia*. Apparently, Chapter 1 is devoted to memory and Chapter 2 to recollection, as though they were separate topics.[390] We will see that they are in fact

---

386 See e.g. *Meno* 81C-D.

387 449b25, above p. 27. Here too we are offered the choice between possession and affection (451a23–24); see also 451a27–28.

388 451a29–30; see above on the perception of time, p. 62. Aristotle (Hist. anim. VII 10 587b10–11) notices a interesting parallel in the case of infants: after 40 days they dream, but their representations are only much later in their memories. This is comparable to modern thoughts about having experiences at a time when one does have the concepts to understand them, and only later acquire the concepts. Thus what one remembers is not the experience as it is interpreted with the concepts but something more primitive.

389 Annas (1992 (1)) interprets the distinction as being between personal memory and memory that is not bound to my experience. This bold claim is meant to solve the problem that Aristotle otherwise leaves himself without a way of accounting for the memory of thoughts and other timeless facts. On accidental memory of thoughts, see above p. 42. Annas' way of distinguishing the two is close to the distinction introduced by Tulving (e.g. 1983) into modern psychology between semantic and episodic memory (and cf. also Bergson 1897). The first refers to content stored with no relation to the self (language, general knowledge), and the second does refer to episodes in one's own life. (Annas' thesis is accepted by Caston 1998: 258 n. 18). van Dorp 1992: esp. 463–76 on De mem. distinguishes the two concepts in another way. Bloch 2007: 74–79 adds to those differences named by Aristotle that memory is passive, and recollection active. The difference in time between memory and recollection (De mem. 2 453a7) may well be simply that while memory remains from the past, recollection is a search from the present. Cf. Scheler 1980, and Buchheim 1997.

390 Bloch (2007: 72–75, with n. 95) sees the two treatments as being largely unconnected. He thinks that De mem. 2 is really about a technique of recollection; in

closely connected and these connections will make it clear that they share much more than simply being common to body and soul. The strict division between the two chapters is not maintained,[391] and we must ask why. One obvious common factor is the cognition of time. At the start of Chapter 1 the perception of time is said to be essential to memory,[392] and in Chapter 2 we have a very difficult section[393] on the cognition of time, which obviously applies to memory as well. In fact, the connection between memory and recollection goes much deeper, since the capacity for memory is involved in recollection, which may, if successful, also lead to active memory.

First, let us consider the distinction between the two. Active memory preserves contents from the past, and recollection recovers them, starting from the present and going back to the past along a series of representations.[394] This distinction has a fundamental agreement as its background namely that both recollection and memory are forms of cognition of the second order, that is both relate to other cognitions that have already been made.[395] Recollection is a form of search, and from this fact follow other characteristics that make it distinguishable from memory:[396]

1. Animals other than humans have memory, whereas only humans are capable of recollection, since it is a form of calculation.
2. Humans may differ in how good their memory or their recollection is. Each of these capacities is associated with different constitutions, memory with slowness and recollection with quickness.
3. Memory and recollection differ in relation to time.

In particular, the second and third distinctions leave questions open, about the relationship between body and these forms of cognition, and between the latter and time. As a first step to understanding how these distinctions are to be understood, let us look at the way recollection is defined (**RD**):

---

fact, he discusses association, and not the system of places so favoured by Sorabji (Ch. 2 Mnemonic Techniques).

391 Annas 1992 (1): 298.
392 See above p. 66.
393 452b7–22, 453a4–14, cf. Annas 1992 (1): 298 with n. 4. See above p. 66 on the cognition of time.
394 For this distinction, cf. that between mediated and immediate remembering in Scheler 1980: II 436, Buchheim 1997: 249.
395 Cf. Caston 1998: 258.
396 The distinction is mentioned briefly at the start of the treatise (Ch. 1 449b6–8), and at greater length towards the end (Ch. 2 453a4–14).

RD: If one recovers some piece of science or a perception or that the possession of which we called memory, then this is the recollection of one of the things mentioned.[397]

This final characterisation of recollection refers explicitly to memory. What is recovered in recollection is that of which the possession (ἕξις)[398] is memory. This underlines the fact that recollection is not merely related to memory, it is dependent on memory. Both phenomena relate to perception and conception, but this does not mean that what we recollect is already in one's memory. In fact, the contrary is the case because only things have to be sought by recollection which are not at that stage in one's actual or potential memory. There may seem to be a paradox here: how does one recollect something that one cannot remember? We will see that there really is a problem here, and the solution lies in the fact that the capacity for memory can be realised in several ways. Either we have some past perception actually in mind without searching for it, or it is necessary to search for it. If the first is the case, then it is simple memory and the capacity for it, and if the second is the case, then it is recollection. The distinction between memory and the capacity for it lies in the fact that there are perceptions I can think of without further ado, although at the moment I am not thinking of them.

In both memory and recollection we are dealing with earlier cognitions; the difference lies in the fact that in the case of simple memory the cognition is ready to hand. For example, Socrates can say he remembers Theaetetus without a search. And if this memory is not ready to hand, then it must be recovered by recollection. This is the reason for the striking parallelism of the Aristotelian formulation of the two phenomena. The distinction lies in the different processes of *saying that*[399] something is the case and *concluding that* something is the case. This is quite evident if one compares the **CF** and the **PD** of memory with an account of what one does in recollection. Compare the following:

---

397   451b2–5. Bonitz s.v. refers to De an. I 4 408b17 for a definition of ἀνάμνησις:
      it starts from the soul and is directed towards changes or remains (μοναί) in the
      sense organs. In recollection, we are looking for a representation arising from an
      earlier perception (Hicks 1907: 275).
398   On ἕξις here, see above p. 34.
399   Or in the case of non-human animals: perceiving that something is the case
      (450a21).

PD The person who is active with their memory says in the soul he or she heard or perceived or thought something.[400]

The person who recollects concludes that he or she saw or heard or underwent something.[401]

The distinction lies in the different processes of saying and concluding: possession or affection in the case of memory is analogous to recovery in the case of recollection.

Memory and recollection are further connected by the fact that successful recollection leads to memory: it is possible to remember by recollecting.[402] Active remembering, however, does not require recollection, that is a previous process of recollection.[403] Recollection is a different process from memory, but it is a search that starts from the capacity for memory and ends in actual memory:[404] If one is able to remember something *via* recollection then one has to presuppose a capacity for remembering the thing in question. What is a capacity for remembering? Aristotle says it is a capacity for change, acquired through a perception. To explain this, let us look again at our example:

(E) Socrates remembers at t2 that he saw Theaetetus at t1.

Memory is acquired after t1: after then, the capacity for memory is established. But between t1 and t2 there does not have to be any actual memory for there to be recollection at t2 which realises the capacity acquired after t1. Now one can understand why recollection is neither the acquisition nor the recovery of memory.[405]

In one sense one recollects what one cannot remember, namely, that which one cannot remember without a search. This dependence of recollection on memory, however, means that memory had to be treated first.

---

400 449b24–25.
401 453a10–12, cf. 451b2–5 quoted above p. 94.
402 Sorabji p. 42 remarks that two processes are called recollection (ἀναμιμνήσκε-σθαι): the search, whether it is successful or not (453a12, 22) and the act at the end of a search, or the search *qua* successful (451a6, b2–5, 452a7–8, a28–9, 453a16–18, a20). This is not an ambiguity of the verb. There are simply different aspects to the process, it may be considered as finished or not, and as successful or not.
403 451a30-b6.
404 Cf. Ch. 1 449b4, Ch. 2 452a10–11.
405 Ch. 2 451b20–1.

The explanation of recollection requires that we have already understood the state it ends in, if successful.

Both memory and recollection are common to body and soul, hence are subjects for the *Parva Naturalia*.[406] One aspect of this status lies in the role of change. We have already noticed the importance of change for Aristotle's theory of memory, something that is ensured by the central role of representations.[407] Now we have a further indication of his use of change to explain distinctions, in this case that between memory and recollection. The distinction between the two is made possible by change because in the case of memory we are dealing simply with a change in the form of a representation, taken as an image of a perception. Recollection is more complicated: the changes, i.e. the representations may form a link from what I am thinking now to the thing I am looking for. The explanation of recollection has thus the task of describing the way in which these chains of change are composed.[408]

Now we must take a look at the way in which recollection actually occurs. We start from something that we now have in mind, and search for something that is within easy distance of the things sought.[409] There is not meant to be any difference in cases which extend over a long period of time and those which occur in short ones. At the outset, one has to have enough of the thing in mind that one can look for it.[410] The search for the thing to be remembered is regulated by the way one representation follows another. The central point is that one representation follows another because they are changes. We are, as it were, moved by representations[411] Changes are set going when one looks, that is, tries to remember. The act of recollection is, to start with, an attempt at memory. The nature of these changes is such that they follow one another when one looks:[412] in Aristotle's own example,[413] from milk to white from white to mist from mist to moist and so to autumn. One representation succeeds another in one's mind. One might say that we are talking

---

406 See above p. 24.
407 Above p. 46.
408 Esp. Ch 2 451b10–22, 452a17-b7.
409 451b18–19, "hence we look for thing which comes in succession to it starting from the now"; ἀπὸ τοῦ νῦν, that is, from the present representation (Michael 26.11–12, Beare). Cf. Ch. 1 450a7–9, 452a2.
410 Michael 19.7–14, cf. Sorabji p. 96
411 Note the passive 451b17.
412 451b10–11.
413 452a13–16.

about the moving causes of recollection.[414] And indeed large part of the explanation of recollection lies in determining how the changes follow one another and how they may be successful or not.

The fact that these representations follow one another in one's mind does not mean that one will be successful in the activity they go to make up. The way these changes follow one another is due to habit, if they mostly[415] follow a certain pattern, or by necessity if they always do. Habit (ἔθος) arises if one is often moved by a guidance which is not innate.[416] Changes establish paths along which later changes will tend to move. Aristotle gives us three ways in which the representations can be connected in recollection: they can be opposed to another, contiguous to one another or similar to one another.[417] One should, I think, therefore talk about *the rules of habit,* rather than the laws of association. The habit belongs to someone; we have noted that part of modesty in memory is that it belongs to someone;[418] and the history of this someone is responsible for the way in which representations follow one another in recollection. Primarily, we are dealing with the ways in which representations in someone follow one another,[419] rather than representations *tout court,* as though your representations would follow one another in the same order as mine do, although our biographies differ widely. Suppose Coriscus is musical and possesses a lyre, and you want to recollect him. If you have the pair of representations "lyre" and "Coriscus", when you see Socrates playing the lyre, you recollect Coriscus' lyre and then Coriscus himself.[420] This process of recollection will only work when the person who recollects knows Coriscus as someone who plays the lyre.

Thus necessity cannot apply to all representations of a certain type, as if the representation of a cat was always followed by that of a dog. For such a series to be established one needs perception, and that of course

---

414 451b20: "Because of this, recollection occurs" (διὰ τοῦτο γίγνεται ἡ ἀνάμνησις).
415 451b13.
416 EE II 2 1220b1–3. On habit and memory, see Morel 2006b, and cf. also Morel 1997.
417 451b18–20.
418 Above p. 9.
419 Note the subject of the sentence 451b11–13: the person recollecting.
420 Michael 24.17–23. Michael suggests that the changes in the soul are like those along a chain. This shows that he is thinking of the experience of one subject. One may well ask if such recollection is intentional or not; on accidental recollection see below p. 100.

belongs to an individual. Habit can modify nature.[421] This then results in what has come to be known as a second nature.[422] Such a nature is naturally the nature of the individual.

Aristotle distinguishes between habitual recollection, in which the representations follow one another for the most part, and a necessary sequence. How is this necessity to be understood? The following change is only necessary, that is to say it is not able to be otherwise,[423] if the previous one occurs. So the necessity here is hypothetical.[424] This kind of series is always so, and not merely mostly, as in the case of habit. But if such series are relative to persons, then how can they be established, if not by habit?[425] Possibly, because not all the fixed forms of behaviour under certain circumstances are entirely fixed by habit, as Aristotle allows for forms of innate capacity for certain activities.[426] However, it is hard to find examples for this kind of necessary sequence, and easy to imagine ways in which any sequence might be disrupted.

The representations have relations to one another because they are representations of things, and as the things relate to one another, so do the representations.[427] This would seem to go against the reading presented here. It is my claim that it is not the things taken in themselves that are decisive for the succession of representations rather it is our perception of them. This does not necessarily mean that a certain chain of representations which arose from the original perception is necessary to retrace one's steps to something one wishes to remember. Many roads may lead to the object of recollection.

The rules of habit[428] formulated after Plato[429] describe the way in which the representations follow upon another, both those that always

---

421 Sorabji p. 93–4, ad loc.
422 See 452a30; for a subtle discussion of this passage see Morel 1997, also more generally McDowell 1994: 84–6, 87–9. I owe the latter references to Thomas Buchheim.
423 451b12; at 451b28–29 necessity is left out. The account of necessity is from Met. VI 2 1026b28.
424 Phys. II 9, cf. also De somn. 2 455b26–28.
425 Sorabji (p. 94) thinks that the necessity has to be without reference to the experiencing subject, and finds no examples of it.
426 For example, εὐφυΐα in relation to truth or the good: Top. VIII 14 163b13–16 and EN III 7 1114b5–12.
427 452a1–2.
428 451b19–20 ἀφ' ὁμοίου ἢ ἐναντίου ἢ τοῦ σύνεγγυς.

do so and those that only do so mostly: they are like one another, close to one another or opposite to one another. These rules have of course some descendents with very important functions in some systems, e. g. being made responsible for the orderliness of nature by Hume.[430] But in Aristotle, they, like the capacity they serve, are modest. They may be taken either normatively or descriptively. They prescribe the way things are associated with one another, insofar as the one person has perceived them. Or else they in fact describe the way representations are reproduced, either always or sometimes, by a certain subject.[431] In the latter case there need be no predictability; and no claim as to why exactly the representations follow one another as they do.

The capacity on which recollection is founded is that to have something in one's memory.[432] Recollection proceeds by changes and ends in memory. Hence the capacity for the latter is capacity for change. But is the capacity to remember the same as the capacity to recollect? Remembering needs no mediation via a chain of changes. It seems that there are simply two routes to memory: indirect, along a path of representations, or direct, "because one originally had the perception".[433]

Changes arise from a principle and so, if one wishes to attain one's objective efficiently, one should pick the right principle.[434] As we shall see there are in fact many ways in which we can follow this recommendation. It is obviously simplest in those cases where the things to be recollected are ordered themselves, as in the case of mathematical sciences.[435]

---

429 Plato in the *Phaedo* (73C-74A) describes things which one recollects as being like or unlike the things that remind one of them. Primarily, of course, Plato is thinking of ideas and their instances (74C), or pictures and their originals (73E9).

430 See *Treatise* I i iv.

431 For criticism of association as a principle of recollection, see Morton 1994: 434–7.

432 452a10: having a memory (τὸ μεμνῆσθαι, to be taken as the capacity to remember something actually (G.Ross, Sorabji, Beare, and Ross' précis), in contrast to re-learning (l. a5–7). Bloch (2007: 88–95) denies that μεμνῆσθαι is the capacity to remember. This seems hard to reconcile with Aristotle's description of it as being the presence of a moving capacity (452a10–11).

433 451b1–2.

434 451b30–452a2. One might translate ἀρχή "beginning" but as every change starts from its beginning, there is not much gain to be had from starting at the beginning. So we have a normative recommendation here. Cf. Ross' précis: 'Therefore the quickest and best way is to start from the beginning since the movements will follow each other in the same order as the original events.' For the principle of change, see 451b30–31.

435 452a3.

The point about this form of organisation, through habitual association, is that it can produce the illusion that people are using a place system[436] (τόποι[437]) to move among the images. Presumably the point is that
natural memory is so good that people think wrongly it can only be achieved by techniques.[438] You can move quickly from *milk* to *white* from
white to *mist* from *mist* to *moist* and so to *autumn*, to give Aristotle's
own example.[439] Obviously, this is an associative chain and the point is
that if mnemonics were really to play an important role, this would di-
minish the importance of the rules of habit.[440] Yet there is no sign whatever that Aristotle wished to do this. What one did in order to use mnemonics was to remember a series of places (cf. τόποι) and to allocate the
things to be remembered to each of these places. Then all he had to do to
recollect the things he had committed to memory is to go along the places
and so be able to reproduce them.[441] If you are doing this, you are not
remembering by using either acquired habits or necessary chains of association.

Recollection is defined as a search, and so it would seem that we can
only recollect intentionally.[442] But then how do we explain the following?
I wish to remember Cebes' face. I try to recollect but fail. Some time later,
while I still have the wish to remember what Cebes looks like, but am not
currently trying to do it, I see Simmias, and because I have seen the two

---

436 452a12–13: "Hence people appear to remember using mnemonics." Aristotle
   mentions mnemonics only in three other places: Top. VIII 14 163b29, De insomn. 1 458b21, De an. III 3 427b19. According to Diogenes Laertius (V 26)
   he wrote a book μνημονικόν, 1 Book. This expression is used for the system of
   places in De an. III 3 427b19, Top. VIII 14 163b29; it could, however, just
   mean μνήμη (LSJ s.v.) (e.g. Xenophon *Oikonomika* 9.11). So this book could
   be De mem.
437 Primavesi (1998: col. 1264) points out that Aristotle's own concept of a τόπος
   (cf. *Top.* VIII 1 155b4–5) was meant to replace that which referred merely to
   a mnemonic framework. Hence, one may conclude, the use of τόπος here for
   mnemonics is not *in propria persona*. On Aristotle's concept of a τόπος, see
   Rapp 2002: II 270–300.
438 Contrast Sorabji p. 44: Aristotle is quite aware that "images" are not naturally
   such as to follow one another, and that they can be influenced by techniques.
439 452a13–16.
440 See above p. 98 on these, and below on the regulated search in recollection
   p. 102.
441 Primavesi 1998: col. 1263; see also Blum 1969, Yates 1966, Müller 1996. Important texts include: Rhetorica ad Herennium III 16–24, Cicero De Oratore
   II 353–60, Quintilian Inst. Or. XI 2.17–26.
442 451b22, cf. 452b2–6.

together so often, I immediately recall Cebes' features. Is that not a possible case of recollection? It seems to me that it is and that we can fit it into Aristotle's theory by calling it *accidental recollecting*. It is like the case of finding a treasure accidentally and, as in other cases of chance according to Aristotle, an aim is reached, which one has or perhaps even merely could have.[443] The intention is there, but is not responsible for the action that, as a matter of fact, fulfils it.

Another distinction needs to be mentioned at this stage, that between recollection and relearning. "Relearning" means in this context that one learns something completely anew, without any recourse to having learnt the thing in question previously. What then distinguishes recollection from relearning is the presence of the principle of change in the subject of recollection.[444] Here again we see the value of the concept of change. Another moving cause, outside the learner is necessary for relearning, a principle of change. For learning is a change in Aristotle's world on an equal footing to other forms of change.[445] Two possibilities of relearning are envisaged, depending on what the moving cause behind the change is, either learning from someone else or else learning something by discovery.[446] The point is that if there is not some bridging presence of a moving cause between the time of original learning and the time of recall, then there is no possibility of recollection, and in fact no presence of memory. That is, there is no capacity for this particular memory. The distinction between relearning and recollection is discussed in the context of the analysis of recollection using change for the simple reason that here at least it is apparent that there must be something in the living thing to cause the recollection to happen.[447]

---

443 Met. V 30 1025a14–19, Phys. II 5 196b33–197a7. Animals and children cannot on this interpretation accidentally recollect, since accidental recollection is parasitic on intentional recollection (cf. Phys. II 6 197b6–12).

444 451b8–10, 452a4–7, 10–12.

445 See e.g. Met. IX 8 1049b29–1050a2, Scott 1995:131–2.

446 Wiesner 1998: 130; cf. also 452a4–12, Sorabji p. 93. Beare's suggestion that "discovery" here means "excogitate" is unhappy, for it is too close to recollection itself, as a form of calculation (see 453a10). But perhaps "excogitate" implies the kind of thought one uses when confronted with the relevant phenomena and facts: there has to be an external moving cause for it to count as discovery, rather than recollection.

447 For the necessity of persistent causes of memory and hence of recollection, see *Introduction* p. 8–9. This, rather than the contrast with the *Meno* (Socrates sets the slave's recollection going with leading questions 82B, 82E, 84D,

To sum up the view of recollection that we have been considering: one has to move along a chain of changes starting from a principle in order to find what one is looking for. The way the changes are organised depends on the nature, or second nature of the person recollecting. This nature determines which representations lead to one another linked by the relations of similarity, proximity and contrariety. Recollecting involves rummaging among the representations.

In a famous passage,[448] Aristotle suggests how such searches may be conducted most economically and successfully. The way this explanation works depends on the rules we have met, and above all on the idea that one representation can lead to or produce (actualise) another. Aristotle uses a row of eight letters (ΑΒΓΔΕΖΗΘ) to stand for a series of representations, associated by the rules we have met.[449] The problem is how to move[450] among the representations in the best way, so that you find the one you are looking for most easily. So the problem is how to best recollect. The representations are changes in the recollecting person. Several searches are envisaged,[451] so the procedure is one one can repeat. Aristotle suggests that one should use the middle as a principle for the search; the eight letters have no absolute middle, and since there are several searches, he must mean the middle of sections of the series, say sections of three letters: of ΖΗΘ, begin with Η, that is, insofar as you do not immediately remember at Θ. The point about a middle letter is obviously that one can move in two directions, e. g. from Η to Ζ or Θ. If you then do not succeed, you repeat the process beginning at Γ to see if Β or Δ is the thing looked for.

The crucial thing about this view of recollection is the way that changes in the recollecting person represent things, and so present a chain of representations along which one can move to find the thing being looked for. When one does so, one then remembers. As we have

---

85D), is, I think, the philosophical point of these remarks (contrast Sorabji p. 37–40).

448 452a17-b7. For a detailed treatment see King 2004: 124–129. I follow Sorabji both in his reconstruction of the meaning of "middle", and in his text, but not in his enthusiasm for mnemonics. Mnemonics are, in my opinion, not readily compatible with a theory of recollection based on the rules of habit (above p. 98).

449 Above p. 99. Compare 452a26–30 with 1–17: the same connections are being talked about in both places.

450 or be moved: passive forms of the verb κινεῖσθαι occur in lines 452a21, a6, a11–12, 25, 27 (bis), 452b3; and twice in the active in line a9.

451 452a22–24.

seen recollection is directed at the same objects as memory, merely through a process akin to ratiocination, not a direct saying or perceiving that something is the case.

2.3 Interim conclusion: Aristotle on the six problems about memory

Let us conclude this chapter on Aristotle by summing up what he has to say about the six problems about memory set out in the *Introduction*:

(P1) The derivation problem. The starting point of Aristotle's enquiry is the **Canonical Formula (CF):** memory is attributed to someone when he says in the soul he has perceived or thought something earlier. Thus memory is derived from thought and perception. Nonetheless it has a class of objects peculiar to itself, namely *past* perceptions.

(P2) The present-past problem. The **CF** points to the connection between memory and time: memory relates to the past perception and thoughts in the life of the person remembering it. The **CF** enables Aristotle to move on to his own view of what happens in perception, and what results from it, namely the representations. In the act of remembering, which consists in saying or perceiving that something is the case, this representation has to be brought together with another representation, namely of the period between the time of the act of remembering (t2) and the time of the perception (t1). That is to say two representations, one of content and one of time, have to be brought together in the act of remembering. The first representation can be similar to the perception for the person who has it. Then it can be used to refer back to the perception, by being taken as an image of the perception. Thus the representation can serve to refer back to the perception not because of any inherent property, for example vividness, that it has but because it fulfils a function. Thus the **Final Definition (FD)** of memory, the possession of a representation as an image of that which it is a representation, encapsulates the use of a representation to represent the past.

(P3) The memory-representation problem. The reference of the representation back to the original perception is of course a reference which connects the present with the past. Hence there is a close connection with the present past problem (P2). For the reference to the past is possible, not by making the past present, but by taking the present representation to be an image of the past. That is what the **FD** says. When one does this one can be deceived or not, be right with what one says or perceives when one actually remembers or not. The distinction between representations in general and representations in acts of memory must be made by means of the intention guiding the action to which they contribute. The same content can occur in either. Thus whether one is remembering or not, is a question of what one is doing, and not of the content of what one then says. A representation can occur and not be taken as anything, but it can also fulfil a function. Thus distinguishing a representation which occurs merely as such, and one that occurs as part of the act of memory, that is with a reference to the past, is to be done on the basis of our awareness of what we are doing, and not because of any quality (such as vividness) of the representations.

(P4) The memory-recollection problem. Recollection can, if successful, end in memory, and is hence a way of using the capacity for memory. This explains why the enquiry into recollection (ch. 2) follows that into memory (ch. 1). But the nature of recollection is also illuminating for memory in that acts of remembering can happen in two ways, either preceded by recollection or not. The capacity for memory is the presence of a capacity for change, either to move from the present contents of one's mind to others, and so to arrive by recollection at the thing one wishes to remember, or else simply to remember at will. Recollection and memory are directed at the same objects, namely perception or conceptions after time has gone by. In both cases, representations are being used to fulfil functions, either of search or else to be taken as present images of the past. Representations are changes, and so can produce further representations. The way they are linked together in the process of recollection is regulated by the character of the person in question, according to the rules of association. For habit, which forms character, is a way of regulating changes. For example, representations, which play a central role in recollection, are ordered by the habits of the person they belong to. Habit establishes series among representations, in such a way that a second nature comes about. Once it is established, it is hard to change. This conception of habit plays an important role in the *Ethics*.

(P5) The self-memory problem. Memory is bound to the perceptions of the animal that remembers. This assumes that there is continuity between the original perception (at t1) and the activity of remembering (at t2). Thus continuity of the concrete living thing forms part of the explanation of memory. Living things are preserved by metabolic activity, and this must also ensure that the living thing preserves a quality suitable for retaining representations from perception. If this does not happen, as in the old and young, memory cannot occur.

(P6) The universal-memory problem. Aristotle's view that memory of thoughts is only accidental is well suited to explain what otherwise would be a serious ambiguity in the concept of memory, namely that some memories require mention of perception and others do not. Primarily, we are dealing with autobiographical memory. Its objects, past perceptions, can then determine the activity of remembering, that is, what one does when one actually remembers, and so the capacity to perform this activity. However, thoughts can also be objects of memory, albeit only accidentally, for the following reason. Because they must be presented to the mind in a representation, thoughts, above all, universals, can only be remembered indirectly, on account of their bearers. An example would be the memory of learning something. The theorem learnt is then only accidentally the object of memory. Rehearsing the theorem is exercising the capacity to think it, and not the capacity to remember.

3 Plotinus

3.1 Against impressions: memory as an active capacity

3.1.1 The context of Plotinus' theory of memory

Plotinus treats memory in two texts, IV 6 and IV 3 25 – IV 4 5. Memory is an activity of the soul in his theory; and because Plotinus' concept of soul is sophisticated, we will begin with a brief sketch of some aspects of this concept to provide the necessary background before we begin interpreting these texts in detail.[452]

Plotinus' system comprises three hierarchically ordered levels of being, which are called the *hypostases*: the one, also called *the good*, intellect (νοῦς) and soul.[453] Plotinus' thought is thus fundamentally concerned with what there is. Each level of being depends on the one that precedes it. Soul is derived from intellect insofar as it is among the things that intellect thinks.[454] It cannot undergo alteration; in the jargon, it is impassible.[455] The fact that the soul is impassible, and possesses active capacities is, as we shall see, central to the theory of memory. As an idea, the soul is on the one hand bound to thought, but on the other hand it can turn away from the intellect and, in the guise of the world-soul, perform the continuous, ongoing process of creating the world.[456] The world soul generates all bodies in the world, both organic and non-organic. The continuous creation of the world is a precondition for the embodiment of individual human souls, when they turn towards the sensible world. In so doing, they are no longer exclusively contemplating ideas, and have imagination, and when they acquire a body they use their faculty of perception to perceive actually. Thus the task of mediating between the perceptible world and the intellect is performed, in different

---

452 For general accounts of Plotinus, see Wallis 1972: Ch. 4, O'Meara 1993, Gerson 1994. For his conception of soul, see Blumenthal 1971, Deuse 1983, Alt 1993 112–120, 219–245. Emilsson 1991, Clark 1996.
453 Cf. the title of V 1: On the three principal *hypostases*, and further, cf. V 2 1 26, V 3 16 36. For the history of the term *hypostasis* see Dörrie 1955.
454 IV 3 1–8.
455 III 6, with Fleet's commentary (1996).
456 IV 3 4 21–30, IV 8 2, 4 4–9.

ways, by both individual human soul and world soul.[457] This double function in the human soul is of crucial importance for the theory of memory, in which the objects of both forms of cognition can be remembered. When the individual human souls turn away from intellect this can lead to embodiment, or else may stop short of a full descent into the material world, and remain in the heavens. Even when the human soul is embodied, it retains its position in intellect, as does the world soul. In both forms of existence, embodied and disembodied, the human soul has the potential for memory.

Each human soul, as such, is individual[458] and governs the body of the individual human. Primarily, a human is the intelligible soul, and secondarily there are phases which depend, for their being, on the intelligible man, namely opinion and perception.[459] Furthermore, each human has two souls, which are united in life and parted at death.[460] One is responsible for the practical life led, and the other is the intellectual soul. The higher, i.e. the intellectual soul only enters the body when it has been formed by the vegetative part of the world soul. The practical soul also has intellectual aspects, and, conversely, the intellectual soul has practical, sensible aspects, when leaving embodied life. This should not be confused with the concept of the soul with its two functions as sketched above, as these two distinctions differ, although both occur in the theory of memory. For the theoretically inclined soul takes perceptual memories with it when leaving the lower, practical soul, which in turn retains some degree of intellectual endowment. We shall discuss at length the chapters in

---

457 The most important Platonic text here is *Timaeus* 35A (see IV 2 2 40, 49–55; cf. also *Parmenides* 155E5, 144E5: V 1 8 23–27, IV 8 3 10 ff): according to Plotinus the soul is indivisible in the intellect but divided, i.e. among individuals, in the sensible world, without thereby losing its unity (IV 3 19 27–35, IV 1 7–10, 14–17, IV 2, I 1 8 10–15.). The unity of soul, and the relation between individual soul and the world/soul is discussed in IV 3 1–8, IV 9, VI 4–5 (cf. Deuse 1983: 118).

458 IV 3 5, VI 4 4 23–4; V 7 argues for forms of individuals. Armstrong 1977 tries to show that this is consistent with the view in V 9 12. See also Rist 1963, 1970, Blumenthal 1966; Wilberding (2006: 45–48), with n. 323 is decidedly contra. The soul is individual through its activity (Deuse 1983: 121–122): VI 4 16 28–35; IV 8 3 13, VI 2 22 25–32; IV 9 5 7–26. Cf. below p. 204.

459 VI 7 6.

460 II 1 5, IV 3 27 1–3 (see below p. 157), IV 4 32 4–13; IV 4 37 11–15, IV 4 43 9–11, VI 4 14 17–31. See Alt 1993: 89–120 for this dualism in the soul in middle Platonism and Plotinus.

which these distinctions are made.[461] Any talk of splitting an entity which
has memory such that two memories come about is of the greatest interest for the theorist of memory.[462] For there is, as we have seen, a group of
crucial questions concerning the relation between memory and the self,
which form the basis of the self-memory problem.[463]

This distinction between the higher and the lower soul leads us to the
question of what "we" are, and Plotinus' answer is clear: the rational
soul.[464] Furthermore, he puts the question in just these terms: "we" are
not the concrete living thing; the living body *belongs* to us, and is not
to be identified *with* us.[465] But then again, if we are our soul and our
soul can perform different functions, above all it can think and it can perceive, and it wants to do each of these, the question arises as which of
these two activities presents my true self. It clearly does not come from
the cosmos.[466] Obviously, in line with the Platonic tradition generally,
Plotinus sees the true work of the soul in thought, but his version is peculiar in that the soul returns to its proper place in intellect by thinking.[467]

Let us now turn to a more specific precondition for memory, namely
perception. Perception is crucial since Plotinus thinks that memory of
perceptions and things learnt is one of the two kinds of memory; here
he is following both Aristotle and of course Plato in the *Philebus*.[468]

We need to give an account of Plotinus' views of perception. Fortu-
nately, we can use the excellent monograph on the subject by Emilsson.
His results can be briefly summarised as follows. Perceptions are judgements, that is, something that the soul does, and does not undergo.
These judgements are intelligible representations.[469] Sensation, the affec-

---

461 IV 3 27–31.
462 See e.g. Parfit 1981: Part Three, esp. p. 221, Shoemaker 1963, Wiggins 2001:
     Ch. 7 esp. 205–225.
463 *Introduction* p. 1–2. For a general discussion of memory and Plotinus' theory of
     the soul, see Brisson 2006.
464 I 1 7 16–24. On Plotinus on the self, see O'Daly 1973.
465 I 1 10 3–10.
466 II 3 9.
467 On the question whether souls choose to stop thinking, and so perceive, see
     O'Brien 1977, and below p. 160.
468 *Introduction* p. 18.
469 Clark (1942: 297–8) translates φαντασία by "representation" with reference to
     the *Sophist* but also to the Stoics, for whom not all representations are sensible,
     some are rational as e.g. the representation of incorporeals. 'In fact a proposition
     may be called a representation' (citing SVF II 61, 65 25). Emilsson also translates

tion of the body in sense perception, is itself not epistemic. Sense organs act as intermediates between the sensible and the intelligible, *via* the soul's power: the sense organ is assimilated to the sensible object. This assimilation is the affection of the body.[470] The immaterial, for example the soul, cannot be affected for it then ceases to exist.[471]

Sense-perception is merely a lower form of intellection: it is obscure thought, and not a new capacity that the soul acquires.[472] In intellect the soul intellectually perceives the ideas, and because of this the embodied human soul has their concepts (λόγοι) in the form of images (ἐν μιμήσει).[473] In the case of beauty, we use the idea just as we use a ruler to judge straightness.[474] Ideas function as standards of judgement.[475] Because of the soul's essential relation to intellect, when it uses the body it forms judgements using the notions of sensible things in the guise of images. In perception we entertain these notions and this depends on our prior possession of ideas.[476] For example, we perceive the harmony in sensibles by fitting it with the intelligible harmony.[477]

Cognition is never merely being affected from outside, the percipient must do something and this act comes from the percipient himself. This is just like the case of discursive reason[478] which is concerned with drawing conclusions, unfolding and manipulating ideas, where perception makes immediate judgements about present affections. Perception judges with νοῦς.[479]

---

both τύπος and also φαντασία by "representation" (1988. 108–9): 'The most important function of *phantasia* is to be the "locus" of these unextended entities that are involved in memory and reasoning, and it is clear that these entities are in some sense representations of things.' Sheppard (1991: esp. 168) argues against understanding φαντασία in Plotinus as representation largely because "not only are *phantasmata* remembered *aisthêmata* [IV 3 29 22–23] but the higher *phantasia* receives thought 'as if in a mirror'" (IV 3 30 10). On this second passage, see below p. 179. She admits that φαντασία in the case of thought cannot be images in the usual sense. The first argument simply assumes that what remains from perception can only be an image.

470 IV 4 23 29–32. Emilsson 1988 devotes his Ch. IV to IV 4 23.
471 III 6 2 49–54.
472 VI 7 5 22–3, VI 7 6 1–11, VI 7 7 28–31.
473 Cf. III 6 18 24–9.
474 I 6 3 1–5.
475 V 3 3 8. See below p. 164.
476 See I 1 7 14–18.
477 VI 7 6 7–11, Emilsson 1988: 134.
478 See V 3 2–4, and Blumenthal 1971: Ch. 8.
479 IV 9 3 26–27.

As we have seen, the soul itself is not affected in perception, only the body is. The affection of the sense organ becomes a form in the soul. Plotinus has a variety of expressions for describing the product of the soul's activity, including τύπος and τύπωσις[480] – in other words he accepts τύποι which are not affections and are incorporeal. The decisive point is that for Plotinus these terms no longer indicate things which the soul undergoes, but rather what the soul does. Since representations are a form of mental language, perception is the realisation that something sensible is there or is the case: the objects of sense perception are sensibles mediated by sensory affections. Affections explain how we perceive things in space: sense organs assume forms of things but without their matter.[481] Plotinus rejects the analogy with sealing with a signet ring, but he does not avoid using its terminology. In effect, his usage is more metaphorical, and closer to our everyday use of terms such as "impression". Insofar as memory is related to perception and what happens in perception, the description of perception using incorporeal impressions is a necessary precondition to understanding his theory of memory.

A central topic in Plotinus' treatment of memory is, as with Aristotle, the role of φαντασία.[482] Unlike Aristotle, he thinks that φαντασία can be

---

480 Stoic terms for φαντασίαι SVF 2 56 (Sextus, Adv. Math. VII 227): Zeno τύπωσις, which Chrysippus rejects in favour of ἑτεροίωσις. Plotinus shows no sign of being aware that Chrysippus rejected this terminology (Emilsson 1988: 131–2, with nn. 7, 8 p. 171). Plotinus is quite happy using the language of impressions as long as there is no implication of material change, *pace* Aristotle and the Stoics (Fleet 1996: 98–9 on III 6 1 8).

481 See Emilsson 1988: ch. 4 above all on IV 4 23.

482 The longest treatment of φαντασία occurs in the texts on memory; there is no separate treatment of the concept. Other important texts are: I 8 15 18–19: 'Representation is brought about by the irrational part (sc. of the soul) being struck from outside. But (the soul) receives the blow on account of its divisible nature.' This clearly echoes the Aristotelian view (cf. Watson 1988: 100), see above p. 46; so too VI 8 3 10–12: 'But as for ourselves, we call imagination strictly speaking, what is awakened from the passive impression of the body.' The role of φαντασία in thought stretches these formulae to their limits; the conceptual aspect of φαντασία is there most important, which also plays a role in perceptual judgements, i.e. opinions: 'φαντασία in the primary sense, which we call opinion' (III 6 4 19–21; see Blumenthal 1971: 92–3). On thought and φαντασία see below p. 179. On Plotinus on φαντασία see Clark 1942, Warren 1966, Dillon 1986, Sheppard 1991, Watson 1988: 99–103, Blumenthal 1971: Ch. 7. Others important functions for φαντασία involve desire and action; see esp. IV 4 17 and 20, Clark 1942: 300–1. The interesting thing is that only in connection with desire is there any treatment of the connection between phys-

actually used without the body, but like Aristotle he thinks that it in some way derives from active perception. A perceptual judgement leaves a τύπος in the soul, an incorporeal, intelligible representation, of what is perceived. These representations are objects of φαντασία. Thus representation is perception that has been internalised by the soul.[483]

3.1.2 Explaining memory using the concept of the soul

After this introduction to the wider context of the treatment of memory, especially perception, let us turn to the question of memory itself. The form of the argument of IV 6 as a whole is:

> Perception is not an impression in the soul.
> So memory cannot be the preservation of an impression in the soul.[484]

This argument provides the structure of the whole treatise. Chapters 1 and 2 are devoted to proving the thesis about perception, and chapter 3 presents the consequences of the argument for the nature of memory. This argument about the nature of memory is based on a thesis about the nature of the soul, which Plotinus describes as the expression of ideas and perception. This thesis allows Plotinus to say that the soul has objects without having them as impressions or having been affected by them.

Of the objections that Plotinus makes to τύποι in the sense of material impressions, the most important for the theory of memory is the following: if we did grasp τύποι of the things we perceive, then perception would not be of the things themselves but merely of pictures and traces. So Plotinus wishes to avoid the problem that if there were impressions in perception, we would then perceive something merely in the mind, and not the things themselves (whatever these may be). If the things were in the soul, then the soul would not have to look out.[485] The objects of perception would be in the soul, so that the soul would not have to go out

---

iology and φαντασία. Since body plays no role in memory, there is nothing to be said here on that score; for Aristotle's view, see p. 75.

483 Emilsson 1988: 110 citing III 6 1 7–11, IV 3 26 and 29; n. 49 p. 167: I 1 7 12–13, IV 4 23 32.

484 IV 6 1 1–8.

485 IV 6 1 21–23. He also asks how one could tell the distance from the perceiver if the thing were in the soul, a question which reminds one of the argument in De mem. against the theory that we stretch our sight out to its objects (above p. 67); cf. also Plotinus' *On why distant objects appear small* II 8.

beyond itself in the process of perception. But in perceiving the soul does relate to things outside itself. This point is relevant to Plotinus' treatment of memory insofar as one central problem concerns the way someone who remembers now may have something in his memory which happened before now and which is correspondingly no longer present. Because this question concerns the temporal relation essential to memory, it forms one of the six conceptual problems with memory sketched in the *Introduction,* namely the present-past problem.[486] Recall our example:

Example (E) Socrates remembers (at t2) that he saw Theaetetus two days ago (at t1).

At t2 the perception of Theaetetus at t1 is no longer present, and the question is how one can then remember it at t2. The fact that a temporal gap is essential to our concept of memory becomes clear if one tries to imagine what it would be like to have a memory where act of memory and thing remembered are simultaneous. Such an argument might take as a model Plotinus' argument that perception takes place at the place where the perceptible is.[487] One might want to develop a theory of memory along these lines: an act of memory takes place when the thing remembered occurs. But such an answer is neither available in the case of memory (our memory of seeing something yesterday is not yesterday), nor does Plotinus use it. So the problem remains how a present memory is of the past.[488]

Part of Plotinus' answer to this problem lies in the way he conceives the preservation of perception. Plotinus does not call into question the basic connection between perception and memory; and that is not the way he argues against the impression theory of memory. So how is this connection preserved in the part of his theory concerned with memory of perception and learning? In Chapter 2, Plotinus describes seeing, which he characteristically chooses as an example of perception.[489] The main point that he makes is that perception is a capacity and an activity directed at an object.[490] As we have seen, he thinks perception consists in

---

486 See *Introduction* p. 1–2, and Aristotle's solution p. 78.
487 IV 6 3 1 14–19.
488 Plotinus is not sceptical about the existence of the past or about the fundamental possibility of being right about the past.
489 IV 6 1 11–14, and the Platonic precedent *Phaedrus* 250D2.
490 IV 6 2 2–3, cf. III 6 1 1–7.

the soul being active, namely saying something,[491] and because of the way in which he understands material impressions they make no contribution to such a capacity and its correlated activity. This is also the central point of the discussion of memory. Memory is an active capacity, and so does not involve impressions. Instead, the capacity for memory is developed by a perception in such a way that in actual remembering the past perception is present. Thus the nature of memory as an active capacity is the way in which Plotinus tries to solve the present-past problem. The way this works will only become clear when we consider the role of φαντασία in his explanation of memory. This role emerges in the chapter we are now considering, but is only treated at length in IV 3 29 and 30.[492]

Let us now turn to the treatment of memory proper. As we have seen, he begins by arguing against perception being a question of material impressions; in the third and last chapter he turns to what he takes to be a consequence of this, namely that memory cannot be the preservation of these impressions. The argument of the first text I wish to discuss in detail, the start of the treatment of memory in chapter 3, is concerned with the relation of the soul to the two kinds of object of memory that Plotinus distinguishes:

> But now that we have said this about sense perception we must next speak about memory; first we must say that it is not astonishing, or rather it is astonishing, but we should not disbelieve that the soul has a power of this kind, if it receives nothing itself and contrives an apprehension of what it does not have. For it is the expression (λόγος) of all things, and the nature of soul is the last and lowest expression (λόγοι) of the intelligibles and the beings in the intelligible world, but first in the whole world perceived by the senses. Therefore it is certainly in relation with both.[493]

Plotinus is giving reasons here for his view of memory which go beyond the rejection of impressions. Here we have a thesis[494] about the nature of

---

491 E.g. IV 6 2 1 and see above p. 109.

492 See below p. 170.

493 IV 6 3 1–8 (AHA trans., modified) Νῦν δὲ τούτων εἰρημένων περὶ μνήμης ἐφεξῆς λεκτέον εἰποῦσι πρότερον, ὡς οὐ θαυμαστόν, μᾶλλον δὲ θαυμαστὸν μέν, ἀπιστεῖν δὲ οὐ δεῖ τῇ τοιαύτῃ δυνάμει τῆς ψυχῆς, εἰ μηδὲν λαβοῦσα εἰς αὐτὴν ἀντίληψιν ὧν οὐκ ἔσχε ποιεῖται. Λόγος γάρ ἐστι πάντων, καὶ λόγος ἔσχατος μὲν τῶν νοητῶν καὶ τῶν ἐν τῷ νοητῷ ἡ ψυχῆς φύσις, πρῶτος δὲ τῶν ἐν τῷ αἰσθητῷ παντί. Διὸ δὴ καὶ πρὸς ἄμφω ἔχει...

494 This is given also as one of the reasons for studying the soul in IV 3 1 6–8. Plotinus does offer an account of the οὐσία of the soul in IV 2 and IV 1, derived from Plotinus' reading of Plato (Timaeus 35A); this account is connected, in

the soul from which its capacity to remember is derived. He is trying to explain how it is possible for the soul to remember things which it "does not have". He does this by establishing a relation between the soul and two classes of being, so providing for its capacity to remember these things. This relation is rooted in what the soul is. Here we see the fundamental dependence of memory on the soul, its modesty, as it was called in the *Introduction*.[495] The other aspect of the modesty of memory, its derivation from perception, is to be seen in the treatment in dependence on a thesis about perception.

What does Plotinus say here about the nature of the soul? It is the λόγος of everything.[496] This is in itself not a perspicuous statement as λόγος is simply too ambiguous. But one meaning that the word has in Plotinus is 'expression'. Just as the words we speak are an expression of the thoughts we have, a λόγος is an expression.[497] On this reading, the soul is an expression of the intelligibles and of the perceptibles. That can be taken to mean that it possesses cognition of both. The soul has two capacities, to think and to perceive. Each of these two capacities must be taken separately. To say that the soul expresses the ideas that are present in intellect is to say that the soul is directed towards ideas. Saying what the soul is has to mention its relation to ideas. In other words, they are already in it, as innate ideas, and so do not have to be acquired, for there to be memory of them. This is why he says that the soul has memory of things which it does not have, i. e. it has not 'acquired' them in experience or learning.[498] This theory of memory is based on a concept of soul that is active both in perception and thought. In it, memory has both sensible and intelligible objects, that is, perceptions and innate ideas which do not have to be acquired by the soul since they are inherent in it. Hence the theory has to go beyond one based on impressions, insofar as these come from outside the soul.

---

some complicated ways, with the thesis offered here. The thesis here is not a definition, but a general thesis, possibly derived in turn from the essence of soul.

495 See above p. 9, 20.

496 Cf. De an. III 8 esp. 431b21–29.

497 It cannot mean "concept", at least if one wishes to maintain the same sense for both intelligibles and sensibles: one might try to defend the view that soul is the concept of, because constitutive of the sensible world; but it is clearly not the concept of the intelligibles.

498 IV 3 25 25, below p. 144; Plotinus nonetheless speaks of acquired knowledge (IV 3 25 11, below p. 143).

Since the soul is immaterial, the representations of that which it expresses, ideas and perceptibles, are not material either, even when the soul is equipped with a body. The fundamental reason that Plotinus is opposed to all forms of material impression is that his theory comprises the requirements of expression and an immaterial soul. The soul cannot have material impressions because it is not material; and impressions cannot explain the soul's expression of its objects. He thinks his opponents, Peripatetics and Stoics, have an inadequate concept of the soul which leads them to make this impossible attribution.[499]

In his view, it is possible for the soul to have a grasp of things without having an impression of them if the impression is seen as something that the soul undergoes rather than something the soul produces, an activity of the soul. The fundamental problem that Plotinus is dealing with here is that the soul "has" objects. It has objects insofar as it is essentially related to them, not in the sense of having acquired them. He wants to explain how it is possible for the soul to have objects without being as it were in the power of the objects. Rather, it is the other way round: the soul has power over its objects.[500] Insofar as the soul has certain powers, such as memory and perception, it is as such related to the objects of these powers. Saying what these powers of the soul are involves mentioning their objects. Thus even if these things are not in the soul, not acquisitions, it is related to them essentially, insofar as it has a power of the relevant kind. And the way it is related to these objects is not by undergoing anything under their influence; rather, it performs an activity in relation to them.

Soul is said to be λόγος of everything, that is, of both intelligibles and perceptibles. It expresses them; and in so doing the hierarchy between them is reflected in their effects on the soul: it is either enlivened, i.e. encouraged to think, or else deceived, i.e. taken in by the similarities which are present in perceptibles. This is a glimpse of Plotinus' pre-occupation with the good. Thought is good for the soul, "quickening" it, whereas sensation is the opposite. The good and bad effects are reflected in the cognitive status of at least sensation which deceives the soul by the (mere) likeness of perceptions.[501] One may wonder what the deception is, and why it leads to a descent, and why it is said to spell-bind the soul.

---

499 For his detailed rejection of materialist conceptions of the soul, see IV 7 2–8³.
500 IV 6 2 9.
501 IV 6 3 8–10.

This means, I think, that the soul takes sensible things to be more real than they are, and so descends to their level.

He goes on to describe briefly what happens when the soul remembers:

> But being in the middle, it perceives both, and is said to think the intelligibles when it arrives at memory (μνήμη) of them if it comes to be near them; for it knows them by being them in a way: for it knows [them] not because they settle in it, but because it has them in some way and sees them and is them in a rather dim way and becomes them more clearly out of the dimness by a kind of awakening, and passes from potentiality to actuality. In the same way [the soul] makes the objects of sense which are, so to speak, connected with it, shine out, one might say, by its own power, and brings them before its eyes, since its power is ready for them, and in a way in travail towards them.[502]

Here memory of both ideas and sensible perceptions is attributed to the soul. Let us begin with memory of ideas. The soul possesses the ideas because potential knowledge of them is constitutive of it. It has them, not because they have been learnt, and so acquired a place in it, but because the soul has them in potentiality, and when it comes to think them actually, then they are in its memory. The process of learning ideas is thus the recall of ideas that are already innate in one: only then, that is, after recall, are they in one's memory. As we will see, he thinks that this conception of memory is not connected to prior time in the way that memory otherwise is.[503] Recalling what the soul always thinks is not to recall something past.

So memory here is a matter of what has been retrieved, and not of what has been retained. Ideas do not need to be retained since they are part of the soul's nature. Plotinus refers here to the Platonist conception of learning which we have already discussed.[504] The soul always thinks,

---

502 IV 6 3 10–19.
503 Below p. 144 on IV 3 25 25. Memory is of the past: IV 4 6 2–3.
504 See above *Introduction* p. 17. No doubt Blumenthal (1971: 97 with fn. 25, 26) is right to point out that Plotinus thinks that Platonic ἀνάμνησις is shown by Plotinus' doctrine of νοῦς to be correct (cf. V 9 5 32), not of course in the sense that Plato meant it. The crucial difference between the two lies in the fact that in Plotinus' view the soul is always thinking. There is less reason to think that ἀνάμνησις for Plotinus is not a discursive process; the passage Blumenthal refers to for an intuitionist recovery of ideas (IV 7 10 30–35), is only about "seeing" ideas, not recovering them. For Plotinus' concept of dialectic cf. fn. 809 and for the recovery of thought by discursive thinking using φαντασία see IV 3 30, below p. 178.

although it is not always conscious of doing so; this is what Plotinus means by saying that ideas are innate.[505] Here it becomes apparent that not all retention, the presence of information over time, is to be attributed to memory: ideas are the innate property of the soul, and remain over time, but their retention is not memory. Nonetheless, the retrieval is recollection, and this is what Plotinus calls "memory" here.[506] The soul is said to recollect the ideas by "coming close" to them. This is of course not to be understood spatially, it is a matter of the attention the soul pays to the ideas.[507]

Parallel to this, perceptibles are "so to speak connected to" (οἷον συναψόμενα) the soul, and it makes them shine out (ἐκλάμπειν). The most obvious, but I think mistaken, reading of the memory of perceptibles here is as follows. It might seem, at first glance, as though the soul produces them as perceptibles through its own power of perception. On this reading, perceptibles would be parallel to innate ideas, by

---

505 As in IV 3 25, below p. 144.

506 See the parallel in IV 3 25 25, where he says that the ancients, i. e. Plato and Platonists, spoke of memory in the sense of recollection. Brisson (2005: n. 458, p 240, and cf. also n. 240) takes the καὶ in that text to be explanatory, and to designate "une identité entre mnêmê et anamnêsis". He connects this to a synonymous use of the terms, when referring to sensible things in the *Meno* and the *Phaedo*; when taken terminologically with a strict distinction between the sensible and the intelligible, in his view the two have nothing to do with one another. But I take it that this distinction is valid in Plotinus' treatment, and at least IV 3 30 is concerned with remembering ideas.

507 This text makes quite clear that there is recollection in Plotinus as a way of coming close to the ideas, that is, not of contemplating them but as learning them. McCumber (1978: esp. p.160) argues that Plotinus uses ἀνάμνησις with reference to forms, and that it plays a part in accounting for ascent of soul, possibility of science, probably not of perception. As McCumber shows ἀνάμνησις is neither all embracing nor trivial for Plotinus, but has a carefully delimited nature and function: soul has a memory of forms, νοῦς has intellection of them, and these memories are recovered as the soul approaches the intelligible realm. His account suffers from not making a distinction between μνήμη and ἀνάμνησις. Hence he seems to say that there is both retention of forms as well as their retrieval. Retention seems to be based on the λόγος – but how that occurs, he does not explain. See below p. 178 on IV 3 30. McCumber agrees with Blumenthal's thesis (1971: 96 ff) that intuition replaces Platonic ἀνάμνησις, insofar as the actual contemplation of ideas is concerned. Of course for Plato recollection is only the learning of ideas not the actual contemplation itself. McCumber does not go into the question of what 'the doctrine of recollection' is that Plotinus is relying on. He merely refers to the *Phaedo* 74, *Phaedrus* 249B (p. 166). On some aspects of Plato's views, see *Introduction* p. 13–16.

being internal to the soul and so not really acquired at all.[508] Soul contains the whole of reality, both intelligibles and sensibles; so all it has to do when remembering is to actualise this potential. Of course, the soul does not *produce* innate ideas, and it does not rely on bringing them in from outside, but it draws them as it were out of itself. The same principle would then be applied to perceptions as follows: if the soul, the individual soul, produces perceptions as part of its activity, then it does not rely on something outside itself to do so. This might seem to be the point of Plotinus' saying that the soul is "so to speak connected" with the objects of sense. These would then be already, prior to actual perception, bound to the soul, so that actual perception would merely strengthen the soul's connection to them. This would enable the soul to make them "shine out" when it remembers them afterwards.

However, the passage should be seen to have a different message: the soul is as it were connected to the perception. What this means is that its power has been modified by the experience in such a way that it can make the experience shine out. In perception the soul *approaches* what it has.[509] How is this to be understood? We have seen that capacities have their objects; the actualisation is seen by Plotinus as the soul getting closer to its objects. In part, the capacity for perception consists in innate ideas, but perception needs more than innate ideas. It must come into possession of them, because Plotinus thinks of cognition as possession of the objects.[510] Perception requires that something is grasped. The parallel with innate ideas is incomplete; for the individual soul does not contain, as part of its make up, all the individuals it perceives. Rather, by an exercise of its capacity, this capacity must be developed. This development occurs through the opportunity for perception offered by individual things outside the soul. Memory is then the calling forth of something that already has entered the soul.[511] The soul is "as it were in contact" with the objects of perceptible memory, because it has come into contact with them.

The same conclusion can be supported by another metaphor that Plotinus uses, giving birth:[512] the soul is in labour with memory. Presumably

---

508 Brèhier vol. 4, p. 170 refers to Leibniz' complete notions of souls.
509 III 6 1, 2 33–42 esp. III 6 2 35–36, Emilsson 1988: 133, "the power of vision already has what is contained in its act", and p. 137 on latent concepts being activated in perception.
510 Emilsson 1988: 68–70 on IV 4 23 6–8.
511 Emilsson 1988: 133 on IV 6 3.
512 IV 6 3 19.

one is justified in completing the sentence, "because it has been impregnated by perception". What this means is that the soul's capacity has been prepared for memory by the actual perception. When you have had the experience, then of course you need no further contact with the things you remember or can recollect since you have had the experience. In this way, a connection between the soul and the contents of its memory has been established.

One can admit that a power of perception contributes to memory of perception, without saying that it produces everything in the perception. Memory of perception presupposes the capacity to perceive. Recall that the soul expresses the sensible world; this does not mean that the individual soul produces the sensible world; merely that it is able to have cognition of it.[513] And only after having cognition of the world, does the soul possess the relevant memory. This memory is not as it were a bodily import from the sensible world, however, because it is produced by the activity of the soul, first of all in perception, and then in the faculty of representation. There is no doubt that Plotinus thinks that we do *acquire* memories.[514] The soul acquires memory of a particular experience by exercising its natural capacities, and also by acquiring something from outside.

Let us recapitulate.

One the one hand, we acquire something from outside in perception, and our ability to remember the perception depends on this. But we do not acquire everything needed for the perception from outside. For innate ideas are necessary. The capacity for perception is nonetheless not to be explained entirely by the possession of innate ideas;[515] it would then seem to be nothing more than the capacity for thought, rather than the capacity to subsume experiences under ideas. Nonetheless, our possession of ideas is partly responsible for our ability to perceive.[516] In an experience, our natural capacity to remember the experience is developed. Here, however, Plotinus is much more concerned with explaining the

---

513 It is, of course, true that the world soul produces the world; but we are not concerned here with the world soul: this has no memory (IV 4 12).
514 A glance at IV 3 25 11 proves this.
515 See V 3 2–3 for the contribution that innate ideas make towards our ability to identify and characterise experiences. On this connection see above p. 109, below p. 164.
516 On perception and innate ideas, cf. above p. 109. Emilsson (1988: 136, 134) points to the latent existence of unfolded ideas in us in three further chapters that are crucial for memory, namely IV 3 26, IV 3 29 and V 3 2.

parallel between perception and thought, rather than with the contribution that ideas make to perception.

What this account of memory does not do is to say how it is that the soul remembers either ideas or perceptions, namely through representation. This task will in part be performed by the definition, which we shall consider next and in part by the extended discussion of the faculty responsible for memory in IV 3 28–30.

3.1.3 Defining memory

Plotinus closes his short, positive treatment of the two kinds of memory by drawing a general conclusion about them:

> Whenever therefore the soul is strengthened with respect to something that appears to it (πρὸς ὁτιοῦν τῶν φανέντων), the soul is disposed to it as if to something present (ὥσπερ πρὸς παρὸν διάκειται) for a long time; the more the soul is strengthened, the more it is always [so disposed].[517]

These lines are difficult and my interpretation is suggested by the translation. An act of cognition equips the soul with a capacity towards something that appears to it, such that the soul can represent the appearance to itself in such a way as though the thing were present. This is the closest Plotinus comes to a definition of memory. Formally, it may seem to have little claim to be taken as a definition. Memory is not even mentioned, let alone a formulation such as "memory is defined as X", and, from the point of view of content, the reader might think that these lines merely describe a disposition being brought about in the soul by something appearing to it. You might argue that it is merely a description of what happens after something appears to one. Something sweet appears to the soul and this strengthens the soul in that respect, i.e. makes the soul *able* to perceive this sweetness, gives it power over this sweetness. This seems too slight as a definition of memory. But these lines in fact offer much more by way of a determination of memory, for the formulation collects the essential aspects mentioned by Plotinus in his treatment of the two kinds of memory, described in the last section. The emphasis in this *quasi* definition, as I shall call it, on appearance and presence should

---

517 IV 6 3 19–21 Ὅταν τοίνυν ῥωσθῇ πρὸς ὁτιοῦν τῶν φανέντων, ὥσπερ πρὸς παρὸν διάκειται ἐπὶ πολὺν χρόνον καὶ ὅσῳ μᾶλλον, τόσῳ ἀεί. In AHA's translation ῥωσθῇ is rendered 'strongly moved', but SP 932.18 translate 'strengthen'. cf. ll. 40, 45, also V 1 7 15, VI 7 22 15.

not lead the reader to see here merely perceptual memory, since as we shall see, the memory of thoughts is a matter of φαντασία, and of the presence of the ideas.

Let us address the difficulties offered by the interpretation of these lines as a kind of definition of memory. The impression that we are not dealing with memory here can be removed simply by pointing to the relations between these lines and their context. This passage presents the conclusion ("therefore") from the preceding lines on the two kinds of memory, as a generalisation about both. But these lines also look forward to the rest of the chapter. For the concept here is offered as a hypothesis which can explain the phenomena which Plotinus goes through in the next fifty lines or so. This can be seen from what he says about his opponents, the proponents of the wax tablet or wax block model of memory, including Aristotle.[518] As we will see in the next section, these posit a concept of soul and fail to see the impossibilities, i. e. contradictions, that follow their hypothesis, whereas, by implication, Plotinus's concept of soul enables him to explain memory, among other things. His concept of memory is explained by his concept of the soul, and further supported by the phenomena which it can explain.

In my view, this passage gives an account of memory. But if this is so, one might want to draw the conclusion that at the time of remembering the object of memory is present. Recall our example:

Example (E) Socrates remembers (at t2) that he saw Theaetetus two days ago (at t1).

This would then imply, if the object of memory is present at t2 that Socrates remembers Theaetetus at t2; and Theaetetus is present at t2. As the account says, "the appearance is always present to the soul". Now, memory is of course connected to time, but I wish to argue that the object of the memory is not present when we actually remember, even if the appearance may be: the soul is disposed towards the object *as though*

---

518 Οἷον γὰρ ἐν πίναξιν ἢ δέλτοις γεγραμμένων γραμμάτων, οὕτως περὶ τῶν αἰσθήσεων καὶ τοῦ μνημονεύειν διάκεινται, καὶ οὔτε οἱ σῶμα αὐτὴν τιθέμενοι ὁρῶσιν, ὅσα ἀδύνατα τῇ ὑποθέσει αὐτῶν συμβαίνει, οὔτε οἱ ἀσώματον. IV 6 3 75–79 There are two groups here, both of whom talk about memory being like writing tablets. They differ in thinking that the soul is material or not. They are thus Stoics and Peripatetics.

(ὥσπερ) it were present, i. e. when it is no longer so.[519] It fits better with the description of a particular act of memory that we are dealing here with a particular capacity. The idea is that we have something in mind as *if it were* present. Clearly this is counterfactual.[520] Well, it may be possible to remember something that is present, but obviously there is a distinction between the grasp of the thing present and remembering it. Socrates remembers Theaetetus at t1, or, rather more precisely, remembers seeing Theaetetus at t1, rather than Theaetetus *tout court.* So what is the point of the presence of the object of memory here? The present-past problem[521] consists in the fact that we must account for the presence of the past. So how does it help to say that the object of memory is *quasi* present? It is the way it appears to me; as a matter of fact it is not. The perception of Theaetetus is *quasi* present; it is as though I am now perceiving Theaetetus.[522] One may of course question this. On the whole I

---

519 Plotinus says here that the soul is strengthened: it has either acquired a new capacity, to remember *this particular perception*, and hence is strengthened; or perhaps it has strengthened a general capacity, and so has a better memory. Cf. IV 6 3 40: the soul can be strengthened either *tout court* or relative to something.

520 IV 6 3 20: ὥσπερ πρὸς παρὸν 'as if to something present' (following AHA, Bréhier): this is counterfactual since, of course, the thing is no longer actually present, as a matter of fact (memory is of the past: IV 4 6 2–3), but one is disposed to it as though it were so. In a certain sense when you remember things, it is as though they are present. Harder translates: "Wenn nun das Seelenvermögen auf irgend eines der in ihm erscheinenden Dinge (*phanenta*) besondere Kraft wendet, dann ist es in einem Zustande, daß ihm dieses Ding auf lange Zeit gegenwärtig bleibt, und je stärker diese Kraft ist, um so länger." This may suggest that the thing is actually present to the soul in the act of memory; but it could mean that it is not actually but merely mentally present. This second use of "present" is also to be found in line 43. One must not of course overinterpret this presence to mean that things really appear as they do when they are present. Plotinus need not be taken to think either that the two situations are identical nor that they are so similar that one can mistake memory for perception or thought. Apart from the word ὥσπερ ("as if") there is no indication that the presence is counterfactual; and it might mean "in the manner such as" or "as if towards". Then Plotinus would be claiming that the soul is related to the thing remembered in the way that it is related to something present. And there are at least two senses in which something may be said to be present – actually, or mentally to someone. In the main text, I discuss the fact that the original perception is no longer present; and the way in which an experience strengthens a capacity to remember, so that one can later remember the original experience.

521 See above *Introduction* p. 1–2.

522 Cf. Aristotle's formulation of the way one can regard a picture as being of Coriscus, although one does not see Coriscus (Ch. 1 450b29–31, above p. 39).

do not tend to think that I am now tasting yesterday's lunch actually or it appears present to me, when I have a good memory of it. But we should allow that *as if* does not specify precisely the way in which the object of memory has to be present, for it to be remembered.

Let us stay with the present-past problem for a moment. We can see in this definition a hint of how Plotinus intends to solve it, along lines which are at least superficially reminiscent of Aristotle. The answer to the question how something past can be present, even if it is only *quasi* present,[523] lies in the faculty of representation.[524] The connection with representation occurs in the definition in the guise of the things that are present, namely the things that appear to me (φάνεντα), since "appearance" (φαίνεσθαι) is, of course, etymologically connected to representation, φαντασία. φαντασία is the way, the capacity in virtue of which things appear to me, and in virtue of which they can remain *quasi* present to me. When Socrates remembers, then there is actually a φαντασία present to him, in virtue of which it is as though Theaetetus is present. Without relying too much on the pun, one might say that representation provides the way things may remain (*quasi*) present to me afterwards. The representation is actually present, and the perception of Theaetetus is thereby *quasi* present, in other words: Socrates has it in mind.

In this definition, Plotinus speaks of the acquisition of memory as a strengthening of the soul, and he elsewhere speaks of memory being a strength or vigour and a capacity.[525] Two remarks here are in order, the first is of perhaps more immediate importance, and the second is fundamental to Plotinus' whole theory of memory. It is of more immediate importance that capacity in this theory is not a mere possibility. It has certain connections with actuality, e.g. that it has been exercised, that we have a tendency to exercise it. The fundamental point is that Plotinus' theory of memory has to do without body. While the other formulations seem informal, calling memory a capacity (δύναμις) has certain implica-

---

523 Bréhier (vol. 4 p. 169) refers to De mem.; see below p. 238.
524 See above fn. 482 for φαντασία.
525 *ἰσχύς* line 55, δύναμις lines 25, 39, 58, 60, 65, 71; cf. δυνάμωσις l. 30. Part of Plotinus' positive purpose is to show that memory is a power (line 55). This is the real aim of IV 6 (Blumenthal 1971: 81). Kleist (1883: 151 n. 2) thinks that there is a large section (lines 29–55) which is meant to prove that memory is the activity of a power of the soul. It is remarkable that in his chapter on memory, Blumenthal (1971: Chapter 7 Memory and imagination) does not even mention the first 21 lines of IV 6 3, which contain the distinction between two kinds of memory and a quasi definition of the phenomenon.

tions for Plotinus, namely that it is immaterial, and it is a capacity to do something. We now have to discuss just how this capacity is to be understood. Part of the aim of his discussion of memory is to show that it is a capacity, and so does not involve material impressions. This is a cornerstone of his account. Being a capacity precludes any involvement of body. The most explicit account of the kind of capacity involved in memory comes in another short account of memory, in the course of the treatment of the impassibility of the incorporeal.[526] Saying that the soul, the first kind of incorporeal, is impassible means that it undergoes no change; this view of the soul is one of the fundamental reasons that Plotinus cannot accept any form of material impressions. So one example of this impassibility is what happens in memory. Just as in perception nothing is laid up in the soul, there is no τύπος, no form as in wax. Instead, here too he uses the concept of a capacity which the soul can "awake", that is, realise in itself and so "have" that which it does not have. He thinks there is an alteration when one actually remembers but only insofar as a capacity is exercised.[527] This is crucial, because it is plausible to demand of any theory of memory that something happens both when we acquire and when we exercise the memory. And one variety of event could be a change.

Plotinus denies that the change occurring when the original perception develops the capacity is a change in substance; and that surely is quite right: a soul does not turn into some other sort of thing when it

---

526 III 6 2 34–54. At IV 3 25 8–9 Plotinus alludes to a definition, and the commentators refer to this text in III 6 2 esp. 42–49. According to Porphyry's chronological list, III 6 was written directly before IV 3 [27]. The reference in IV 3 25 cannot be to IV 6, since that was written long after IV 3. It is n. 41 in the chronological order (HBT II b 441 ad loc.). III 6 2 34–54 cannot be *the* text where Plotinus tackles the task of defining memory, because the reference to memory is passing, and there is in turn here a reference to another treatment. The passage on memory starts at l. 42: "we must remember that it was said that memories too are not of things laid up [in the soul]…" HS refer to IV 7 6 43, where, however, Plotinus is arguing against the soul being a body: for if it were then there would be no possibility of something *remaining* insofar as body is something in flux; cf. IV 3 26 52–54. The point in the passage in III 6 is, however, a different one: material things can change, e. g. the body-soul composite; but the soul cannot (see esp. lines 39–40).

527 III 6 2 45–46. HBT II b 442 ad loc. note a) that alteration here may refer to Aristotle, De an. II 5 417b5 ff (so too HS); I discuss this reference below; and b) that εἰς ἐνέργειαν ἐλθεῖν is a formulation that is to be found in IV 6 3 16 for remembering ideas.

acquires an individual memory, nor indeed does it become a different individual of the same kind. The problem that Plotinus has with this fact is
that he cannot see how a soul can be in one state and then in another,
without changing its identity. He thinks that any change in an immaterial
thing involves the change of the whole thing.[528] Thus if the soul were to
change, acquire a new modification or something of the kind, then Plotinus is of the opinion that it would no longer be the same soul. This is in
contrast to material things which can undergo change. The nub is that
Plotinus does not accept the corporeality of the subject of memory. So
he has to work out a way that the soul can do something in memory,
without losing its identity. Presumably, however, his opponents[529] are
thinking not of substantial change but of something more modest. The
subject undergoes some kind of modification when he has an image
(φάντασμα); and that refers us to a rather different discussion, namely Aristotle's. For Aristotle considers memory to be the possession of a kind of
affection, one that is in part due to the material nature of the subject of
memory.[530]

The way Plotinus hopes to get out of the difficulty in having the soul
do something, without losing its identity originates in the distinctions
about the kinds of capacity and actuality, made by Aristotle in *De
anima* II 5, which we have already discussed under the soubriquet "the
triple scheme".[531] In Aristotle's view, while perception is a kind of alteration, it is one that does not involve change between contraries. Change
between contraries is necessary, however, to establish such capacities as
perception. Capacities of living things are first established by the growth
of the living thing, and this involves change. Exercise of the capacities so
acquired does not require change. This is what is explained by the triple
scheme: things change from first capacity to first actuality by undergoing
changes which involve the loss and acquisition of attributes. First actuality
is also a capacity (so-called second capacity), and exercising this capacity
requires no further changes that consist in the loss and acquisition of attributes. An example Aristotle gives is of a child having a capacity to act as
a general. Of course, only when he has gone through the requisite series
of changes, of growth and training, is he in possession of a capacity which

---

528 III 6 2 50–54.
529 Both Aristotle (above p. 46) and Chrysippus (above fn. 480) thought of φαντασία
    as forms of change.
530 See above pp. 20–21, 35, 73.
531 Above p. 30.

he can then exercise, and when he does so, he does not change his nature; rather the ensuing event is an exercise of his nature.[532]

This passage is a help for the general definition of memory in Plotinus because it makes clear what kind of capacity Plotinus means when he talks of memory being a capacity or a strength. It is not a capacity to undergo a material change. The trained general does not lose any quality when he exercises his capacity; he merely acts out that which he is, his nature or disposition. The difference between a general in capacity and an active general is one that is bridged merely by a change of a sort, not a change that runs between contraries. So too with Plotinus' conception of memory.

However, Plotinus use of first and second potentiality from *De anima* II 5 is not Aristotelian, because the preliminary account of perception offered there is predicated on the Aristotelian definition of the soul in II 1; and that is a conception of the soul Plotinus roundly rejects.[533] He cannot accept that soul is the primary actuality of a body, nor that perception is a capacity established by the growth of a perceiving animal. The main point is that Plotinus wants to ensure that the soul does not change and he thinks that by using *De anima* II 5 and its conception of alteration of a kind, he can have mental activity without physical realisation and hence affection. That is not something Aristotle wants at all: for him the soul is the form of the body, and as a form is not subject to change, although the concrete living thing can be affected.

Let us sum up the fundamental points about the capacities of the soul which we have been able to gain from this discussion of Plotinus' use of the Aristotelian distinctions made in *De anima* II 5. The importance of this latter passage for Plotinus is that it allows him to talk about changes without any recourse to material change. The decisive difference to Aristotle lies in the fact that as far as living things are concerned any capacity developed presupposes a process of development, the living thing must acquire its organs and so on, through a process of growth characterised by passage between contraries. This is not true for Plotinus, for the soul alone has these capacities, and obviously does not do so by going through organic development. Only the body does that. Instead, he

---

532 De an. II 5 417b2–16, see also III 6 2 49–50, 60, IV 6 3 16, words which are perhaps echoed in III 6 2 48–49. Fleet 1996: 96–101 on III 6 2 34–54 refers Plotinus' use of the triple scheme to Aristotle, without suggesting that there are fundamental differences.

533 IV 7 8[5].

sees the exercise of memory as the exercise of a capacity that undergoes development in the original experience. The original experience makes the soul ready to have the memory later. How can this be possible without the soul changing?[534] Precisely by the exercise of a second capacity; its development is not a change. Thus memory of something particular is a capacity to do something. This is true whether it is a thought that we remember or a perception. It is the capacity to make something that appeared to the soul present to it, after the original thought or perception is past. The way this task is performed, in both perception and thought is through φαντασία. Before we turn to discussing φαντασία, we shall try to follow Plotinus' in the arguments he gives in support of this conception of memory. They take the form of explanations using the concept.

3.1.4 What memory as a capacity can explain

Plotinus defends his thesis that memory is a capacity by using it to explain a wealth of phenomena, which all require a dynamic concept of memory rather than impressions, which he regards as entirely static. One example is that children's good memories cannot be explained by impressions; another is that memory can be improved by practice.[535] He claims that (material) impressions cannot, in contrast, do the explan-

---

534 Lloyd Gerson pressed me on this point.
535 The rest of IV 6 3, lines 21–79. The thesis is repeated e. g. in line 55. This strategy explains the fairly emphatic start of this section with διό. Kleist 1883: 149–50 distinguishes between the metaphysical exposition of the first part of the chapter (which he ends at line 25, but the argument about children lines 21–25 is clearly not part of the explanation of the concept of memory itself), as opposed to the empirical-psychological exposition of the second part. He does not explain how he thinks the two parts are related. In his translation (or rendering) of lines 67–70 he says, 'Gerade die bekämpfte Thesis würde eine Erklärung dieser Erscheinung unmöglich machen', which suggests that he sees the function of the second part of the chapter in a similar way to the present interpretation: the thesis that memory is impressions makes the explanation of certain phenomena impossible. The arguments run as follows: children have good memories (21–33); impressions that remain cannot explain delayed or partial recollection (33–40); impressions cannot explain the improvement of memory by practice (27–33, 40–55); memory is a form of readiness which requires time for its preparation (55–63); clever people and people with good memories are not the same ones (63–70).

atory work required.[536] In this section I wish to discuss some of these arguments, since they are of interest for any theory of memory. Furthermore, they document very clearly Plotinus' interest in the cut and thrust of philosophical debate about everyday phenomena. Underlying the mass of arguments is a fundamental view that a capacity is immaterial and cannot be explained by any material configuration. Thus memory requires something quite different from impressions as an explanation.

The simple example that Plotinus begins with is the following. Children have a good memory because the contents of their memory remain present to them, since they do not have so many memories. If the capacity is related to many different contents, as it is in older people, it is dissipated and can no longer keep the experiences present. If one supposed that memory was (caused by) impressions, he argues this would not be true; a mass of impressions would not cause loss of memory.[537] There are two kinds of reply to this argument worth mentioning. The first challenges the argument directly, the second draws attention to Plotinus' rather too brisk approach to his opponents. First, the immediate problem with the argument. One could certainly argue against the conclusion that, as a matter of fact, a lot of impressions could make one another illegible, so to speak, through contamination, like a muddy footpath which many people use. The individual footprints are no longer discernible.[538] Secondly, as to Plotinus' approach, it must be said that the model need not be taken quite this literally. Plotinus takes the model out of context, and pays no attention to the appropriate way it may serve the purpose of illustrating an explanation. At the very least, one must always bear in mind the purpose of such a comparison. As we have seen, Aristotle's use of the wax block image in connection with memory is different from his use of it to illustrate the process of perception.[539] In the case of memory, he is interested in the change that occurs when the original perception occurs; when he is talking about perception itself, the central

---

536 Arguments against impressions: 25–27, 27–29, 33–40, 55–57, 67–70, 71–79; arguments for power 29–33, 40–55, 57–63, 63–67, 70–71.

537 Διὸ καὶ τὰ παιδία μνημονεύειν λέγεται μᾶλλον, ὅτι μὴ ἀφίστανται, ἀλλὰ κεῖται αὐτοῖς πρὸ ὀμμάτων ὡς ἂν ὁρῶσιν οὔπω εἰς πλῆθος, ἀλλὰ πρὸς ὀλίγα· οἷς δὲ ἐπὶ πολλὰ ἡ διάνοια καὶ ἡ δύναμις, ὥσπερ παραθέουσι καὶ οὐ μένουσιν. Εἰ δέ γε ἔμενον οἱ τύποι, οὐκ ἂν ἐποίησε τὸ πλῆθος ἧττον μνήμας. IV 6 3 21–27.

538 Plotinus himself uses a variant of this argument in IV 7 6 41–49 to show that the soul cannot be a body. Chrysippus used the same argument against the signet ring comparison (LS 39 A, Diogenes Laertius 7 49–51 = SVF 2 52, 55, 61).

539 Above p. 23, 69.

point is the separation of form and matter. Either way one might make a case for saying that memory could be like the impressions in wax. But of course either way, supposing there are no others, Plotinus would want to reject the model.

Another of Plotinus' arguments against material impressions in memory is that if memory were caused just by the remaining of impressions then one would not need to look at them in order to recollect them. Indeed there would be no need to forget them and then remember them because they are there the whole time.[540] Recollection here is everyday recollection, not the technical Platonic variety. Curiously, he does not mention memory without any need of recollection.[541] The contrast between these two phenomena is one we encapsulated in the memory-recollection problem.[542] The point is that some past experiences are in mind without searching (memory); others require a search (recollection). In effect, Plotinus denies that his opponents are able to describe this problem, and yet fails to discuss it in his own theory. On behalf of his opponents, "being in mind" is understood by Plotinus as simply the presence of the impression in the wax. Since the impression is there, no process of calling to mind, nor the temporary forgetting which may precede this, are explicable. Plotinus is pleading for a dynamic concept, whilst his opponents, in his view, emphasise the static remaining.[543] This argument shows how simple minded, or strict, Plotinus' understanding of the impressions is. He does not allow that they are potential. This seems to make good sense: either the impression is there or it is not. However, among the many ways of taking the model, Plotinus chooses an all too literal reading of impressions. His opponents might well want to claim that the presence of the impression in the living things need not be identified with the actual presence in the mind of the remember. Aristotle certainly thinks that one can have the capacity to recollect something which one does not now have in mind. That is the point of his whole conception of recollection. Aristotle's position here contrasts strongly with one of Plotinus' central convictions. In Plotinus' view materialist views of the mind do not have a concept of capacity or power, since these are immaterial.

---

540 IV 6 3 27–29: Ἔτι, εἰ τύποι μένοντες, οὐδὲν ἔδει σκοπεῖν, ἵνα ἀναμνησθῶμεν, οὐδὲ πρότερον ἐπιλαθομένους ὕστερον ἀναμιμνήσκεσθαι κειμένων.
541 He would seem to be following here a *Phaedo* like concept, which allows for recollection with or without memory. See above *Introduction* p. 16.
542 See *Introduction* p. 2.
543 Cf. the Stoic account of memory as "permanent and static printings" in LS 39 F, SVF 2 847 (Plutarch comm. not. 1084F-1085A).

Mnemonics[544] plays an important role in Plotinus' theory, but not at
all in the way one might expect, namely because of the images that mnemonics uses. On the contrary, the nature of memory as a capacity is proven by the fact that it can be strengthened. Exercising one's memory,
mnemonic gymnastics as it were, shows that memory is a matter of
strengthening, 'empowering', the soul. The idea is that practising recalling things shows that memory is a power. He compares the process with
the preparation of hands or feet for (athletic) feats, which they otherwise
would not be capable of.[545] Memory requires preparation for its exercise
since without going through the relevant training – thinking of ideas,
learning things – the soul is in no state or position to perform the relevant
feat. What he does not show here or anywhere else is that such powers do
not require a body to exist.[546] And he can be criticised here on account of
the capacities he uses as a comparison for his concept of supposedly incorporeal memory. Athletic abilities obviously do include the capacity
of the athlete to undergo changes, namely of the parts of the body
that have to undergo changes in the course of training.[547] Plotinus uses
the idea of practice to support his conception of memory, but it is by
no means clear that the phenomenon need be understood in such a
way as to support him. For Aristotle's procedure shows how at least
one impression theorist thinks that he is able to use practice of one's
memory as a support for his theory. His final definition has it that memory is taking a representation as an image of that of which they are representations. This is confirmed by the way he understands exercising one's
memory, namely repeatedly regarding the representations one has in
mind as copies of that of which they are representation.[548]

The capacity of memory is used by Plotinus to explain imperfect
memory performances.[549] He argues that since memory is a power that

---

544 For the concept of mnemonics see above p. 100.
545 IV 6 3 29–33: Καὶ αἱ εἰς ἀνάληψιν δὲ μελέται δηλοῦσι δυνάμωσιν ψυχῆς τὸ
     γινόμενον ὑπάρχον, ὥσπερ χειρῶν ἢ ποδῶν τὰ γυμνάσια εἰς τὸ ποιεῖν ῥᾳδίως, ἃ
     μὴ ἐν ταῖς χερσὶν ἢ ποσὶ κεῖται, ἀλλὰ πρὸς ἃ τῇ συνεχείᾳ ἡτοίμασται. "Prepara-
     tion": l. 33 ἡτοίμασται. For "preparation", see also lines 18, 60.
546 See below p. 152 for the arguments that the soul, and hence memory, can exist
     without body.
547 See IV 6 3 51–52 for a related point about training. On δύναμις see also IV 7 8¹
     11–28. For the relation between capacity and organ, cf. Aristotle De an. II 12
     424a24–28.
548 Cf. De mem. 1 451a12–14, above p. 81.
549 IV 6 3 33–40: Διὰ τί γὰρ ἅπαξ μὲν ἀκούσας ἢ δεύτερον οὐ μέμνηται, ὅταν δὲ
     πολλάκις, καὶ ὁ πρότερον ἀκούσας οὐκ ἔσχε, πολλῷ ὕστερον χρόνῳ μέμνηται

requires preparation for its exercise, one can understand why only things that one has often heard, for example, stick. And the phenomenon of a memory that one has, but for a long time is unaware of, points in the same direction. Memory has been prepared, yet requires time to mature completely.[550] Impressions cannot, according to this argument, be divided, in order to explain partial memory for then one could remember the parts. The examples of partial memory that Plotinus mentions here are various. One is only being able to recall something after having heard it several times; another is the case in which something not retained (οὐκ ἔσχε) from an earlier hearing (presumably: as far as one can immediately tell) is remembered much later. It is only then clear that it was retained when recollection has been successful. This example counts against impression theorists, since, on Plotinus' reading, they hold that either the impression is there or not, either it can be recalled or not. He does not allow them any degrees of intensity in the impressions.

The other example of an imperfect memory performance we mentioned above was the sudden recall of the memory content, and Plotinus ascribes this phenomenon to the exercise of the soul's capacity responsible for memory. Quite how he imagines that this happens is not explained. He skates lightly over the complicated question of the structure of recollection, a question which Aristotle and Plato had at least approached with their different conceptions of the association of ideas.[551] It seems that for Plotinus there is no more to be said than that a capacity of the soul is called on, activated, for instance by something that one hears. This capacity may be strengthened further by training. And for it to be a capacity of memory, a previous act of strengthening has to have happened, as was described in his account of memory.[552] In our example, an original per-

---

ἤδη; Οὐ γὰρ δὴ τῷ μέρη ἐσχηκέναι πρότερον τοῦ τύπου· ἔδει γὰρ τούτων μεμνῆσθαι· ἀλλ᾽ οἷον ἐξαίφνης γίγνεται τοῦτο ἔκ τινος ὑστέρας ἀκροάσεως ἢ μελέτης. Ταῦτα γὰρ μαρτυρεῖ πρόκλησιν τῆς δυνάμεως καθ᾽ ἣν μνημονεύομεν τῆς ψυχῆς ὡς ῥωσθεῖσαν ἢ ἁπλῶς ἢ πρὸς τοῦτο. Note the γὰρ in line 33.

550 IV 6 3 34–35 are difficult, but this is at least a possible interpretation. The argument may be connected to the point made in lines 57–59: memory is not simultaneous with the experience of which it is the memory, but only happens afterwards (cf. De mem. 2 451a21–30). If, however, the relatively complicated phenomenon of a memory that remains unconscious for a long time is meant in 34–35, the point may be the entirely negative one that material impressions certainly cannot explain it, even if Plotinus is not claiming to have a successful explanation himself.

551 Above p. 98.

552 See above p. 120.

ception at t1 leads to a later act of remembering at t2. The act of strengthening is this original perception at t1 and it prepares the soul with a view to a particular content, for an individual later act of memory.

The view of memory that Plotinus attributes to his opponents is that the impression is there, and that is actual memory; there is no room for a chain of representations, "association of ideas". The whole of memory is exhausted by actual impressions. They leave no room for the capacity of memory. We have seen that this is not true for Aristotle.[553] The power of Plotinus' arguments is derived from his insistence that his opponents' theories only allow them the use of impressions, without any prospect of a power being constituted by them, at least in part. But this is not convincing, unless one is committed to the view that powers are immaterial, and that they are not necessarily (as powers) associated with any material things. If one does not share this view one might think that being able to remember involves the possession of an impression, in some sense. This could be understood along the lines of Aristotle's theory. This possession of a representation, like the impression in some matter, forms part of the capacity, which is thus in part materially constituted.

The idea of a generally good capacity to remember leads on to the next point, about trained memories.[554] The conclusion of the argument is a repetition of the main claim that memory and perception are a "strength and a capacity". The capacity to remember is obviously not merely good with a view to isolated contents but is connected to one's habits.[555] Plotinus' example is of learning and repeating re-

---

553 See above p. 98. Plotinus does not, unlike Plato and Aristotle, discuss the way memories are recalled by certain relations between our perceptions or representations.

554 IV 6 3 40–55: Ὅταν δὲ μὴ μόνον πρὸς ἃ ἐμελετήσαμεν τὸ τῆς μνήμης ἡμῖν παρῇ, ἀλλ᾽ οἵπερ πολλὰ ἀνειλήφασιν ἐκ τοῦ εἰθίσθαι ἀπαγγελίαις χρῆσθαι, ῥᾳδίας ἤδη καὶ τῶν ἄλλων τὰς λεγομένας ἀναλήψεις ποιῶνται, τί ἄν τις ἐπαιτιῷτο τῆς μνήμης ἢ τὴν δύναμιν τὴν ῥωσθεῖσαν εἶναι; Οἱ μὲν γὰρ τύποι μένοντες ἀσθένειαν μᾶλλον ἢ δύναμιν κατηγοροῖεν· τὸ γὰρ ἐντυπώτατον τῷ εἴκειν ἐστὶ τοιοῦτον, καὶ πάθους ὄντος τοῦ τύπου τὸ μᾶλλον πεπονθὸς τοῦτό ἐστι τὸ μνημονεῦον μᾶλλον. Τούτου δὲ τοὐναντίον φαίνεται συμβαῖνον· οὐδαμοῦ γὰρ ἡ πρὸς ὁτιοῦν γυμνασία εὐπαθὲς τὸ γυμνασάμενον ποιεῖ· ἐπεὶ καὶ ἐπὶ τῶν αἰσθήσεων οὐ τὸ ἀσθενὲς ὁρᾷ οἷον ὀφθαλμός, ἀλλ᾽ ὅτῳ δύναμίς ἐστιν εἰς ἐνέργειαν πλείων. Διὸ καὶ οἱ γεγηρακότες καὶ πρὸς τὰς αἰσθήσεις ἀσθενέστεροι καὶ πρὸς τὰς μνήμας ὡσαύτως. Ἰσχὺς ἄρα τις καὶ ἡ αἴσθησις καὶ ἡ μνήμη.

555 line 42 εἰθίσθαι.

ports.[556] This habit enables the practised messenger to remember other things easily too.[557] "Remember" here is presumably an amalgam of retention and retrieval. The messenger learns easily and can reproduce successfully. This performance can only be attributed to the capacity of memory and not to actually existing impressions. Here again the point is that the actuality of the impressions is meant to exclude their relation to any conception of power. And on this point, in fact, Plotinus has the better of the argument, at least if one uses a fairly simple minded interpretation of the wax model. It really is so that if memory were to consist only of actual impressions, then the whole idea of practice would make no sense. Wax cannot practise taking on imprints.[558] Impressions, he thinks, can only weaken their owners, since the receptivity of that which takes on the impression lies in its yielding nature.[559] And so the best memory would lie in the most yielding nature; and that would go against the general idea of practice or training, which never makes people good at yielding or undergoing change, but rather good at doing things. Here we see one of the roots, or perhaps offshoots, of Plotinus' conviction that there is no passive capacity. What he is mainly thinking of are the things people do, and the training necessary so that they can do them.[560]

---

556 What kind of messenger is meant here? Is there any connection with mnemonics? Note that an obvious example of a trained memory – the orator's – does not feature here.

557 AHA, following HS, refers the use of τὰς λεγομένας ἀναλήψεις here to De mem. 2 451a20: but see also the use at line IV 6 3 29; and for the μελέται see also De mem. 1 451a12 (and Brèhier vol. 4 p.171).

558 He still does not argue that the realisation in a body cannot be part of what a power requires, merely that actual impressions cannot make sense of the phenomenon of training.

559 Contrast the idea in De mem. (above p. 73) that there is a functional optimal mean between hardness and softness for memory. Plotinus echoes this idea in IV 7 6 38–42.

560 He offers an explanation for the weakness of the old in perception and memory (IV 6 3 53–55): perhaps a competing explanation to that in De mem. 1 450a32–450b11 (above p. 73). But it is very unclear how the explanation here is meant to work. He says simply that the old are weak in memory and perception; hence both are forms of strength. For an explanation of failing strength in the old (including the power of memory) using the state of material organs, see De an. I 4 408b18–29.

The last argument had as its conclusion the general thesis that memory and perception are capacities. Now[561] we return to the connection between the two. Plotinus goes on to raise an objection to the view[562] that since perception is not caused by impressions, memory cannot be the retention of impressions. Put positively this view is the general claim that memory is a capacity. The objection is that if memory is a capacity and "a preparation for readiness",[563] then why do we only later (that is, than the original experience) have the capacity to bring back (ἀναπόλησιν[564]) the contents of the memory? In his answer, he turns to the phenomenon of preparing a capacity for exercise. We have a capacity, but only when this capacity has been bundled (συλλέγεσθαι)[565] is it established. Talk of bundling a capacity is pretty unclear, but it might mean the following. The various parts of the capacity to ride a bicycle (balancing, pedalling, steering) just need to be brought together to bear on the act of riding this bicycle. It can then be exercised immediately. This is the point of Plotinus' distinction between those powers that require time between their establishment and their exercise and those that do not.[566] Thus some capacities need time, to mature, as it were, perhaps like being a skilled sailor. In such capacities there is a temporal element involved. There is a connection between the concept of time and memory which there is not in the idea of a capacity such as riding a bicycle. Memories need time to mature, before we can say that we really remember something we have experienced. But Plotinus lays himself open to the objection that, unlike Aristotle,[567] he nowhere justifies using the relationship between memory and time, which this argument turns on. Furthermore,

---

561 IV 6 3 55–63: Ἔτι τῶν αἰσθήσεων τυπώσεων οὐκ οὐσῶν, πῶς οἷόν τε τὰς μνήμας κατοχὰς τῶν οὐκ ἐντεθέντων οὐδὲ τὴν ἀρχὴν εἶναι; Ἀλλ' εἰ δύναμίς τις καὶ παρασκευὴ πρὸς τὸ ἕτοιμον, πῶς οὐχ ἅμα, ἀλλ' ὕστερον εἰς ἀναπόλησιν τῶν αὐτῶν ἐρχόμεθα; Ἢ ὅτι τὴν δύναμιν δεῖ οἷον ἐπιστῆσαι καὶ ἑτοιμάσασθαι. Τοῦτο γὰρ καὶ ἐπὶ τῶν ἄλλων δυνάμεων ὁρῶμεν εἰς τὸ ποιῆσαι ὃ δύνανται ἑτοιμαζομένων καὶ τὰ μὲν εὐθύς, τὰ δέ, εἰ συλλέξαιντο ἑαυτάς, ἐργαζομένων.

562 See IV 6 1 1–5.

563 AHA's trans.

564 Cf. *Philebus* 34B10-C2, above p. 19.

565 IV 6 3 63. What does it mean? To collect, gather one's strength, so that it can be exercised? See LSJ s.v. I 2 F. Euripides *Phoenissae* 850, Plato, *Phaedo* 83A: the soul collects itself from the distractions of the body (cf. Plotinus I 6 5 7), Plato, *Axiochus* 370E: rally oneself from weakness.

566 IV 6 3 61–63. Are there other powers that require time like memory – or is it *sui generis?* Pregnancy – ripening?

567 Above p. 32.

at this point he is apparently thinking of perceptual memory, that is memory of a temporally fixed perception in one's life. And this too needs arguing for, like the use of time. For he thinks that there are two kinds of memory, namely also one for ideas.[568]

However, Plotinus does not use the relationship with time to isolate memory from other capacities, for he thinks that there is a whole range of capacities which require time for them to be exercised at all.[569] Nonetheless, his phrasing here reminds one of the account of perceptual memory. The capacity is there said to be "in labour and ready with" the objects of memory.[570] And it would seem to be true that the capacity for memory cannot be exercised without some perception happening beforehand.[571] Here we touch on the derivative nature of memory, as it was called in the *Introduction*.[572] We all have the capacity for memory, but without actual, previous perception, memory cannot be exercised. A first experience could never be a memory.[573] However, as we have seen, that is not the way Plotinus justifies the time-dependence of memory.

The next argument equates capacity with a talent or developed disposition. Memory and quickness of mind are not the same capacity, just as being a good boxer and being a good runner are not.[574] In some people the one talent is dominant, and in others, it is the other one. Plotinus as-

---

568 But perhaps it is possible to see some form of preparation for the use of concepts, leading to the realisation of this power which is comparable to the later recall of previous experience and which could be described as collection or bundling namely, the whole business of learning the articulation of concepts that dialectic constitutes. Plotinus does think that the recollection of ideas occurs without reference to time (IV 3 25 33–34, below p. 144). On his conception of dialectic see fn. 809.

569 Cf. perhaps IV 6 3 34–35; Cf. for a time elapsed between perception and recall De mem. 1 449b15–18, 2 451a29–30.

570 IV 6 3 19–20 above p. 118.

571 Cf. IV 4 6 2–4, see above p. 70 for Aristotle's account of the previous perception.

572 P.1.

573 See above on first perceptions in Aristotle p. 70.

574 IV 6 3 63–70 Γίγνονται δὲ ὡς ἐπὶ τὸ πολὺ οὐχ οἱ αὐτοὶ μνήμονες καὶ ἀγχίνοι [πολλάκις] ὅτι οὐχ ἡ αὐτὴ δύναμις ἑκατέρου, ὥσπερ οὐδ' ὁ αὐτὸς πυκτικὸς καὶ δρομικός· ἐπικρατοῦσι γὰρ ἄλλαι ἐν ἄλλῳ ἰδέαι. Καίτοι οὐκ ἐκώλυε τὸν ἀστιναοσοῦν ἔχοντα πλεονεξίας ψυχῆς ἀναγινώσκειν τὰ κείμενα, οὐδὲ τὸν ταύτῃ ῥυέντα τὴν τοῦ πάσχειν καὶ ἔχειν τὸ πάθος ἀδυναμίαν κεκτῆσθαι. Plotinus is continuing a discussion about the relation between memory and other intellectual capacities: HS cf. De mem. 1 449b7, also (HBT), along with IV 3 29 16, n. on ἀγχίνοι *Republic* 495B5.

sumes that capacities are like potentates that always strive for dominance over each other, so that only one can rule.[575] However, the examples of boxer and runner are not suitable as comparisons with memory, since the difference between two talents does not mean that the whole basis for the talent is a capacity in Plotinus' sense. There can be, for example, parts of the body which are also responsible for a talent, indeed the examples Plotinus gives are surely due in part to physique. One might well see an attack against materialism here: for example the mix of the body does not need to be appealed to if the simple difference of capacity between memory and sharp wits explains their dominance in different people. Plotinus wishes to draw the conclusion that if memory was merely imprinting then a talent such as quick-mindedness would not hinder the person concerned from reading off the impressions and so having a good memory.[576] Since he thinks that the two capacities compete, and one of them has to win, he has an argument against the impression theory of memory.

Plotinus is here tackling an old and important question, the relation between intelligence and memory, so a few words on the background is in order. The question is important, because the capacity to learn is obviously closely connected to memory, and it is debated in Aristotle and Plato. Plato thinks that the abilities occur in parallel: those able to learn (εὐμαθεῖς) are the same as those with a good memory (μνήμονες).[577] This leaves open the possibility that the connection between the two capacities is actually quite weak. Aristotle denies that there is a parallelism when he draws a distinction between the slow people who have a good memory and the quick people who are good at calling things to mind.[578] His position here is also dependent on his view that it is the concrete living things we are talking about. For there would appear to be a causal connection between the bodily constitution of each kind of person and their memory or their quick wittedness. Apparently, slow people preserve impressions better than those who are quick; and the quickness of the latter may be connected to the role of change in recollection. They

---

575 Kleist 1883: 151, 'die Herrschaft der einen Kraftform schließt die der anderen aus'.

576 He seems to shift from arguing that the people with a good memory and a quick mind are not the same, since the power is different, to saying that a quick mind interferes with a good memory, and this would not be the case if memory were impressions.

577 *Theaetetus* 194D2–3, cf. *Laws* IV 710C6.

578 See De mem. 1 449b7–8 and cf. 2 451b14–16.

recollect better because the representations follow one another more quickly.

As we have seen, Plotinus denies any connection between body and memory. We have been discussing the consequences of his view of memory, as revealed in his explanations of phenomena using a capacity for memory. We can now turn to some of the assumptions on which these explanations are based. Plotinus explains the concept of memory using that of the soul, without any mention of body, and this enables him to argue for the non-material nature of memory. For he has a peculiar view of the way that the soul, and its attributes, are related to its activities and capacities. The most important attribute of the soul is that it has no magnitude, or, in a more modern idiom, it is not extended, unlike body.[579] This quality applies to all further attributes of soul, and this is one aspect of Plotinus' thought that one has to grasp before approaching the next argument.[580] The other aspect is that capacities in general are not extended, even in those cases where they require body for their exercise.[581] While the organ of seeing is extended,[582] because it is corporeal, the ability to see is not, and is not, for example, spatially divisible. Put more generally, because soul is not extended, any attribute of soul is also non-extended, and capacities are prominent among the attributes of souls. Therefore memory as a capacity which is not to be explained by material impressions fits well into the wider perspective of Plotinus' psychology. Clearly, he is arguing here from the immateriality of the soul for the thesis that memory is a capacity. This argument simply assumes his concept of a capacity.

At the end of the chapter, and hence of the whole work on perception and memory, he makes some more general observations about the status of his views on the soul as the result of his investigations, as opposed to the more usual views which are, in contrast, due to deception by the senses.[583] He thinks that it is a mistake to conceive of the soul as analo-

---

579 See IV 1 and IV 7 1–8; on the relation between the unextendedness of soul and other attributes of soul, see Emilsson 1991.

580 IV 6 3 70–71.

581 See above fn. 494, 547.

582 Cf. Aristotle's remark, De an. II 12 424a25 ff.

583 IV 6 3 71–79 Καὶ ὅλως τὰ περὶ ψυχὴν πάντ' οὐ θαυμαστὸν ἄλλον τρόπον ἔχειν, ἢ ὡς ὑπειλήφασιν ὑπὸ τοῦ μὴ ἐξετάζειν ἄνθρωποι, ἢ ὡς πρόχειροι αὐτοῖς ἐπιβολαὶ ἐξ αἰσθητῶν ἐγγίνονται δι' ὁμοιοτήτων ἀπατῶσαι. Οἷον γὰρ ἐν πίναξιν ἢ δέλτοις γεγραμμένων γραμμάτων, οὕτως περὶ τῶν αἰσθήσεων καὶ τοῦ μνημονεύειν διάκεινται, καὶ οὔτε οἱ σῶμα αὐτὴν τιθέμενοι ὁρῶσιν, ὅσα ἀδύνατα τῇ ὑποθέσει αὐτῶν

gous to something material, such as a piece of wax which can take on impressions. His opponents, materialists or Aristotelians, who think that soul is a body or the form of a body, are said to use the model of letters written on tablets or panels for perception and memory. But they fail to see the impossibilities, i. e. contradictions, which arise from their hypothesis. As we have seen,[584] this passage is useful because one can use it to understand what Plotinus thinks he himself is doing in the last long part of Chapter 3, namely showing how his hypothesis does not give rise to contradictions, because the phenomena which he wants to explain do not contradict his hypothesis. Put positively, the concept of the soul is assumed, and then used to explain the phenomena.[585]

If we assume these arguments are directed against Aristotle among others, how successful are they? Plotinus' strategy is weak in that he does not argue that the involvement of body in memory need not preclude memory being the capacity of a living thing. Only if he can be sure that soul is not the form of a living thing, can he assume that his arguments for memory being a capacity are effective arguments against the Aristotelian position. And indeed, this proof forms part of his important early treatise proving the immortality of the soul.[586] Nonetheless, Aristotle's view of the soul as an actuality which includes capacities remains tenable on his own assumptions. For just as he thinks that the perceptive organs are identical with the capacity to perceive, but different in being, in the case of memory he can hold the view that concrete living things do have the relevant capacity, which is identical with their body, more exactly with the central organ, and so require the existence of the body, without depriving himself of the concept of capacity and its actualisation.

συμβαίνει, οὔτε οἱ ἀσώματον. His opponents are both those who have conducted no investigation (non-philosophers) but also the materialists, who have been deceived by the senses. Kleist (1883: 152) points out that in IV 7 the thesis that the soul is not a body is both proved and serves to prove further theses about the soul.

584 Above p. 121.
585 The procedure is thus a variant of the *Phaedo's* (99D-102A) hypothetical method.
586 IV 7, against the Peripatetics Ch. 8$^{4-5}$.

3.2 The subject of memory in life and after death

3.2.1 The soul as the subject of memory and as the reason for its two objects

We have seen that Plotinus distinguishes two kinds of memory by their objects, namely experiences and ideas. This distinction recurs as the first move in his treatment of the question of what the subject of memory is.[587] He is interested in this problem because in his view the soul continues to live after death without a body until it is reincarnated.[588] The question is which stages of the soul's post-corporeal existence have memory, and which do not. His main interest lies in showing that it is the soul that is the subject of memory, in fact only the soul which passes between states, that is to say those souls which sometimes are embodied and sometimes not. Souls, like those of the stars, which remain in a certain form of existence, are without memory since they do not migrate. So it is migratory, human souls that are the subject of memory.

At the outset of the enquiry,[589] Plotinus says that the definition of memory has often been given elsewhere, and so needs no further discussion. Since there is no discussion of the definition either in *The problems about the soul*, or in any work which predates it, this is probably a reference to the philosophical tradition of investigating memory. However, Plotinus did go on to define memory later, as we saw in the last section, where we considered two texts which should be considered as defini-

---

587 Plotinus' longest treatment of memory comes from the important work which Porphyry gave the title *On problems connected with the soul* (περὶ ψυχῆς ἀπορίων), IV 3, 4 and 5. In his *Life of Plotinus* (Ch. 5), Porphyry gives them the numbers 27, 28 and 29 in the chronological series. He also gives them the simpler titles *On the soul I, II and III*. The idea that the work is aporetic in character is derived from the first four lines of IV 3. Porphyry split this treatise in three, for his own reasons. The first important division, between IV 3 and IV 4, falls more or less in the middle of the treatment of memory in the human soul. This investigation runs from IV 3 25-IV 4 5. Thus we restrict ourselves to the treatment of memory in human souls, and do not discuss the question of memory in the other souls (souls of heavenly bodies, the world soul) in IV 4 6–17. Our exposition will follow its course, since the discussion is systematic, and programmatically follows the human soul in its peregrinations from corporeal existence to contemplation of the ideas.
588 IV 3 24.
589 IV 3 25 8–9.

tions.[590] Before turning to the enquiry into the subject of memory it is worth recalling the main features of memory according to the definitions. Apart from anything else, we will then see what the connection is between the soul as the subject of memory and the two objects of memory. I think that the definition is not merely compatible with the discussion of the subject of memory. The latter deepens our understanding of the way in which Plotinus conceives of memory. Core aspects of these *quasi* definitions are that memory is a capacity of the soul which is related to the two basic activities of the soul, perceiving and thinking. Furthermore, memory relates to things that appear to the soul, and can make these things 'shine out', that is, I take it, the soul can call them to mind.[591] A large part of our discussion will be concerned with the way the soul does this, namely by using φαντασία. The definition leads us to expect the use of φαντασία in memory because of its relationship to things that appear to us, that is, things represented to us. In due course, we will review the arguments that Plotinus appeals to for the use of φαντασία, and so, of course, we will be concerned with the nature of φαντασία.

The idea that there is a connection between the subjects of memory and what memory is, is one that we have met in Aristotle. Several aspects of the relation between subject and memory from Aristotle's treatment may be mentioned. At the most trivial, or least explanatory, level he says that people with good memories are slow, as opposed to good recollectors, who are quick. More serious is the restriction of memory to animals which can perceive time; and the exclusion of animals from possession of recollection on the grounds that it is a kind of deliberation. Turning to his definition of memory, it mentions representation, and representation is a change arising from perception and perception is a change in the soul mediated by the body. *Ergo* memory implies body. Since memory is one of the subjects of the *Parva Naturalia*, we should anyway

---

590 Above pp. 120, 124.

591 There are, however, two puzzles about this mention of a definition of memory in IV 3 25. On the one hand, none of the questions about the subject of memory, discussed in IV 3 25–4 5, as far as humans are concerned, are apparently made superfluous by the definition. This is surprising, since one would expect a definition of a predicate to make clear the kinds of things it can be attributed to as its subject. On the other hand, although in this discussion mention is made of the definition, it appears to do no work in the investigation. Why even mention the definition, if it apparently needs not to be called on to decide important questions in the enquiry itself?

expect it to be common to body and soul.[592] For Plotinus, in contrast, if memory can be defined without mentioning or implying any mention of body, then there is a prospect that the soul alone can have memory, at least in some stages of its existence.

Looking back at what we have already found in Plotinus' work, we notice that several other aspects of the treatment of the definition in IV 6 3 are of importance here. Firstly, there was the distinction between two kinds of memory, memory of perception and of ideas; Plotinus envisaged furthermore the possibility of finding a definition common to both kinds, explaining why both fall under the concept of memory. The question about the unity of memory will crop up in various forms in the discussion we are now beginning. There are two fundamental ways in which this unity may be challenged: by the division either of the subject or of the object of memory. Either what is remembered is not unitary, or what does the remembering is not.

An aspect of the relation between the subject of memory and memory itself is the modesty of memory. Memory includes some form of reference to what happened earlier. This fact has important consequences for the possible subject of memory. It entails subjects existing through time. These subjects must be able to grasp time, and hence be involved in and aware of different cognitive states. Plotinus uses this aspect of memory to exclude the souls of the heavenly bodies' and the soul of the cosmos from being subjects of memory.[593] Despite the fact that for Plotinus time is very closely related to the soul,[594] in that it is the life of the soul, he excludes the souls of heavenly bodies, and of the cosmos from having memory, although they are temporally organised.[595] In the case of these souls, the contemplation of ideas and god is uninterrupted. Since they have lost nothing, that is, have forgotten nothing, for example, though involvement with body, they do not have to recover anything through ἀνάμνησις. Thus Plotinus tries to show that they do not fulfil the conditions for being capable of memory. This is the case although, of course, they are involved in process in a very broad sense, in that the heavenly

---

592 Above p. 24.
593 IV 4 6–17.
594 III 7 11, but also IV 4 15 and 17. See Smith 1996, 1998, Beierwaltes 1967.
595 in IV 4 6–15. AHA (ad loc. p. 113) refers to IV 4 16–17 for the discussion of the question whether divine beings have memory; this seems too restrictive; the discussion begins at ch. 6.

bodies revolve. Nonetheless, he does not think that the succession they experience is suited to giving them memory, because of its regularity.[596]

Soul possesses thought and perception as characteristic capacities and activities at different phases in its existence. It is with reference to these phases that Plotinus proposes the investigation of memory.[597] He asks: just when do "the souls themselves" have memory? In order to answer this question he turns to the subject of memory. That is, in sentences of the form "X remembers Y", we want to know what kinds of things can take the position of X. In answer to the question, Plotinus will offer us the following possibilities.[598] The composite being, and so all involvement of body, is dismissed. Turning to the soul itself, Plotinus distinguishes between two candidates, the higher soul and a "less clear soul" in us, which we have from the cosmos, and he then asks which is the subject of memory.[599] His answer is that both have memory. Since we will be following the course of his exposition we will discuss this answer at length when we come to it.[600]

Further questions[601] raised by Plotinus at the outset give the enquiry more detailed aims, to wit, which part or capacity of the soul explains memory, and what the nature of the "animal" is, should it be responsible for memory.[602] The final question is whether the same faculty is responsible for the apperception (ἀντιλαμβάνεσθαι) of thoughts and percepts, and hence might serve to remember them. These questions provide the rationale for key steps in the enquiry, in which Plotinus tries to prove that soul, and not the body or the concrete, is the subject of memory,

---

596 IV 3 25 20–24
597 IV 3 25 1–5.
598 HS (ad IV 3 25 35–37) cite an important Aristotelian text (De an. I 4 408b13–18) in which Aristotle says that the soul is not the subject of psychic activities but rather the composite with the soul. See esp. I 1 for Plotinus' discussion of the subject of different mental states and activities.
599 The composite Ch. 26, below p. 146.
600 The two souls Ch. 27, below p. 157.
601 The final section of IV 3 25, lines 34–45, provides a more precise version of the question what the subject of memory is; it is explicitly an improvement on the start. At the start of the chapter, lines 1–3, the question is merely when, in their different phases, which souls themselves have memory, and for how long. In contrast, the end of the chapter develops the question anew, offering the prospect of a serious discussion of the possibilities.
602 IV 3 25 41–44. The nature of the living thing is the subject of I 1.

that both souls have memory, and that it is φαντασία which is responsible for memory of both perceptions and thoughts.[603]

Let us now turn in a little more detail to the distinction between two kinds of memory which Plotinus makes before turning to the question of the subject of memory. The distinction is based on the objects of memory,[604] as already mentioned. Firstly, there is memory of things acquired (ἐπακτός), experiences and things learnt, and secondly memory of one's own thinking.[605] How is one to explain the first kind of memory? The central point is that the object of memory is acquired. If both experiences (παθήματα) and things learned, theorems (μαθήματα), can be remembered, it would seem that the decisive point about the content of memory in this sense is that there is a time when one was not in possession, and then a time when one was in possession, of the relevant cognition.[606] The content of the cognition itself may be temporally characterised or not (for example: Socrates was pale last summer and: pale is a colour). Plotinus talks of experiences (παθήματα) here: Are these of the body or the soul or the composite? That is, does this kind of memory actually require a body insofar as the original perception requires one? Yes, the experiences are bodily. We perceive only when we have a body,[607] and presumably, insofar as learning usually requires sense organs, we cannot learn when not in the body.[608] This view seems to be made necessary by the fact that neither the impassible, here: νοῦς, nor things which are not in time have this kind of memory. So the acquisition of this kind of memory is something related to the past.[609]

---

603 The concrete animal is a mixture of body and soul and is not responsible for memory (Chapter 26). The capacity of soul responsible for memory-percepts is φαντασία (Chapter 29), and also for that of thoughts (Chapter 30).

604 Chapter 25.

605 IV 3 25 10–24 and 25–40.

606 Cf. IV 4 6 2–3.

607 Cf. IV 3 26 46–50.

608 He does seem to think that spirits (δαίμονες) and souls hold conversations, nonetheless (IV 3 18 20–24).

609 This kind of memory is the same as that in IV 6 3 16–19 in which the capacity towards some perceptible (αἰσθητά), is strengthened, thus enabling the soul to make the perceptible shine out in itself. They have no cognition of the before and after, and so are unable to remember such things. See above p. 117. Plotinus excludes certain subjects (god, being, intellect) from being subjects of memory (IV 3 25 11–14; it is strange that he speaks of the impassible here, since this of course includes the soul, and yet these memories must belong to the soul, at least insofar as it is in a body). The point cannot be that there can be no mem-

When we turn to the second of the two kinds of memory, we notice something curious, namely, "the other form of memory" (ἕτερον εἶδος μνήμης)[610] is, to begin with, said to be not memory at all. Plotinus says that one should not say that one has memory of one's own thinking.[611] The reason for this is that the soul is always thinking; and so thinking is not acquired in contrast to experiences and things learnt,[612] and nor does thinking have to be retained, so that it does not go away. Further, since this thinking is not dated there is no time involved in this kind of memory. This would seem to be the decisive point: memory is always of the past[613] and eternity is not in any temporal relation to what is in time. Plotinus does, however, weaken his objection to speaking of "memory" here to the extent that he says that it is not memory in the same way; "hence"[614] he can allow that it is memory *in some sense*.

What is this sense? Plotinus says that the ancients were accustomed to attribute "memory in the sense of recollection" (μνήμην καὶ ἀνάμνησιν) to those who actualised their capacity to think.[615] We will turn to the question of the identity of the ancients in a moment. What is Plotinus claiming here? It is an attractive thought that in Plotinus' view exercise of such

---

ory of god, being or intellect, since this kind of memory is defined by its object. That there cannot be memory of these things, at least not in the same sense as there is of acquired knowledge, is the point of the second part of the chapter. Intellect is excluded from being an object of memory in IV 4 1; on eternity and being cf. IV 4 1 13, II 5 3 8.

610 IV 3 25 33.
611 IV 3 25 25–35. There are other passages where Plotinus speaks of the process of retrieving one's thought, and hence one's eternal nature, through recollection III 7 1, V 1 1, IV 8 1, V 3 2 13–14 (this last one seems to be a concept of ἀνάμνησις that includes recollection of experiences). Memory of the self, i. e. of our experiences, will be discussed at other stages in the soul's cycle. See below p. 201 on IV 4 2.
612 IV 3 25 25.
613 IV 4 6 2–3; on timelessness and νοῦς see Beierwaltes 1967: 72–3, n. 45., Merlan 1963: 72–77, esp. 76 n 2.
614 τοίνυν l. 27.
615 IV 3 25 31–33. I take καὶ as epexegetic. Warren (1965: 258) translates lines 31–33 as follows: "the ancients seem to have attributed memory in the form of (καὶ) recollection to those activating what they have." He thinks that Plotinus (in contrast to McCumber 1978) rules out Platonic ἀνάμνησις and confines himself to memory proper: the re-cognition of a prior event, sensible events in ch. 25, 26, 29, concepts of discursive reason in ch. 30 and 31. On IV 3 30 see below p. 179. There is no need to see the present text as excluding recollection, if this is just the task of getting back to thinking Forms, rather than the thinking itself. Getting back to the Forms of course requires the exercise of discursive reason.

a capacity would be recollection of what is in one's nature, that is, the retrieval of what is innate. It is *re*collection because it is *re*covery of what is already in the soul. Thus memory here is not due to retaining something. As already noted, we do not need to do that in the case of our thinking ideas because that is in our nature. The soul always thinks even if it does not do so consciously. But what we do need to do is recollect that thinking is in our nature by exercising this capacity. That is to say, we become conscious of our thinking the ideas. We can awaken this capacity, which has its basis in what we are, and bring the ideas to clarity by exercising it.[616] This exercise of the capacity is recollection, and Plotinus is talking about this as a form of remembering here (μνημονεύειν). Although Plotinus' wording here – "the ancients were accustomed etc." – suggests that he does not accept this way of speaking, this appearance is deceptive. For he does go on to talk at length about memory of thoughts,[617] and he does in the end say that it is a form of memory, just not the same as that for experiences.

Let us turn to the ancients. Before asking who they are, it is worth noting the authority they are invested with, and also the fact that no name is mentioned. Plotinus clearly thinks that tradition is a guide to truth, quite independently of any particular thinkers.[618] So the question of who exactly is meant here is not so urgent. Nonetheless, a comparison with Plato is instructive, especially the *Phaedo*. There are, as a matter of fact, decisive differences between Plotinus and Plato. To begin with, the condition that this kind of memory, memory of ideas, is not connected to time seems to fit none of Plato's accounts of memory or rather ἀνάμνησις. The concept of ἀνάμνησις in the *Philebus* has no particular connection to ideas.[619] In the *Phaedo* there is no explicit theoretical distinction between memory and recollection, in the sense we found in Ar-

---

616 This is the concept of recollection from III 6 and IV 6 3 10–15, above p. 120, 124.

617 IV 3 30.

618 Boys-Stones (2001) argues that in post-Hellenistic philosophy, above all from the second century AD, thinkers looked for traces of the privileged wisdom of the first generations of mankind. Platonists were then those thinkers who thought Plato presented a reliable reconstruction of this wisdom. This is the point of V 1 8 10–14 where Plotinus says he relies on Plato's writings as evidence that the views are old. V 1 8–9 provide a doxography justifying Plotinus' own views; see Atkinson 1983: 191–2. Cf. also III 7 1 13–14, II 9 6 37, 51–52, VI 4 16 4–7.

619 See above p. 18. On the *Phaedrus*, where there is a distinction between recollection and memory, and recollection is related to ideas, see above fn 22.

istotle, that is a distinction between the immediate availability of past experiences without a search in memory, and recollection as the deliberate search for experiences which are not available.[620] In the *Phaedo*, the point of departure is the parallel between retrieval of experiences and retrieval of ideas. Both processes have the same structure. In both cases recollection presupposes prior cognition, and, usually, also the forgetting of the thing to be remembered.[621] The main difference is that in the case of ideas, forgetting plays a crucial role. There is of course no suggestion that *really* we are thinking the ideas all the time. Yet this is the idea behind the way Plotinus conceives of innate ideas, and is of course one reason that he is so concerned to distinguish recollection of ideas from the memory of acquired experiences. Ideas are in us because we are thinking them the whole time, even when we are not conscious of doing so. So we can understand Plotinus not making such a direct reference to Plato.[622]

Now we have distinguished the two forms of memory, we can turn to the question of what it is that plays the role of the subject of memory.

3.2.2 Against the corporeality of memory

We now turn to a crucial aspect of Plotinus' concept of memory, to wit that body plays no role in it. This aspect of his theory has been touched upon in his arguments against impression theories of memory.[623] His support for his theory and attack on impression theories was based partly on his view of soul and partly on phenomena connected with memory. The arguments we shall now discuss are of a more fundamental nature, connected directly to how we understand the soul, the body and the concrete living thing. In this section we will review his arguments for the thesis that neither body nor the concrete living thing are suited to being the subject of memory, and then turn to his positive arguments for the thesis that only an unalterable ("impassible") soul can account for memory, and the associated phenomena connected with awareness. Finally, we will show that the treatment of memory is the only place where Plotinus

---

620 HS refer here to *Phaedo* 71E2–7. On the *Phaedo*, see *Introduction* p. 14.

621 *Introduction* p. 14: Condition 1. 73C1 and condition 4. 73E1–3. For condition 4 cf. 76A1–4.

622 Contrast e.g. IV 8 1, where he turns to Plato explicitly, after running through rapidly other accounts of the soul's ascent, but notes that Plato does not always say the same things.

623 Above p. 124.

may be held to mention what is sometimes called an "astral body" for the soul, a vehicle that carries it when it is not in an earthly body. We shall see that there are good reasons in the concept of memory for him to make this radical deviation from his normal doctrine.

Now for the first step towards proving that the soul, indeed a certain capacity of the soul, is responsible for memory. Plotinus must show that body cannot perform this task, either on its own or in company with the soul.[624] He proceeds by presenting his opponents' arguments and then refuting them. The first argument for memory being common to body and soul[625] starts from the idea that perception is common to body and soul. The implication is that because perception is common to body and soul, and because memory builds on perception, therefore, by preserving it, memory must also be common to body and soul.[626] Plotinus obviously thinks, mistakenly, that his opponents have to admit a change in the soul, if body and soul are involved in memory.

Hence Plotinus wants to show that the soul can use bodily instruments without being changed. In his argument against his opponents, Plotinus compares functions common to body and soul with weaving or boring. The craftsman uses his tools[627] and the tools undergo change, and serve the craftsman. The craftsman serves as the soul in the comparison. The soul then receives the imprinting of the body, either from the body[628] or in form of the perceptual judgement which the soul makes on the basis of the affection of the body. The argument against attributing memory to both body and soul is that, even if the imprinting initially

---

624 The chapter is best divided in two: lines 1–40 shows that various possibilities of memory being common to body and soul do not work as explanations of memory; and lines 40–56 show that soul is an independent nature, some of whose capacities require organs for their actualisation.

625 IV 3 26 1–12.

626 This line of argument has much in common with Aristotle, who argues that the most important phenomena connected with animals are common to body and soul, just because they stand in a variety of relations to perception. See above p. 24.

627 IV 3 26 3–4; HS cf. De an. I 4 408b13.

628 This is puzzling, in view of the fact that the soul cannot on Plotinus' view undergo such experiences; hence Emilsson's conclusion that perception for Plotinus *is* the formation of a judgement on the basis of bodily affection (above p. 108). On judgement (κρίσις) see Emilsson 1988: 78–82. Also see the parallel in IV 4 23 37–40. The most important texts on perception are IV 4 23, IV 5 and IV 6 1–2. Which of these possibilities is actually the case need not be decided here, since all that is at issue is the involvement of body in memory.

came through the body, that does not mean that the preservation of the imprinting requires the body. It is the soul that preserves or casts off the imprinting.[629] Hence memory does not need to be common to body and soul.[630] Quite how[631] soul is meant to preserve the "impression" in memory Plotinus does not say. Presumably he has his own theory in mind according to which psychic impressions are involved. Thus this argument claims that the impressions needed for memory are entirely non-corporeal, they are purely psychic. Hence the argument is compatible with Plotinus' own theory that memory consists in an active strengthening of a psychic capacity.

The second argument for memory belonging to body and soul which Plotinus counters here starts from the idea that different mixtures of the body may influence the capacity for memory. An example for this kind of theory is Aristotle's one for explaining that the old and the very young have bad memories because of their bodily constitution. Hence bodily mixtures can only influence memory because memory is common to body and soul. Plotinus uses two strategies against this view. To start with, he allows that body can be a hindrance, but he maintains that even if we have a concrete living thing with memory, its memory is due to soul not body. Quite how he envisages body being a hindrance to memory, he does not say; clearly he does not think that the soul is literally hindered by body, for it cannot be affected. Presumably, in Plotinus' own view the hindrance is in the form of a distraction, a bodily interest that diverts the soul from the memory in question. For example, a banquet might distract an orator from remembering a speech. Secondly, he points out that his opponents have no answer to the question of why the body should be responsible for the memory of things learnt (μάθησις). The idea is presumably that while body is involved in perception, and hence may be involved in the memory of perceptions, there is no prima facie reason whatever for body being involved in the memory of propositions (e.g. theorems) which cannot be perceived.

Plotinus' next two arguments[632] against the corporeality of memory discuss the question of just what the concrete living thing is,[633] so that

---

629 IV 3 26 12 αὐτήν. HS interpret this as τὴν τύπωσιν.
630 This view of memory is very close to what Plato says about recollection in the *Philebus*; see above p. 18.
631 Cf. IV 3 25 43, p. 178.
632 IV 3 26 18–22, 22–24.
633 A question asked at the end of Chapter IV 3 25 43–44.

it can be excluded from being the subject of memory. He denies that the living thing is a third thing besides the body and soul. The most important reason is that he does not accept a mixture between body and soul, as though soul were only potentially in the living thing.[634] This argument should be seen in the context of the Stoics' view that body and soul are mixed in such a way that they constitute a living thing. This form of mixture (κρᾶσις) represents one way of constituting things in Stoic theory, whereby something new comes about from the mixture, leaving the ingredients only potentially present. Plotinus' first objection to this view is that body and soul cannot make a third thing, because then soul would only be potentially in the mixture, and that is to say no longer actually there; and for Plotinus it is obvious that a living thing has an actual soul. The second argument concedes for the sake of argument that the living thing is a mixture, but denies that even then the concrete thing would be what remembers. For[635] even if there were a mixture, soul would be responsible for remembering, in the way that the sweetness in honey-wine is due to the honey.[636] Plotinus' understanding of mixture is such that one can still attribute some quality, for example, to one of the ingredients and not the whole. This represents a weakening of the idea of mixture, in that then soul is actually present, not merely potentially there.

The weakness of the comparison with honey-wine lies in the fact that sweetness is merely an attribute due to the honey, and the honey can exist independently. Remembering is something like an attribute; and if Plotinus goes on to say that it is due to soul, *which, he implicitly assumes, can exist independently,* then of course he has assumed part of his position. For his opponents want to say that soul *only exists* in a body-soul compound, and so the body plays at least the role of a contributing cause to memory. Hence, body is necessary for the soul's existence and so plays a causative role in all the soul's activities.

Plotinus goes on to use a thought-experiment to show that body need have no role in explaining memory.[637] He suggests a way the soul could need body in order to explain memory using impressions, only to deny

---

634 Cf. De gen. et corr. I 10 327b15–22. For Aristotle, soul cannot be affected by body, and so too for Plotinus. A prime example of mixture ("blending") for the Stoics is that of the soul in a living body (LS 48 C Alexander On mixture 216,14–218,6 = SVF 2 473). An extended critique of Stoic views on the soul is to be found in IV 7 2–8².
635 IV 3 26 22–24.
636 For other relations between body-soul and ἐντελέχεια, see IV 7 8⁵.
637 lines 25–35.

that there is really any need for body, if one understands the impressions correctly. He puts forwards the hypothesis that it is the soul that is responsible for memory but that by being in body it is "impure" and has acquired a *quasi* quality[638] that enables it to play this role in the explanation of memory. In this way, having a place by being "with body", it can take on impressions.[639] To have impressions (τύποι), on a materialist view, one needs more than mere extension, one needs a material that offers at least some resistance to the pressure from the ring. So the thought experiment is to suggest that this quality of resistance might be given to the soul by being in the body, and the answer to this suggestion is simply to deny that there is really any "pushing", even in the case of sense perception, where clearly the body is involved. So impressions in perception, and other psychic activities, are not like seal-impressions, where there is a counter-pressure. Perception is like thinking, and there is no pushing or counter-pressure in thinking, nor is there, for Plotinus, any need for body or a bodily quality.[640] In this way he is able to defend his concept of psychic impressions, which can be involved in perception, thought and memory, without any pushing or resistance, and hence without any reliance on the body.

We have seen that Plotinus is not an all-out opponent of impressions, merely of material ones.[641] According to this passage, two attributes do not belong to impressions, extension and (limited) resistance to change. It is striking how literally he takes the image of sealing and impressions to derive arguments against his opponents. One may well doubt whether any serious proponent of impressions in memory attributed a kind of resistance to them, with the implication that something material takes on the impression and exerts a counter-pressure. Plotinus himself is quite

---

638 ὥσπερ ποιωθεῖσα, AHA: "a kind of special quality". This peculiar formulation would seem to be due to Plotinus, and not the Stoics, for whom the idea that the soul is modified presents no problems; on their view of perception see SVF I 484, II 343.

639 Of course, one of the problems with the idea that the soul takes on impressions for Plotinus is that the soul is not extended, and if one applies the seal model strictly, then impressions are extended. However, Plotinus is not operating here at this basic level; the *quasi* quality is not extension, although he does point out that τύποι are not extensions (IV 3 26 29). For this basic character of the soul see IV 1 and 2; and cf. IV 7 2–8³.

640 IV 3 26 26–34.

641 Above p. 110.

happy talking about impressions,[642] merely he thinks that they are possible without the soul undergoing change. Rather the soul in having impressions is just as active as it is in thinking. In fact, the argument we have just considered shows how closely allied he thinks thought and perception are.

None of the arguments so far has tackled the fundamental problem of soul not existing without a body. Neither does the final argument[643] for attributing memory to the soul alone. It is possible, says Plotinus, for the soul to have memory of its own impulses (κινήματα), and this shows that memory belongs to the soul. His example of such an impulse is a desire,[644] and the soul can have a desire without this desire reaching the body, i.e. resulting in action or physical satisfaction, and the soul could then have a memory of this desire. This memory, since the desire never reached the body, cannot be attributed to the body. And, as a final blow against ascribing memory to body, Plotinus asks how one could in any case attribute cognition to body, since it is not in body's nature to know anything at all. This last *petitio principii* is hardly more than a rhetorical flourish.

Finally, we come to the crucial question of the nature of the soul itself, and its ability to exist alone.[645] He proceeds by dividing activities[646]

---

642 See esp. I 1 7 9–17 (AHA trans.): "And soul's power of sense-perception need not be perception of sense objects, but rather it must be receptive of the impressions produced by sensation on the living being; these are already intelligible entities. So external sensation is the image (εἴδωλα) of this perception of the soul, which is in its essence truer and is a contemplation of forms alone without being affected. From these forms, from which alone the soul receives its lordship over the living being, come reasonings and opinions and acts of intuitive intelligence; and this is precisely where 'we' are." Cf. III 6 1 8–11 (AHA trans.): "But it would, all the same, be possible to say also about what are called the impressions, that their character is quite different from what has been supposed (AHA cites SVF I 141, 484, II 55), and is like that which is also found in acts of thought; these too are activities, which are able to know without being affected in any way; and in general our reasoned intention is not to subject the soul to changes and alterations of the same kind as heatings and coolings of bodies" (AHA cites SVF I 234, III 459). Plotinus talks of impressions in the soul, also of εἴδη, εἴδωλα; s. Emilsson 1988: 162 n. 24 who cites also IV 6 1 38, V 5 1 18.

643 IV 3 26 34–44.

644 The moral effect of a desire is the subject of IV 3 28. The memory that a desire occurred seems to be what Plotinus has in mind here.

645 IV 3 26 44–56.

646 IV 3 26 39–44.

of living things into those that are mediated by the body and end[647] in the soul, and those that are merely activities of the soul itself. The point is that the soul is an (independent) nature (τι καὶ φύσιν τινα) with its own functioning (ἔργον τι), which can have striving (ἔφεσις), such as the desire (ἐπιθυμεῖν) just discussed, and hence memory of this striving and its fulfilment (or non-fulfilment) can be present in the soul without any involvement of the body. How does Plotinus prove this decisive point, that is, that the soul is an independent nature? The crux of the argument is that the nature of the soul is not in flux. For if it were, according to Plotinus, then there would be no memory. This touches a point which we have referred to several times, and which goes to the heart of Plotinus' treatment, namely the demands that memory makes of its subject. His thesis is that the subject of memory is not subject to change, in other words it is, in the jargon, "impassible". How is this thesis to be taken? The train of thought leading to the conclusion that impassibility is necessary for memory is complicated and can be summarised very roughly as follows. The idea is that only impassibility can preserve identity, and identity is necessary for various forms of awareness, and so too for memory. The main point about memory here is the ability to ascribe a past experience to oneself.

Let us now turn to this train of thought in more detail. The interesting questions can be divided in three. The attribute that soul is said to have is "not flowing" or "remaining".[648] What does this mean? The second question concerns the attributes that are said to depend on this "remaining". They are co-perception, συναίσθησις, awareness, παρακολούθησις, synthesis σύνθεσις, practical understanding οἷον σύνεσις. What do these terms mean? And the third question is: how is the soul's remaining connected to these attributes?

Two obvious possible meanings for "remaining" are: not subject to (any) change or maintaining a stable identity. In fact, it seems that for Plotinus, these are not two distinct possibilities in the case of immaterial things. We have already seen[649] any change whatever in immaterial things

---

647　λήγειν. HBT cf. I 1 5 11. On perceptions ending in representation see below p. 173 on IV 3 29 25.

648　IV 3 26 52–54. Brisson (2005: 492) notes the presence of the play on words remaining (μονή) and memory (μνήμη) in De an. I 408b18, and De mem. 2 453b3

649　In a passage from III 6 2 50–54, see above p. 124. Actually remembering something requires that something happens, but Plotinus, by implication, does not think that this realisation of a capacity is a change.

would cause their perishing. The contrast with body seems to support this view, for body changes and flows, and hence is the cause of forgetfulness.[650] Thus for Plotinus, the identity of the soul depends on its complete changelessness. This view of the subject of memory may be contrasted with Aristotle. For the latter does think that living things are involved in change, and yet preserve their identity. Indeed, it is through the regular change of their metabolisms that they preserve their identity. The soul itself is not subject to change, only the concrete living thing.

What about the four terms? I will discuss these difficult concepts briefly in turn, and suggest tentatively in each case how they are connected to the idea of identity. The first two (συναίσθησις, παρακολούθησις) are concerned with consciousness, the third (σύνθεσις) is very ambiguous, and the last (οἷον σύνεσις) is "something like" practical understanding. συναίσθησις is a general term for awareness, which sometimes[651] belongs to νοῦς but not to the soul, and sometimes[652] the soul is said to have it. Here it is obviously being attributed to the soul, in combination with the latter's changeless identity.[653] We can try taking it here as meaning "co-perception". Any perception is at least potentially accompanied by a per-

---

650 On body as the cause of forgetting when the soul enters a new one see Aristotle *Eudemus* Fr. 5. On forgetting and dullness being caused by bodily process cf. *Timaeus* 87A7.

651 V 3 5 45, 6 33, 13 12–14: νοῦς thinks itself and has awareness of itself thinking. For the co-perception of the beast see I 1 11 11: it has an image of the soul along with the body. For another passage in which co-perception, along with understanding, is attributed to nature as a kind of soul, at rest in itself, see III 8 4 18–20.

652 IV 4 2 32.

653 On consciousness and unconsciousness in Plotinus see Schwyzer 1960, Lloyd 1964, Warren 1964, Smith 1978, Schroeder 1987; and the studies of V 3 by Beierwaltes 1991 and Halfwassen 1994. Schroeder (1987: 687), when discussing VI 9 6 50–52: "συναίσθησις and σύνεσις as consciousness of self may also involve a concomitant awareness of the ground of self and being." He goes on to suggest that this awareness is designated by σύνεσις in I 6 2 3, where there is talk of the soul remembering itself. Similarly, with συναίσθησις referring to IV 4 2 24–32 (on which see below p. 201). The terms may well have this connotation in our passage; after all the point is the independence of the soul, its having its own function – which is, I take it, to turn to thinking, that is the ground of the being. Brisson (2005: 242, n. 489 ad loc) has a much more down to earth approach, with which I am in general more in accord: συναίσθησις refers to the association of the soul with its own perceptions, παρακολούθησις is attention to a process bringing the soul information, and σύνεσις is a synthesis, sharing ("mettre en commun") of information.

ception that it is my perception. There is here then not strict consciousness of oneself,[654] but merely the possibility of ascribing a perception to oneself. If this is the right way to take συναίσθησις here, how is it connected to the changeless identity of the soul? The obvious connection lies in the fact that the soul can only perceive that a perception belongs to itself if the soul has an identity. For if the boundaries of its identity were not circumscribed, if they were fluid, there would be no possibility of the soul saying which perceptions belong to it and which do not.

This basic form of self-ascription is distinct from παρακολούθησις which is the awareness of what one is doing while one is doing it.[655] Plotinus conceives of it as an accompanying action, alongside what one is doing, and a distraction from the main action. As to the connection between παρακολούθησις and the soul's identity, the same may be said here as before about co-perception. As an example, let us consider me reading. I can only know that I am reading if there is a fact of the matter that I am reading or not. There has to be a subject with a boundary for the sentence. With both of the reflexive forms of understanding (συναίσθησις, παρακολούθησις), the move from a distinct identity to the possibility of reflection is fairly clear.

Let us turn to the second pair, synthesis and σύνεσις. The first would seem to refer here to a cognitive act of synthesis on the part of the soul, and the second, some form of practical understanding. In order to connect these terms to the idea of the identity of the soul I think that a mediating step should be taken *via* the idea of unity. A bounded self is a unity, and only if there is a unity, can any forms of synthesis such as acts of perception or understanding be performed.[656] Either subsuming an individual under an idea or bringing together two ideas presupposes the identity of the soul performing the action. The same holds of σύνεσις, which may be connected to the idea of unity,[657] but is here

---

654 On this term see Graeser 1972: 126–137, especially of the soul (p. 135–7), and he thinks it is a kind of inner sense, a perception of the body perceiving, in our text as well as in IV 4 24 21–22, V 3 2 4, IV 4 8 20.

655 See I 4 5 2, I 4 10 28, II 9 1 44, III 9 9.

656 Schwyzer (1960: 368) suggests it means "Kombinieren" in our text; I take this to be an act of cognitive synthesis.

657 Plato in the *Cratylus* 412A derives it from συνιέναι, "go together", whereas it comes from συνίημι, I perceive or understand (LSJ s.v.) Cf. the crux at VI 9 6 52, and Schroeder 1987: 687. See also EN VI 11 esp. 1143a5–10, 16–18. At V 1 4 7 it occurs with ἀΐδια and ζωή of primary being; see Atkinson 1983:

best seen as a form of critical understanding directed at practical decisions.[658] The connection between practical understanding and identity is straightforward enough. The soul's identity is a pre-requirement for practical decisions. My interest in and concern about decisions rests on my continuing identity.

So much for the four attributes of soul which are said to depend on its completely unchanging identity. One may well ask what these concepts are doing in a treatment of memory. The decisive point is that a distinct identity of the soul is assumed for the treatment of memory, and these phenomena are taken as guarantees for the existence of such a distinct identity. Memory cannot underwrite identity, but identity is a precondition for awareness of oneself, and for those cognitive operations that involve forms of synthesis. In the context of a theory of memory, proving that the soul has an identity of its own serves the function of demonstrating its independence. Then memory can be ascribed to the independent soul. The soul possesses some functions even when on its own, and it receives the organs for others, above all perception, along with the body of which they form a part. But memory does not belong to the second group of functions since the soul can remember whether it has a body or not. We might interpret Plotinus as saying that there is no organ of memory as the eye is for sight. Indeed, body is destructive of memory since it is in flux. Memory is a form of remaining[659], just as forgetfulness is a flux.[660] Plotinus excludes body from any involvement in the permanent identity of the subject of memory.

What are the problems with excluding body from identity? There can be no doubt that it is Plotinus' intention to exclude all body from the constitution of the subject of memory. But if the subject is incorporeal, one can also ask if the object of memory has a body or not. This is another way in which body could be necessary to memory, for example, for

---

76–7. Schwyzer (1960: 349–352) in his sketch of the term's pre-Plotinian history denies that it is a philosophical term.

658 Another possible translation for this term is of course also "consciousness" (SP s.v.), and see VI 9 4 1, where it refers to cognition of the one, see Hadot 1994: 148. O'Daly 1973 argues that Plotinus' interest in the self is largely influenced by ethics and above all the idea of knowing thyself.

659 IV 3 26 52. HBT refer to De an. 408b18, De mem. 453b3; on the connection with science, cf. Anal. Post. II 19 99b35–37, Met. I 1 980a27–29; cf. also the Ps Platonic definition of memory (414A8–9); and Plato's derivation of μνήμη from μονή in the Cratylus (437A3).

660 IV 3 26 52–54.

the re-identification of individuals. In general Plotinus thinks that souls, when outside their earthly body, have no body. And we have just reviewed a series of arguments against the involvement of body in memory. But he is concerned that when we are in the heavens, we will be able to re-identify human souls we have known, and to do this he seems to suggest that they have a "shape", by which we could know them.[661] And if they have a different shape to the one we are accustomed to, well then, Plotinus seems confident that character and conversation will be enough to re-identify individuals, even without their familiar bodies.[662] This is the tricky question of "astral bodies" in Plotinus. The topic is tricky, because there are very few texts that even suggest that the soul has some such vehicle.[663] He seems to assume that this "astral body" in some way resembles the body the soul was in previously, so as to allow one to use it to recognise the soul or prevent one from recognising the soul. Furthermore, if character and conversation are enough for recognition, then the role of the astral body in recognition seems to be redundant. It is difficult to judge precisely what Plotinus has in mind in these passages; but it is clear that these texts represent an acknowledgement that for souls to be remembered and recognised, they need some vehicle by which they can be known, perhaps by being the means of conversation and expressing character, even if Plotinus has made a great effort to show that souls, alone and without body, can be the subjects of memory.

---

661 IV 3 18, IV 4 5 15.

662 On individual forms and souls see below p. 204.

663 See Alt 1993: 225 and Dodds 1962: Appendix II. The Astral Body in Neoplatonism, on Plotinus p. 318, Sorabji: 2004: 221–243 for translations of sources. Alt cites IV 3 24 5, IV 4 5 15, IV 3 15 1 as the only possible references to astral bodies, and notes that they are all from IV 3-IV 4. Add IV 3 18 13–22. There is in IV 4 5 no suggestion that a body is in any way a hindrance, as Alt sees. Brisson 2005: 245, n. 2 and 3: IV 3 9 1–9; 15 1–5. Brisson divides the career of the soul into three – with a vehicle of fire or air in the sky, with an earthy body on earth; and no body when contemplating. If one is to assume that the soul always has a body except when actually thinking ideas, it is odd that there is no explicit mention of this in the text. Note also that, as Brisson sees, the capacity for memory is preserved by the soul when contemplating. Toulouse (2006: esp. 119) rightly describes the doctrine of the soul-vehicle as hypothetical and allusive. Cf. below p. 217 for the relevance of body to memory.

3.2.3 Memory and the world soul and the thinking soul

Step by step, Plotinus is isolating the explanatory factors of soul responsible for memory. So now that the body has been excluded from memory, he has to decide which soul, and then which part of soul, has memory.[664] This is surprisingly complicated on account of a central aspect of his psychology, namely that humans have two souls, one of which is derived from the soul of the world. In the generation of a human, a vegetative soul is added to the already existing rational soul. For Plotinus thinks that the soul of the Whole, nature, is responsible for nutrition, or vegetative activity.[665] That is, the world is an organism, in which individuals are constituted from their environment by nutrition. The body produced in this way, and equipped with a lower soul, is then requisitioned by a rational soul that turns towards the sensible realm.[666] If the human, that is, the rational soul turns away from contemplation, it acquires a habitation, that is, a body, from nature, which provides it by nourishment.[667] This theory apparently has the effect of giving each human two souls. In generation, the soul comes to "illuminate" a body living by virtue of activity of the world soul.

The question that concerns us is whether memory belongs to the vegetative soul we have from the Whole[668] or to our rational soul, by virtue of which we are ourselves.[669] Plotinus considers the problem of what each soul remembers in connection with some lines of Homer,[670] which de-

---

664 In Chapter 27 he picks up on a question from IV 3 25 35–37.
665 IV 9 3 11–29.
666 See esp. VI 4 14; the vegetative soul is also responsible for anger IV 4 28.
667 "habitations", οἰκήσεις IV 3 6 15.
668 See Blumenthal 1971: 86 n. 8, who cites Plutarch fac. orb. lun. 944 f. Plotinus speaks here of the soul which comes "from the whole" (AHA) (τοῦ ὅλου), as in IV 3 8 3, as opposed to IV 3 7 2 where it is the soul "of the all" (τοῦ παντός). For the world soul see II 9 18, cf. II 3 9 11–24, II 1 5 19 for the contrast with the true self. Blumenthal (1971: 94, n. 21): IV 3 27 shows that Plotinus thought the lower soul immortal; see also IV 7 14 12–13, VI 4 16 40–44, I 1 12; but only IV 7 suggests according to Blumenthal that there is potential existence of the lower soul; and all the other texts suggest that *if it continues to exist* it does so separately from the higher soul.
669 The more divine soul: cf. VI 7 5 21–23, the true self: see II 3 9 1, 4 ff, IV 3 7 25–29, I 1 7 17: that which masters the passions through knowledge of forms. In Chapter 25 35–37 the question was put in terms of "that soul" or a "dimmer" one.
670 Odyssey XI 601–2. As Blumenthal notes (1971: fn 8, p. 86) the passage is a later addition. Blumenthal sees the use of Homer here as a mere illustration; if one

scribe the double afterlife of Heracles. He himself (αὐτός) is with the Gods, whereas his shade or image (εἴδωλον) is in Hades, as Homer says. It is crucial for Plotinus that the shade in Hades, in other words the vegetative soul, is the image of the rational soul, in that the shade is thus obviously dependent on the soul. Plotinus asks which of the two has memory, and answers that both have memories, some of which they share, and some of which belong to only one of them. Before going into the details of the answer, we must discuss the division of the two souls, since it is none too clear. It sounds as though we are dealing with two distinct entities. This would be problematic if the two are to share memories, as Plotinus thinks they do. For, as we have seen, there is prima facie a close connection between the self and its memories, such that only one individual subject, with a fixed boundary, can have just those memories it does have.[671]

So what about the shade and the soul? On a grammatical level, it does appear that there are two souls.[672] But the lower soul, what Plotinus, following Homer, here calls the shade (εἴδωλον), is merely a reflection of the last embodied life lived by the higher soul. For it is dependent on the higher soul. So I think that Plotinus' division is basically an ethical one, in the sense that ethics is a matter of the kind of life one should lead. Thus the distinction depends on the different values of kinds of life or activities within a life. There are practical and intellectual aspects to the life that shade and soul, when joined together, lead. The practical aspects are connected to the lower soul, since the need for food determines the whole of our practical lives. And the intellectual aspects belong to the rational soul. After life, soul and shade separate, but this does not mean that they are really two separate, independent entities, one is just the image of the other. The ethical division between shade and soul can be understood along the following lines. We are really our reason, a common enough view in the Platonic and Aristotelian schools, but we also lead practical lives, which of course requires a body. Such lives are of less value than theoretically orientated ones and in fact present

---

compares I 1 12 31–39, one might see in the story rather the explanandum of the theory. Clearly, one philosophical point here concerns the separation of practical life from theoretical life; the division is really of great importance since it determines the whole discussion from IV 3 27 up to IV 4 1.

671 See *Introduction* p. 1–2.

672 Especially in IV 3 27 1–6: here there are "souls" in the plural, and talk of them separating and coming together.

only a pale reflection of reason. Despite this lack of value, we are the shade as well as being our higher soul.

Now that the division between shade and soul is a little clearer we can ask just what it is that each of them remembers when they separate. Discussion of this question takes up the remainder of the treatment of human memory, together with the discussion of the capacity of the soul involved in memory, and before we go on it may be helpful to give a sketch of the rest of the enquiry into memory after death. The first part of the answer that Plotinus gives to the question of what each soul remembers is that, while the upper soul can remember everything that it has undergone, the lower one, the shade, is confined to what happened in the last life,[673] along with the degree of intellectual knowledge necessary for the practical life. Their memories are "together" as long as the soul and the shade are together, and separate when these do. We will discuss these memories briefly later in this chapter.[674] He then explains why we do not notice, in normal life, that we have two souls and hence two sets of memories, by suggesting that we do not notice the distinction between the two as long the higher soul controls the lower one in such a way that there is harmony between them.[675] This is then presumably what "being together" means: the two sets of memories harmonise, and so cannot be told apart.

Turning to the fate of the souls after death, Plotinus can use Homer's account of what the shades say in Hades, but he has to work out for himself what the soul, when separate from the shade, will remember.[676] He thinks the souls have their memories as long as they exist, although some memories may be hidden when they come to be in a new body, and they may cast off other memories, insofar it is good for them to do so.[677] He then goes on to describe at length[678] the absence of actual memory, of its previous lives and of itself, when the soul is actually contemplating ideas. Despite the lack of actual memory during actual con-

---

673 IV 3 27 7–13.
674 And at some length below, 3.2.6Shared memories and their loss, p. 187.
675 IV 3 31, below 3.2.6.1Shade and soul: shared memories, and an ethical separation.
676 IV 3 27 13–25. He then in Ch. 28–30 turns to the general question of which part of the soul is responsible for memory (IV 3 27 24–25), before going back to the problem of the two souls in Ch. 31, and what the higher soul will remember in Ch. 32 and IV 4 1–5.
677 IV 3 32 esp. 17–18.
678 IV 4 1.

templation, he thinks that memory does explain the course the soul takes, whether towards embodiment, or to contemplation or something in between. Here, then, memory plays a decisive role in the fate of the soul.[679]

Let us go back to the shade and the soul. I have already suggested that the talk of separating the two souls[680] should not be taken to imply two identities,[681] in that both are Heracles, and are aspects of the one soul, the one an image of the other. The shade is parasitic on the soul. From the point of view of a theory of memory, the interesting aspect of the story of Heracles being divided between a shade in Hades and a soul in heaven is the idea of splitting memories. For it is a crucial question if two individuals can have the same memories, not that is merely shared memories of the same events, but memories which suggest that they relate to perceptions of one person. For Plotinus explicitly denies that, as it were, the one soul has all one kind of memory, all intellectual memory, and the other one, the shade, practical memory. That way, there would be two "living things" with nothing in common.[682] Rather, each does have its peculiar memories but some memories are also shared between the two. The contents of the memories of the shade and the soul have been mentioned above, namely the soul can remember everything that shade and soul together remember, and the shade's memories are restricted to the last life, along with those intellectual memories necessary for the practical life. The point now is that among the memories of the shade are also intellectual ones, and among those of the soul are also those of things undergone. Explicitly, the shade is said to remember justice, and the soul to remember all that the man did or underwent.[683] Even if it is unclear exactly what "memory of justice" implies,[684] some form of sharing of memories be-

---

679 The account of the separation of the shade and the soul in I 1 12 18–24, 27–39 is not compatible with that in IV 3 27–32.

680 I 1 12 31, IV 3 27 5. Cf. HS, "de anima nostra quatenus mundo sensibili afficitur". This makes the second soul – the dimmer soul – sound merely like an aspect of the one soul. But there is no doubt about the phrasing, which suggests that two souls are in play – world soul and our soul; for the relation of the two see IV 9. For the doctrine of two souls, Emilsson 1988: 155 n. 14 cites besides IV 3 27 1–3, II 1 5 18–24, 3 7 25–31, IV 4 32 4–13, 37 11–15, 43 9–11, VI 6 15 12–13.

681 The two souls are not two entities, because they mix. Soul is a continuum, and only differentiated by its present concerns (Emilsson 1988: 27, 29).

682 ζῷα IV 3 31 5–8.

683 IV 3 27 13, 15–16.

684 One might think that e. g. the work done by Plato in the *Republic* is implied in such knowledge, but is it also in a *memory* of justice? And it is not clear to me

tween shade and soul does exist; knowledge of what justice is, is an intellectual feat, and so implies dependence on intellect. If shade and soul are not really two distinct entities, then the problem of the shared memories is not so acute. They are not really two entities since the shade is purely a product of the soul's inclination towards the sensible world. And they share memories because they share a past. As it were, insofar as they share memories they are not distinct individuals.

Plotinus finds himself having to answer the question of what the soul itself will remember,[685] since Homer said nothing about this, and his answer is long,[686] because he of course tends to identify our real selves with rational aspects of our souls. However, besides the true self, we have a practical self involved in the sensible world and that too is us, so we should not separate ourselves from it entirely.[687] The shade has memory of everything that was done according to our way of life, since our "career"[688], the differentiating characteristic of our biography, belongs to the shade especially. In other words, the choice of a life is something that the shade must answer for since it is particularly associated with the shade, and not the soul itself, the essence of soul.[689] Memory of our earthly life, i.e. very roughly what is usually called *autobiographical memory*, is not a function of the intellectual soul, except insofar as the latter drags something of the body along with it.[690] We may not be *really* our shades, but we are them *too*. Their memories are ethically organised, in that they correspond to the way of life chosen by the soul. What shades do not do, is talk about thought or ideas. Indeed, Plotinus takes Homer to be saying that the shades besides Heracles' only talk about their earthly lives,[691] which also requires intellectual capacities. And he is quite right to

---

what such a memory would be – of a just act or of learning justice or of what justice is. Perhaps it is the recollection of the idea of justice. HS refer to Odyssey XI 570, but that is merely about the judges in the underworld, not the capacities of the shades. For that Ajax' memory of his unjust treatment is more relevant (XI 549–565): justice is part of practical life.

685 IV 3 27 13–15.
686 IV 3 31-IV 4 2.
687 IV 3 27 7–10.
688 Cf. MacK. s trans. of lines 9–10: "since that career was mainly of the hero's personal shaping."
689 See I 1 12 esp. 17–27 for the shade answering for the life led, even if the inclination to the corporeal world is not culpable.
690 IV 3 26 15–16, 19–20. In Plotinus' theory, death is not the separation of body and soul, but of two souls, i.e. the intellectual and the shade (IV 4 29).
691 IV 3 27 10–13 adopting HS' emendation of the text in lines 10–12.

do so, since it is certainly true that the other souls in *Odyssey* XI talk exclusively about their lives, and some of what they say requires memory, and indeed understanding, of justice. An obvious example is Ajax's attack on Odysseus for the unjust distribution of Achilles' armour. Thus the shades' memories are mainly concerned with the interests of the lives they have led.

So much for the shade. Now let us turn to the soul. When Plotinus talks about the soul "when it has come to be alone",[692] that is, exists without a shade, I take this to mean that he is concerned with a soul that only thinks. Perhaps unsurprisingly, the claims of post-corporeal existence will stretch Plotinus' conception of memory to its limits and beyond. As an approach to this question,[693] he discusses the parts of soul with which we remember. The next sections are devoted to this discussion. Before that, three phases in the career of the soul after death are distinguished, in which "the soul dragging something of the body along with it" shares the memories of the shade.[694] Firstly, it will have a complete memory of all that *the human* did or underwent in the last life. Clearly, the soul can remember what happened to the human, only if there is body still attached to the soul in some way. Secondly, with yet more time, earlier lives, that is, autobiographical memories of earlier lives, come to the surface and are cast off.[695] Finally, in a new incarnation, the soul again busies itself with "external" life, that is its new practical life, but it still retains much from the earlier life. Thus it is clear that Plotinus believed in reincarnation. One soul has a series of lives and, in time, comes to remember them, and then forgets them. The memories of such lives are acquired memories.[696]

---

692 IV 3 27 14–15, 23–24.
693 IV 3 28 and 29. This question in its various ramifications will accompany us up to the end of IV 4 5.
694 IV 3 27 15–16 following H S reading ἐφελκομένη l. 15 as middle, cf. HBT II b 502.
695 IV 3 27 16–19.
696 ἐπακτά IV 3 27 23 (for this word being used to refer to perceptions which can be remembered see IV 3 25 11). Brisson (2005: 243, n. 507) suggests that this apparently refers to those things that happen to the soul on account of the body. On Plotinus on reincarnation, see Rich 1957. For Aristotle's denial of memory, either to souls after death, or in life of previous existences, or to the agent intellect see De an. III 5 430a23–5, and Hicks 1907: 507–8 ad loc., Wedin 1988: 182–198, Frede 1996, Burnyeat 2008a: 40 with note 55. Plotinus does seem to believe in a memory of a former existence: χρόνου δὲ προιόντος ἐπὶ τῷ θανάτῳ καὶ ἄλλων μνῆμαι ἂν φανεῖεν ἐκ τῶν πρόσθεν βίων, ὥστε τινὰ τούτων καὶ ἀτιμάσασαν

For the theory of memory, a crucial point is mentioned by Plotinus in this connection, namely that the soul *says* (λέγειν) things which are in its memory.[697] The characteristic performances of memory are propositional performances.[698] So it is impossible to ascribe to Plotinus the view that acts of memory consist in the presence of a picture before the mind's eye. There are of course certain problems here, due to the fact that it is the soul or the shade which says things. And how are they to do that in the absence of a body? Here we meet a point touched on at the end of the last section, namely the problem of a theory of memory which has to do without body.[699] I think that this problem is insuperable for Plotinus, and that it is more profitable to look more closely at the memory performance itself. In order to see more clearly what is involved

---

ἀφεῖναι. Σώματος γὰρ καθαρωτέρα γενομένη καὶ ἃ ἐνταῦθα οὐκ εἶχεν ἐν μνήμῃ ἀναπολήσει· (IV 3 27 16–20). The question is whether the soul only after death remembers previous existences, when it loses the memories of the last existence, or whether the human, approaching death, becomes increasingly free from the body and so has access to memories that were covered over. The phrasing is ambiguous: ἐπὶ τῷ θανάτῳ might mean at death or after death, and 'at' might mean approaching death (SP 409.9, LSJ B II 1 or 2 s.v. ἐπί). The last sentence quoted, however, suggests strongly that we do not have such memories "here" (line 19–20) but only when the soul has become purified of body. This is the way MacK. translates. However, AHA translates: "it will go over again in its memory what it did not have in this life" – that is: the memories are ones we have here, but of things we do not have here, i. e. bits of previous lives. HBT II b 502–3 understand the lines similarly (as had Brèhier before them), namely as concerning the "erinnerungsstarke Zeit des Heraustretens". They then have difficulty with lines 20–22, which they apparently see as a doublet from an earlier version.

697 IV 3 27 11, 14, 21 as well as in IV 4 1 1.
698 Cf. 'Memory and Imagination belong … to the Discursive reason' (Inge 1968: 226). Blumenthal (1971: 92) argues against Inge that memory cannot be identified with discursive reason, because "the faculty of memory" remembers the products of discursive reason: a few pages later Inge admits that the faculty of forming images is so independent of the judgement that illusions frequently occur. But Plotinus does not think there is a separate faculty of memory, and of course it would be an exaggeration to identify the capacity for memory with discursive reason. But they have at least the capacity to entertain propositions in common.
699 IV 3 18 22–24. Sometimes Plotinus does ascribe voices to souls and spirits in the air ("because they are living things"), while denying them to souls who are thinking "in heaven", even if they have bodies: there, communication happens, mysteriously, "in understanding" (ἐν συνέσει). (IV 3 18 14–15. Note HBT's variant punctuation of the passage, contrasting their possession of being with the question of whether they have needs there too.)

in the propositional nature of remembering something, let us look at a
very useful text, in which he summarises what happens when we make
a perceptual judgement:

> Well then, sense-perception sees a human being and gives its impression
> (τύπος) to understanding (διάνοια). What does understanding say? It will
> not say anything yet, but only knows and stops at that; unless perhaps it
> asks itself 'Who is this?' if it has met the person before, and says, using
> memory to help it, that it is Socrates. And if it makes the details of his
> form (μορφή) explicit, it is taking to pieces what the representative faculty
> gave it. If it says whether he is good, its remark originates in what it
> knows through sense perception, but what it says about this it has already
> from itself since it has a norm (κανών) of the good in itself.[700]

Plotinus is describing how the soul acquires understanding of perception
and ideas. In this text, he begins from the simple case of seeing a man.
Perception sees a man and the impression (τύπος) is given to the understanding a) which recognises it. This is the simple act of seeing something
as something, without saying anything about it. b) Understanding may
then go on to ask, and answer, a question about it: It may ask who it
is? And give an answer: Socrates, calling on a memory if one is present.[701]

The understanding can then go on to explicate the τύπος, analysing
what representation has given it. If an idea is applied to the perceived
man, then it is relying firstly on the deliverances of perception and secondly relying on what we i. e. our souls are, namely a norm (κάνων).
The point is clearly that the ideas are not derived from perception but
are already in us, capacities which can be realised by their application
to cases. And such application implies some way of distinguishing what
they apply to and what they do not, for instance, distinguishing what
is a man from what is not. Innate ideas form a complex network, as suggested by the talk of classification, which enables distinctions in the cases
they are applied to, to be made. Assuming that representations provide
information and that innate ideas serve as a norm, judgements are possible.[702] These judgements are perceptual judgements, and so presumably
those that the soul will remember from its past life. They are dependent
on the presence of innate ideas, but not to be confused with the recollection of these.[703]

---

700 V 3 3 1–9.
701 Cf. Alcinous, Didaskalikos 154.41–155.13.
702 On the question of the norm, or canon in Plotinus see Blumenthal 1989,
    esp. 258–267.
703 Cf. IV 3 25 25.

3.2.4 Memory and the modification of desire

The question is now which part of the soul we remember with. Plotinus begins by considering the Platonic tripartition of the soul into the learning part, the desiderative part and the spirited part, and then goes on to discuss the last two as candidates for the explanation of the memory of desires and ambitions.[704] He comes to the conclusion that experiences in these two parts do not lead to memories, rather they modify the relevant capacities. In effect, he explains the origin of habits, in that our desires and ambitions become fixed by previous experiences of desire and ambition. But this phenomenon is distinguished by Plotinus from memory.

Now, we may ask the following question. If the career of Heracles is due to what he wanted, and to his ambition, one might think that the faculties which guide him in these respects preserve the experiences which have made them the way they are. This preservation might reasonably be thought to be memory. Thus ambition would preserve the experience of having striven for honour, and this preservation would be memory of such an ambition. However, this is not Plotinus' view. For he goes on to show how desire or ambition is modified by experience in such a way that memory is not involved. Nonetheless, he does think it possible to remember the experiences that form our sensual desires or commitments. But this memory is not what moulds desires and commitments.

Now, back to the question of which part of the soul remembers. As already mentioned, Plotinus apparently uses here the classic Platonic division into three parts of the soul:[705] something we learn and perceive with[706], something we desire with and something we are angry or ambitious with (the spirited part, θυμοειδές). This use is remarkable since his own positive theory of memory is more Aristotelian, and uses φαντασία. As a matter of fact, he does not explicitly try to connect these disparate theories.[707] Nonetheless, in order to get to φαντασία as the capacity responsible for memory, he first excludes desire and ambition.

---

704 IV 3 28.

705 IV 3 28 1–3. For Platonic tripartition of the soul, see *Republic* 439–440, *Timaeus* 44D-45B, 69C-70B, *Phaedrus* 253D; see Johansen 2004: ch. 7.

706 Learning and perception belong together as memories that can be acquired (IV 3 25 11).

707 Images play a certain role in the *Timaeus* 71A-B, but are there connected with desires being based in the liver. A concept of φαντασία as a mixture of opinion and perception is offered in the *Sophist* 264AB.

In a sense this is a diversion from the theory of memory proper. But the theory of modifying desire (or ambition) without recourse to memory is very interesting in its own right. It is in effect an analysis of habit.[708] What Plotinus wants to do is have the information acquired, for example winning races is honourable or apples are tasty, passed onto desire or ambition from some other faculty.[709] The different faculties of the soul have to communicate with one another, because he thinks that the subject of some such experience is not the concrete animal or even the whole soul, but rather the separate faculty. So he would say that perception perceives. Part of the explanatory power of faculty psychology might be thought to lie in the (trivial) fact, that any act of perception, e.g. of seeing is due to a capacity to see; and one might want to express this by saying that (the faculty of) perception is the subject of any act of perception, despite the fact that it clearly cannot be considered as independent, in the sense that it does not occur on its own. One is thus pointing to a part of the soul to explain an aspect of the whole soul's behaviour. In order to make such explanations possible, Plotinus is prepared to make a fairly radical revision in the Platonic theory, by saying that the division into faculties is not absolute, rather each faculty is only named after its dominant element,[710] while actually containing the other faculties as well.[711] So if these aspects of the whole communicate with one another, perception (the faculty) sees, and passes this information onto desire, and desire perceives, but "unconsciously"[712]: "it cannot say what sort of a perception it is". Plotinus uses a comparison with a shepherd and his dog to illustrate this relation. Whereas the shepherd sees the wolf, the dog merely smells or hears it. The shepherd is compared with perception, and the dog with desire. The comparison is imperfect (the dog does actually perceive the

---

708 The question is not whether the memory of a pleasure is a function of the same thing that had the pleasure in the first place. Warren 1965: 255 Fn. 2 quotes Chaignet 1862: IV 188, 'C'est le commencement de l'habitude, l'habitude naissante.' Brisson 2006: 24 sees memory here as the foundation of ethics.

709 "by a sort of transmission" (AHA). The word for this transmission is διάδοσις; cf. the criticism of a materialist theory of transmission of pain in IV 7 7 esp. 7.

710 IV 3 28 7–10.

711 This may be Plotinus acknowledging the fact that each faculty has its own pleasures, and hence desires; see *Republic* 580D-E.

712 IV 3 28 12–13; on "unconsciously" ἀπαρακολουθήτως see above on concepts of consciousness p. 153.

wolf, even if not by sight),[713] but the point is clear. The dog is excited but is unable to say what it has heard. Just as desire cannot say what the perception is, neither can the dog. Not a very plausible picture of shepherds and their dogs, perhaps, but the picture is more successful in describing the relation between perception and desire:

> And the desiring power certainly enjoyed and has a trace (ἴχνος) of what happened implanted in it, not like a memory, but like a disposition and affection; but it is another power which has seen the enjoyment and of its own motion retains the memory of what has happened.[714]

Thus instead of a conscious memory, there is a modification of the desire, a trace of the past event, which is not conscious. The clear contrast between memory and disposition in this text allows one to draw the conclusion that Plotinus sees memory here as conscious. When active it is accompanied by the ability, for example, to say what the perception was like. This faculty, which is not named here, is presumably the faculty responsible for perception, i. e. φαντασία. Its performance is saying something, in contrast to the inarticulate modification of desire.

Another example that shows that memory is not to be attributed to a disposition of desire is the phenomenon of memory of pleasant experiences, which Plotinus turns to as a final confirmation of his theory that desire does not have memory of having desired.[715] For he points to the fact that not all memories of pleasant experiences are then pleasant to confirm the theory that it is not that which enjoys the experience which later remembers it. In this way, desire would not have the memory of having desired something. It is not clear how this proof would work in detail. It is perhaps more illuminating to think of memories of painful experiences, which are themselves not painful.[716] Thus the conclusion is that the experience of the original pain and the memory of the painful experience are not to be ascribed to the same faculty. What Plotinus needs is an argu-

---

713 'The point of the simile is that the faculty which acts is made aware of the stimulus to action in a different way from the perceptive faculty'. (Blumenthal 1971: 86–87)

714 IV 3 28 16–19 (AHA trans.) Καὶ τοίνυν ἀπέλαυσε μὲν τὸ ἐπιθυμοῦν, καὶ ἔχει ἴχνος τοῦ γενομένου ἐντεθὲν οὐχ ὡς μνήμην, ἀλλ᾽ ὡς διάθεσιν καὶ πάθος· ἄλλο δὲ τὸ ἑωρακὸς τὴν ἀπόλαυσιν καὶ παρ᾽ αὐτοῦ ἔχον τὴν μνήμην τοῦ γεγενημένου.

715 IV 3 28 20–22. For a defence of the Ms. reading in line 20 see HS.

716 This shows that Plotinus does not think that memories of painful experiences are painful or perhaps just unpleasant. Nor need memories of travails be unpleasant: forsan et haec olim meminisse juvabit (Virgil, *Aeneid* I 203). Cf. Rhet. I 11 1370b1–8.

ment such that the memory is not simply the renewed activity of the enjoying part, but the activity of another part which thus does not, indeed cannot, enjoy in the same way as the original experience. Pleasurable memories are pleasurable, he must say, in a completely different way to original experiences.[717]

The theory, that memory is not a disposition of desire might seem to conflict with two passages, one of which we have already discussed, the *quasi* definition of memory,[718] the other of which is still to come; it discusses the effect of memory on the wandering of the soul. In the *quasi* definition, it is said that in remembering the soul is disposed (διακεῖσθαι) as if towards something present. And here memory is contrasted with a disposition (διάθεσις). We have to find a way of taking the two passages in such a way that memory can be one kind of disposition, and be contrasted with another. The obvious way of doing this is to say that memory is not a disposition of desire, that is to say not a desire that is thus and so because of a past experience. Memory is rather a disposition, i.e. an acquired capacity, of the representative faculty. This is a way of taking the *strengthening of the soul* of which the *quasi* definition speaks. The strengthening is the acquisition of a disposition on the basis of a capacity. After the experience the representative faculty (φαντασία) is disposed in such a way to be able to remember the experience. Quite how the φαντασία is disposed so as to cause memory is something we shall have to discuss in the next section. For our present purpose, it is enough that memory is not a disposition of desire, but a disposition of φαντασία. Thus the *quasi* definition and the theory of habit are compatible.

Let us turn briefly to the second passage which is apparently inconsistent with the denial that the desiring faculty is responsible for the memory of desires. The passage, which we have not as yet discussed, suggests that memory is not always to be considered as a conscious perception that one is remembering, but as a disposition (διακεῖσθαι) of the soul which corresponds to past experiences or things contemplated.[719] On the one hand, this conception fits well with the *quasi* definition, in that there too the soul is disposed in a certain way; on the other, it seems that in the text quoted above from IV 3 28 memory is contrasted with unconscious dispositions, rather than being identified with one. Desire is modified by

---

717 Hadot (1960) connects this with Anaxagoras' "naming by predominance". Cf. Aristotle Phys. I 4 187b1.
718 Above p. 120.
719 IV 4 4 7–11. See below p. 213.

experience, and the modification is unconscious. The difficulty can perhaps be dissolved by pointing to the two levels at which the soul is being discussed by Plotinus in each of the passages. Here, we are discussing how habit forms character; in the later passage we are talking about the determinants of the wandering of the disembodied soul after death, e. g. what makes it decide to descend to the sensible world rather than ascend to the realm of thought. Here, the point is that character is formed not by acquiring memory of decisive experiences, but by these experiences forming our desires. Later, the point is that at an unconscious level we can be influenced in what we are really interested in, that is, when we come to make the choice of a new life. This influence is said to be a matter of memory.[720] A further difference lies in the fact that the latter theory does not deal with accessible aspects of our existence, that is: we are not aware of them, whereas the view that the formation of habit should be ascribed to a disposition of desire most certainly does refer to aspects of the soul that it can be aware of while this formation is happening.

What is meant by saying that memory helps regulate the wandering of the soul after death? It influences the desires and ambitions of the soul, insofar as the latter can then move towards the sensible world or towards the contemplation of ideas. When the soul turns towards the sensible, it falls; how this happens, and how a soul can escape sense perception is a major topic of Plotinus' work.[721] And there are obvious roles for memory in this story. One might ask, for example, what the soul takes with it when it falls, or what keeps it in the sensible realm or makes it leave perception behind. The answers to these questions are: memories of sensual experiences on the one hand, and memories of ideas on the other. These functions of memory are the subject of our final section on Plotinus.[722] While he is very concerned to limit memory strictly, he allows it a controlling function in the peregrinations of the soul. In many respects this forms the core function of memory in his thought.

Now that Plotinus has given this account of the formation of habit as the modification of desire, he can turn to the faculty responsible for memory.

---

720 IV 4 4 5–10.
721 E.g. IV 3 13. Cf. above p. 160.
722 Below p. 193, 3.3 "The soul is and becomes what it remembers."

3.2.5 Explaining memory using representation (φαντασία)

3.2.5.1 Representation in perceptual memory

Plotinus explains memory both of things acquired and of innate ideas, using φαντασία, representation. His account begins with[723] memory of things perceived. We have already met the distinction between types of memory, but nonetheless before we turn to this explanation, a quick sketch of some of the distinctions between types of memory and the different subjects of memory will be useful.

As we have seen, Plotinus insists that there are different kinds of memory: of things acquired, experiences, perceptions, and of recalling ideas, that is, when we remember what is innate in us.[724] A further distinction also threatens to multiply the kinds of memory, namely that between the shade and the soul. Note that he does not think that the distinction between shade and soul is that between the perceptible and the intelligible. If that were the case, the distinction between the two kinds of memory would coincide with that between soul and shade: there would be two animals with no memories in common, and he denies this alignment explicitly.[725]

It is against the background of these distinctions that Plotinus approaches the question of the faculty that is responsible for memory. He can exclude the perceptive faculty on the basis of the first distinction. Since he is going to go to explain memory of ideas as well, perception would have to be responsible there too, and he wishes to avoid that.[726] An alternative might be that there is a single faculty responsible for both kinds of memory, apperception (τὸ ἀντιληπτικόν), which might be able to play this role because it is (partly) responsible for both perception and thinking. Again, he denies this possibility, perhaps because he thinks that apperception is directed either at one or at the other of these two, and not at both.[727]

---

723 IV 3 29.
724 See above p. 144–145.
725 IV 3 31 5–8 οὐ γὰρ δὴ τὸ μὲν τῆς ἑτέρας τῶν νοητῶν, τὸ δὲ τῶν αἰσθητῶν· οὕτω γὰρ ἂν παντάπασι δύο ζῷα οὐδὲν ἔχοντα κοινὸν πρὸς ἄλληλα ἔσται.
726 IV 3 29 6. See below p. 179 on memory of thought and φαντασία.
727 On ἀντίληψις see IV 3 30 11. His denial of a single faculty which unifies perception and thought is strong evidence that apperception (IV 3 29 8 τὸ ἀντιληπτικόν) does not play the role in his system that we might expect. Perception and thought are not unified in the one person by both being the activities of (the one) consciousness. Interestingly, the idea that if a single person thinks and per-

As already mentioned, the two distinctions, that between the shade and the soul, and that between perceptive and intellectual memory, force Plotinus, at least to start with, into admitting no less than four faculties of memory, as both shade and soul have both kinds of memory. But in what follows he suggests the solution to the problem lies in a single faculty that is in itself Janus-faced, namely φαντασία. Thus intellectual and perceptual memory are different functions of one faculty. Plotinus is able to make this step because he thinks that knowledge of x need not be a function of the same faculty as memory of x. He offers no positive argument, but merely asks the reader what necessity there is for the two to coincide. Thus he comes close to identifying a special faculty of memory, but he only comes close, since in fact he makes a faculty with other distinct functions beside memory responsible for memory.

The faculty Plotinus makes responsible is φαντασία, the faculty of representation. What kind of argument does Plotinus have for thinking that perception is remembered by the representative faculty? Purely a negative one: There is nothing to prevent the percept ("the sight" ὅραμα) being present to the person remembering as a representation (φάντασμα). This is the argument as far as perception is concerned, while thoughts and the memory of thoughts are the subjects of the next chapter.[728] He also requires that the remembering faculty, i.e. the representative faculty should be distinct (in some sense) from the perceptive one.[729] This distinction is important to Plotinus for two reasons.

---

ceives, then there must be some unity underlying these different activities is not one that surfaces here; or indeed that our possession of ideas (that is: our ability to think) is partly responsible for perception. Both of these views are, however, in the background. See IV 7 6 14 for the thought that there must be something like the centre point of a circle (cf. also IV 3 3 20), and see Henry 1960, Emilsson 1991, and 1988: Chapter 5 on the unity of the perceptive faculty. See also I 4 10 – where the term is used for conscious activity; it is however also used for the different grasp of things through the different organs (IV 3 3 18). On consciousness, cf. above p. 153.

728 IV 3 30, below p. 178, 3.2.5.2 Representation in the memory of thought.

729 From another point of view, Emilsson (1988: 111) doubts that there is a very sharp distinction between representative capacity and perceptive capacity. The reason he gives is that the act of sense-perception and the first apprehension of this image by the faculty of representation are simultaneous: 'For at what previous point could the remembering power have perceived what it is later to recall, if not when the thing was originally perceived?' So for Plotinus, perhaps perceptual judgement 'involves in itself the apprehension of the representation that constitutes the judgement. If this is so then there is no sharp distinction between rep-

Firstly, it follows from the argument he has given for saying that there is
no necessity for the perceptive faculty to remember perception, nor for
the intellectual faculty to remember thoughts.[730] In this way, he is able
to move towards a distinct faculty of memory.[731] Secondly, the soul without the body has no actual perception;[732] but in Plotinus' view it certainly
may have some memories.

The claim that memory is to be explained by reference to φαντασία is
not new. We have already seen that, and why, Aristotle had assigned
memory to representation, although with the vital difference that representation is in its turn assigned to the perceptive system, specifically to
the common sense.[733] In contrast for Plotinus part of the point of assign-
ing memory to representation lies in the possibility of explaining memory
without the body.

Plotinus tries to separate memory both from perception and from
thought by pointing out that different people excel in each, a form of argument that we have met, both in Plotinus and when used by Aristotle[734]
to distinguish between recollection and memory. But there the excellence
in memory and recollection was correlated with different bodily constitutions. Plotinus, however, denies that the body plays a part in determining
or explaining the soul's faculties at a fundamental level.[735] He thinks that
body has a merely disruptive function. In other words, he thinks he has
proven, at least for the sake of this argument, that only distinct faculties
are responsible for the different levels of achievement in each of the activities. Activities are explained in part by faculties. The fact that different
people show different degrees of competence in memory, thought and
perception, shows that the faculties explaining the competence are different. What he wishes to prove is that memory of perceptions and memory

---

resentation and sense-perception:' Still, one might say that, while in actual perception there is no distinction between perception and representation, the real
distinction only comes into force when the soul has no body since it then has
representation but no perception. In contrast to Aristotle's conception of φαντασία above p. 46.

730 IV 3 29 13–16.

731 τὸ μνημονευτικόν IV 3 29 2, 4–5.

732 See IV 3 26 46–50.

733 See above p. 42. Of course, the Stoic theory will also have played a part in forming Plotinus' views (see LS 39 esp. e and f, Scott 1995: 187–210), as well as
other Platonists, see e. g. Alcinous 4.4–6.

734 IV 3 29 16–19, see above p. 130, cf. p. 2, Aristotle's distinction: p. 94.

735 He of course thinks that organs explain perception; but the soul has the faculty of
perception independently of the organs.

of our studies can be divorced from perception and thought. He will do this by identifying the faculty of memory with the faculty of representation.[736]

At first, Plotinus' strategy of using a purely negative argument for turning to the representative faculty seems very weak. Could he not, after the manner of Aristotle, have made the positive assertion that perceptions produce representations? In fact, when one considers his argument more closely, this seems also to be his opinion, at least if that is what he means by saying that perception ends[737] in representation,[738] which is what he goes on to say. The argument then is perhaps not as weak as it appears on the surface in that there is a background theory of representation, according to which for example, a sight, i. e. what was seen, is present to the representative faculty when the (actual) perception has ceased to exist. This, however, lets in a lot, as many remains of perceptions may be there without one saying anything about anything. A picture of Theaetetus may go through Socrates' mind without anything being said about it.

---

736 IV 3 29 2 μνημονευτικόν, 23–24 φανταστικόν.
737 IV 3 29 25 λήγειν. On the meaning of λήγειν here, see Emilsson 1988: 111: 'Given that representation is operative in memory and reasoning, there must lie some path from perception to the faculty of representation since we can obviously remember and reason about what we have previously seen or heard.' And cf. Blumenthal 1971: 85 'all information that comes through the body ends (λήγειν) in the soul'.
738 Three readings are: 1. perception causes representation; 2. perception is unified in the representative faculty; 3. perception becomes conscious in the representative faculty. In Emilsson's view the representative faculty and perception are inextricably intertwined (1988: 111): perception consists in the formation of an image, in this case a judgement. But it is problematic how Plotinus can distinguish between the formation of the image or judgement and the apperception of the image by the representative faculty. In his view IV 3 29 suggests that the two are simultaneous. The faculty of memory i. e. the representative faculty, must immediately grasp the perception, since perception, i. e. the perceptual judgement includes the grasp of the representation, which constitutes the judgement. But *in that case* there is not a great distinction between φαντασία and perception: they meet in perception itself (R.K.: i. e. actual, conscious, perception). Emilsson's view is clearly strongly influenced by his major preoccupation, perception. But it is worth remembering that the most important passages on the representative faculty occur in the treatment of memory, not perception. And for the sake of the theory of memory, it is very important indeed that the representative faculty is separate from perception, both in actuality, and also in the function of representing concepts.

So we have to restrict representation to those remains of perception which are relevant. As we have seen, for Plotinus[739] as for Aristotle[740] memory performances consist in saying that something is the case. So if representation explains memory, it would be advantageous if representation could explain this aspect of memory. A central feature of the concept of representation here and in the next chapter is that it provides the capacities for a performance that is an utterance. Obviously, not all representations provide part of the ability to make assertions, but it is a consequence of Plotinus' theory of memory that representation does provide at least part of the basis for them.

So much for the distinction between representations in general, and those aspects of representation which are suited to providing a capacity to make assertions in active memory. Another distinction which must be made is between the mere retention of a representation and its use in memory. In the lines immediately preceding,[741] Plotinus has said that memory and retention (κατοχή)[742] are present in the representative faculty as something distinct sc. from the perceptive faculty: and one may ask whether in Plotinus' view retention and memory are meant to be the same, or whether retention is merely one condition of memory. The identification of memory with retention may be thought to be asserted in the next lines. They can be translated as follows:

> If then the representation of the absent thing is present in this [sc. the representative faculty] it [sc. the representative faculty] already remembers, even if it is only present for a short time.[743]

Plotinus seems to be saying here that if the representation is in the representative faculty, then it is a case of memory. So a possible interpretation of 'memory and retention',[744] would be that retention *is* memory. Simply through representations remaining, we have memory. We can call this "a naive reading". As we shall see, however, further conditions are necessary for memory.

---

739 See above on V 3 3, p. 164. This, of course, does not mean that the assertions are made on the evidence of the appearances or representations.
740 See p. 32.
741 IV 3 29 23–24.
742 Cf. IV 6 13, 3 57, and μονή see IV 3 26 52, 30 11. On the question of κατοχή in Plotinus' theory, see Taormina 2010.
743 IV 3 29 26–27.
744 Previously mentioned IV 3 29 24.

One further condition is that memory, when actualised, is an activity, and the simple remaining of a representation has no claim to being an activity. He hints at the rest of the explanation, I think, when he gives two conditions for memory taking place, in the text just quoted:

a) when the representation is present in the faculty of representation,
b) when the representation is of the "absent thing" i.e. past thing, i.e. the experience of the thing.

What these additional conditions demand is that the representation is present to the mind, and that it is *of* the object. That is, two actual relations can be asserted of it – to the subject's mental activity, and to the object of memory. This could be called "the sophisticated reading".

In order to see how the sophisticated reading works, we have to see how memory goes beyond mere retention. We have just seen that the sophisticated reading required that in a memory the representation is present to the subject of the memory and so related to its object. Of course, retention is also required by memory. The weak relations between the object that caused the representation, and between the representation itself and the subject it is in are necessary conditions for memory, but they are not sufficient. They only make up retention. So how does Plotinus conceive of that element in memory which distinguishes it from mere retention? The trouble is he does not say how an act of memory is related to its object. One way that is worthy of consideration, is that the soul delivers a judgement using the representation. Recall our example:

Example (E) Socrates remembers (at t2) that he saw Theaetetus two days ago (at t1).

Socrates can say the sentence, "I remember I saw Theaetetus two days ago", either aloud or not, without any image occurring. In some cases he may have an image of Theaetetus, but this is not necessary. Nonetheless, he can only do this because of a capacity in part constituted by a representation. Confirmation for this reading of Plotinus comes from his arguments against impression theories of memory: some are based on the idea that an occurrent impression cannot explain many of the things we wish to say about memory.[745] In general terms, mere retention cannot explain the propositional nature of memory.

---

745 See above for arguments against impressions in memory p. 127, 3.1.4 What memory as a capacity can explain.

We have already discussed a text[746] which points in this direction. The present reconstruction of his argument admittedly goes beyond what he says there, most importantly in attributing a role to saying things, i.e. predication in memory.[747] But it is clear that there memories, although differently structured from (E), can take the form of saying something. Equally, when we turn to the relation between memory, in the sense of recalling, and ideas, it will be clear that *saying that* is involved in memory. Further confirmation is to be found in passages where he asks what the soul after death will *say*, when recounting its memories.[748]

Plotinus summarises his investigation into perceptual memory as follows:

> Memory and actual remembering of such things belong to the representative faculty.[749]

Activity and capacity of memory have the same object, perceptible things. The sentence then says that actual memory and the capacity for it, in the case of perceptual things, belongs to the representative faculty. In this way, memory has as its objects not mere representations in my mind, but the objects of perceptions, via the representations remaining from those perceptions.

Let us turn back to the status of the representative faculty. We said that it has to be distinct from the perceptive faculty, that is to say, it must be able to act separately. Perception is a capacity of the soul which it possesses even without the body; but obviously it cannot actually perceive anything without the organs to do so. Apparently this is not true

---

746 V 3 3, above p. 164.
747 See above p. 163 for texts in which actual remembering consists in saying something.
748 E.g. IV 4 1 1.
749 IV 3 29 31–32: Τοῦ φανταστικοῦ ἄρα ἡ μνήμη, καὶ τὸ μνημονεύειν τῶν τοιούτων ἔσται. I translate with Bréhier ("La mémoire des choses sensibles appartient donc à l'imagination."), not AHA ("Memory, then will belong to the image making power, and remembering is of the mental-image kind"), HBT, MacK who take τῶν τοιούτων "of such things" to refer to "images" or "Vorstellungen" apparently as the objects of memory. This reading, however, runs entirely counter to the investigation set up in Chapter 25, namely into two kinds of memory, distinguished according to their objects, namely experiences and things learnt on the one hand, and one' own thoughts on the other. See above p. 143, 144. Chapter 29 is a continuation of this investigation, asking about the memory of sensible things; the next chapter then asks about thought. It is therefore impossible that memory should have images, representations or whatever as its objects.

of memory, in that it can be exercised without body, that is, it does not require an organ. This is part of the importance of the proof that perception, and hence memory, requires no imprinting. One of the things that theories of imprinting can do is to explain the excellence of memory in terms of the mixtures in the body.[750] Plotinus is concerned to show, I think, that his purely psychic explanation can do as well. Hence he closes his account of perceptual memory by offering three factors that explain people's different memory performances. Firstly, a good memory is constituted merely by the long remaining of the remains of the perception, and a bad one by short preservation: then the power will be strong and not allow memories to be "shaken off".[751] Further differentiations among different people's active memories are to be accounted for using, firstly, their different capacities to represent things to themselves,[752] as already mentioned; and also by other factors, their attention[753] and, perhaps rather surprisingly, their bodily mixture. "Surprisingly" because, of course, part of the general direction of Plotinus' explanation is towards a purely psychic account of memory; it is furthermore obscure how the body can have any influence on a psychic power, unless by diverting its attention.[754] The strange thing is that here bodily mixture and attention are counted as distinct factors, along with changes in the bodily mixture. It appears that the expression is merely misleading, and bodily disturbances are active in changing our capacity for memory because they catch our attention rather than because they are the existential basis for memory.[755]

In the course of setting up his enquiry into the subject of memory, Plotinus poses a question which, while it is not entirely perspicuous, is of the greatest importance for a theory of memory. He asks if the living thing remembers, how does it do it (τίς ὁ τρόπος)?[756] Now, Plotinus does *not* think that the living thing remembers; his view is that the soul is the subject of memory. So he may not think that he owes us an answer to the question. However, the reason that the question is interesting lies in the

---

750 See Aristotle's view of the impairment of memory in old age and extreme youth p. 73.
751 IV 3 29 28–31.
752 IV 3 29 33: αὐτῆς scil. τῆς φαντασίας (HS, app. crit.).
753 Reading in IV 3 29 34 ταῖς προσέξεσιν with RJU (followed by HS, HBT, AHA), not ταῖς πράξεσιν with wBC (MacK, Bréhier).
754 Cf. on body as a hindrance to memory, p. 148. For a discussion of Plotinus on body-soul interaction see O'Meara 1985.
755 See above p. 73.
756 IV 3 25 43.

fact that Plotinus' opponents do apparently have an answer to it: The living thing remembers in the way that wax takes on a form. In contrast, Plotinus presents a representational theory of memory which does without a material basis.[757]

3.2.5.2 Representation in the memory of thought

In IV 3 30, Aristotle's view of thought is, again surprisingly, Plotinus' starting point for his consideration of the memory of thought. What he wishes to prove here is that representation is the key to memory, and he considers two entirely different models, without, apparently, deciding which one to accept. The first is Aristotelian, and the second seems to be his own.[758] The first (lines 2–5) has it that a representation follows thought and if the representation remains then there is a memory of the thing cognised, that is, of the thought.[759] He then passes to the second possibility saying merely that if the first is not right then one has to find another way. The second possibility (lines 5–11) is that the reception of the thought into the representative faculty happens through a formula (λόγος). The task of the present section is to explain just what these suggestions mean.

Plotinus offers us two possibilities, without, on the face of it, deciding which to accept. There are a variety of ways of interpreting this. We might remember that the start of IV 3 describes the project of this

---

757 See Blumenthal 1971: 83: Plotinus nowhere gives an account of how the soul does retain and store information. He does not go beyond the somewhat unhelpful statement that memories are not of something stored up inside, but that the soul stirs up [wakes up] the relevant power so that it possesses what it does not have This, he says, involves no change [ἀλλοίωσις], unless one is to regard as such that from potency to act, and no addition [οὐδὲν προσγενόμενον] (III 6 2 42–49). On this account of memory see above p. 124; on the transition between capacity and its realisation as not being a change, see p. 30 on the triple scheme in Aristotle, and on Plotinus' use of it. p. 125.

758 Cf. below p. 185.

759 On Aristotle's view of the memory of thoughts, see above p. 42. McCumber's (1978) thesis is that, according to Plotinus, the soul needs images to think forms, which it achieves by recollection; he actually thinks that recollection is merely the path towards forms, i.e. learning, not what you do when you actually think. See p. 164: Memory of intelligibles (i.e. recollection – R.K.) is distinct from νοῦς; when the soul is purely in νοῦς IV 4 1, because soul when purely in νοῦς cannot change (IV 4 2 24 ff). Thus, I think we should conclude that IV 3 30 is also a discussion of the first form of memory from Ch. 25 and not just the second (see above p. 143–144).

work not as providing the solution to all problems concerned with the soul, but merely to those which can be solved,[760] and the implication would be that we, Plotinus' readers, might find ourselves confronted with an insoluble problem, in which case the discussion would remain aporetic. So the point behind the two suggestions would be that Plotinus sees no rational way of deciding between them.[761] A second way of proceeding would be to suggest that lines 5–11 effectively refute the suggestion made in lines 2–5, by pointing to forms of thought that are in fact *not* accompanied by representation.[762]

---

760 IV 3 1 1–4.
761 Cf. Blumenthal 1971: 88–89 who sees in lines IV 3 30 1–5 a first possibility: if all thought is accompanied by an image (φαντασία), the persistence of the image could account for memory here, as well as in the case of perceptual memory. Besides this, Blumenthal allows the second possibility to stand (lines 5–16): the discursive sequel to the act of intuitive thought is taken into the imagination: the λόγος deploys the thought and shows it to the imagination (Blumenthal thus takes εἰς τὸ φανταστικόν with ἔδειξε in line 10; but it goes with ἐπάγων as in AHA's translation) through these images we become aware of the thought that is always in progress. He sees a similarity to the treatment in I 4 10 of consciousness: intuitive thoughts are reflected onto a mirror, which is probably to be identified with the faculty of imagination. Thus he reads the second possibility not merely of the process of learning but of the actual contemplation of ideas: ἀνάμνησις is the conscious contemplation of eternal thinking of soul. But one should hold onto the distinction between learning, that is the recollection of ideas, and the actual contemplation of them. I take recollection to be a discursive process.
762 Warren (1966: 280–2) thinks IV 3 30 1–5 presents Aristotle's theory, which Plotinus does not explicitly reject, but it is unacceptable to Plotinus since he denies that an image accompanies each thought: διάνοια can happen unconsciously. The rest of IV 3 30 gives Plotinus' theory. So too Brisson 2005: 243 n. 508. This is also the view of McCumber 1978: 164, who sees the chapter on the one hand in connection with the question whether there is "memory of intelligibles": Denying that Plotinus held a doctrine of the memory of intelligibles implies that all memory 'will consist in after-images of sensation' then the 'logos which accompanies the act of intellection' in the sentence l. 5–8 will have to be equated with the 'imagination remaining on' in the sentence 2–5 (n. 11 p. 163:). This equation is Blumenthal's (1971: 89), who notes that the 'translation' of pure thought into images is difficult. But of course it is not Plotinus' view that all thinking is accompanied by images (I 4 10 10–27): intellection proceeds even more strongly without images than when we are aware of it. McCumber does not mention the possibility that νοῦς is without representation, where discursive thought requires it. Above all see the end of ch. 3.30 for νοῦς being without representation. The second context McCumber sees here is the division into the two souls from chapters 27 and 29. This distinction plays no role in Chapter 30; furthermore,

In this section I will argue for a third form of interpretation, according to which Plotinus in fact thinks that there are two ways in which one can speak of the memory of thoughts. In order to understand this interpretation, we must tackle a simple fact about IV 3 30, namely, that we are dealing with two kinds of memory. These are required here because there are two kinds of thought, acquired thought and innate thought. The two kinds of memory of thoughts can be derived from the fundamental distinction made in IV 3 25 between memory of things acquired, that is learnt or perceived,[763] and of innate ideas. The striking thing is that the first form of memory, perceptual memory, is also responsible for memory of thoughts, namely acquired ones, theorems which we have learned.[764] The second kind of memory[765] is concerned with the thoughts that we always have, i.e. those of ideas and which do not, therefore, have to be acquired. The question then is whether IV 3 30 is concerned with the retention of thoughts or with the recollection of ideas.

The first would suggest that we are dealing with the means of retention and the second with the means of retrieval. From the point of view of a theory of memory the following question has to be asked: is the function of representations here to retain (acquired) thoughts or is it to retrieve (innate) ideas? The first model might be taken as follows:

McCumber misses the point entirely that the shade has intellectual memories, and the soul sensual ones. A further problem lies in his failure to distinguish recollection from memory. There may be recollection of ideas, but no memory of them (see IV 4 1), there may be recollection of discursive thoughts, and also memory of them (see IV 3 25 25, above p. 144).

763 Above p. 143, IV 3 25 10–11 τὸ τῆς μνήμης ἐπικτήτου τινὸς ἢ μαθήματος ἢ παθήματος.

764 The question looks like a simple one to answer, assuming that the borders between what one learns and that which is innate are easy to establish. But one just needs to think of what one might learn about triangles, to ask, if the concept of triangle is innate, is the fact that the sum of their angles is equal to two right angles not also innate? What else could be a μάθημα? The example of a triangle may seem to be contentious, since all we can know about triangles is necessary, and so in some sense part of the concept (but note that at I 3 3 5 μάθημα means "mathematical studies"). IV 6 1 3 speaks of the retention of perceptions and μάθημα. This may be a reference merely to the first kind of memory in IV 3 25, or include both the first and second kind. At IV 3 29 6–7 he denies that the faculty of perception can be responsible for the memory of μαθήματα and thoughts (διανοήματα); this coupling confirms the problematic status of thought.

765 Mentioned at IV 3 25 25–34, above p. 144.

R1: you retain the representation of the thought, and hence you remember the thought.

And the second model as:

R2: you form a representation of the thought, and hence recollect the thought sc. which is in you.

Apparently, the two models are suited to the memory of different kinds of thought, namely of discursive thoughts and of ideas, respectively. This opens the way to my interpretation of the chapter. The two ways in which the representative faculty may be responsible for the two kinds of memories of thoughts are both permissible, but must be ascribed to the relevant kind of thought. Lines 2–5 described the retention of discursive thoughts. For these acquired theorems Plotinus utilises Aristotle's theory whereby representations follow, that is, accompany, thoughts. Because this is so, the retention of the representation is the retention of the thought. Lines 5–11 then describe the way in which ideas are recollected using λόγοι. In many ways, this is the most comfortable reading of the chapter. We can then account for the fact that the first way is not refuted, namely, because Plotinus holds it to be right. The memory of thoughts (διανόησις) is also attributable to the representative faculty. If a representation accompanies every thought, then when this representation remains there is memory of this cognition.

What is Plotinus' relation to Aristotle here? This passage is of cardinal importance for an assessment of the relationship between the two theorists. Bréhier[766] thinks that Plotinus is inspired by Aristotle's view[767] that there is only accidental memory of thoughts. He understands this to mean that while memory is only of sensible images, but can also be applied to thought accidentally through sensible images, in the form of "des formules du langage". But Bréhier's view does not really explain why Plotinus follows Aristotle here. I think it can be explained on the following lines. We can take Plotinus to be giving qualified assent to Aristotle. He thinks Aristotle is right about thought being accompanied by representation, if thought is taken to be discursive thought, but straightforward representation cannot be applied to νοῦς, rather, as we shall see, representation articulates the ideas in recollection, and this goes beyond

---

766 Vol. 4 p. 169.
767 Above p. 42.

Aristotle's theory. A more fundamental discrepancy lies in the fact that Aristotle clearly says that there is memory of thoughts only incidentally. Even if Plotinus thinks that both discursive thoughts and ideas are retained and recollected respectively using representations, he does not say that this relegates thoughts to accidental objects of memory.[768] Nonetheless, in his view ideas are primarily objects of thought, and not the objects of memory, so there may be agreement under the surface of the text here.

Now that we have discussed Plotinus' method in his treatment of the memory of thought, the next thing we have to discuss is the role of φαντασία here. The memory is of the thing cognised,[769] and here that is not the representation, but the thing thought of. It is important that Plotinus does not think that we remember the representation, properly speaking, but rather the thing that the representation is a representation of. We have already seen that perceptual memory has the object of perception as its object, mediated by the representation remaining from the perception.[770] Plotinus is more concrete than Aristotle in his expression of the relation between the representation and the thought. For Aristotle, it is simply that there can be no thought without a representation. Plotinus says that a representation follows (παρακολουθεῖ) every act of thought; the same expression is used for the λόγος which accompanies every thought,[771] and one may well ask:

i)   Is the relation of accompanying the same in both cases?
ii) What is it in each case?

On the one hand, one reason for thinking that accompanying is different in each case is that the λόγος unpacks the thought, articulates it, in a way which a representation need not. On the other hand, both representation and λόγος may serve in some sense as a vehicle.[772] In the case of the λόγος this refers to making the thought in each case divisible, namely into subject and predicate[773]:

---

768 HBT (II b 504 ad loc.) compare Aristotle's De mem. 1 449b31 and De an. III 7 427 b16. An additional difference from Plotinus emerges in the first passage in that it also is concerned with the perception of time, which is not treated anywhere by Plotinus.
769 IV 3 30 4–5.
770 Above p. 176.
771 IV 3 30 2, 6.
772 Cf. HBT II b 504 ad IV 3 30 6.
773 This is Emilsson's suggestion (1988: 136).

> Perhaps the reception into the representative power would be of the λόγος which accompanies each thought. For the thought is without parts, when it has not, as it were, come out, and escapes our notice inside.[774]

Besides showing Plotinus developing Aristotle's view of thoughts, this discussion of the memory of thought is crucial because it makes clear that φαντασία cannot simply be understood as a faculty of images. This is clear when we consider λόγος serving as the way in which thoughts are present in φαντασία. If the first lines of the chapter did not offer us much of a clue as to the function of representation here, this is certainly not true of the second part.[775] The first part does in fact suggest that the representation is a kind of image of the thought,[776] but the second part is one of the chief witnesses for Plotinus' view that representation is a conceptual or logical faculty, in some sense. This must be the case, since it is able to take up, "receive" (παραδοχή) the λόγος which accompanies the thought. The λόγος here has the function of developing, "unfolding", the thought, which until then is "inside", and escapes our attention. How are we to take these metaphors? One way would be to say that we are dealing with thoughts of ideas, which are innate in us, and we have here a description of the way in which discourse (λόγος) makes explicit our mastery of these concepts by making them manifest, for example, in definitions. Another way of putting the same point would be to say that in recollecting our innate thinking of ideas, we are exercising a capacity to think.[777] But what does all this have to do with memory? The λόγος is said to display the thought "as if in a mirror", and this is the way that "remaining and memory" of the thought occurs. So once we have displayed the concept using λόγος, we are able to grasp it consciously, that is, there is apperception (ἀντίληψις) of it.[778] Whereas before it was "inside", but unconsciously so, and thus it escapes our attention (ἔνδον ὂν λανθάνει),[779] now it is available to our conscious thought. Plotinus does not say so explicitly, but as we have seen the process of retrieval

---

774 IV 3 30 5–7. Emilsson (1988: 135–6) refers the thoughts here to perception; but they do not contribute to perception (in contrast e.g. to the concepts in V 3 3 see above p. 164); they represent another activity which can disturb perception (IV 3 30 13–16).

775 IV 3 30 5–11.

776 διανόησις, IV 3 30 1, οἷον εἰκόνος οὔσης τοῦ διανοήματος lines 3–4.

777 Cf. the way in which the second kind of memory is described in IV 6 3 15–16.

778 IV 3 30 13, 14.

779 IV 3 30 8.

is ἀνάμνησις.[780] Innate ideas are retrieved and so made conscious using representations. We have here a broad conception of memory in that innate ideas are always in us, so that in a certain sense, time is not involved.[781] Recollecting something that always happens is in that sense not temporal, but in another sense, of course, our recollection, from the perspective of the embodied soul most certainly is temporal as there is a before and an after with respect to the process of recollecting the ideas.[782]

So in some sense, representation involves λόγος. We are explaining here why the memory of thoughts involves representation, and the present suggestion is grounded in the fact that, in order for there to be consciousness and memory of thoughts, a λόγος enters the representative faculty and displays the thought. But in what sense are we to take λόγος here? A preliminary point is that the turn of phrase "the λόγος displaying the thought as if in a mirror"[783] need not mean that in some way the λόγος is pictorial.[784] Rather, λόγος contributes to the representation of the thought in φαντασία, which in turn might be regarded as a pictorial representation. But this last claim is still one that requires discussion. For the point of the metaphor of the mirror may well be that something is being represented, not that something is being pictorially displayed.

So how is λόγος to be taken here? If what we have said so far is right, we are dealing with an articulated presentation, articulated at least in the sense that it can now be divided into parts. Here at least, λόγος is 'the representative of a superior kind of reality at a lower level'.[785] Ideas, that is, the intellect, is being represented in the embodied soul. There are still, however, questions that remain unanswered. To start with, there is the intuition that lies behind Bréhier's view, which has proved to be widely appealing, that what we need here is *a verbal formula*. In

---

780 Cf. V 3 2 13–14, III 7 1 20–24.
781 Cf. the discussion of the memory of ideas in IV 3 25 25; and also the universal memory problem, *Introduction* p. 3.
782 Cf. Merlan 1963: 76 n. 2.
783 IV 3 30 10.
784 Warren 1966: 282, 'The image in conceptual imagination is *not* a picture whereas that of sensation is.' Warren refers to Clark 1942: 306–7 for non-pictorial images (i. e. representations) in Plotinus. For judgements and φαντασία see above fn. 482. Cf. I 4 10 esp. 10–21, also V 3 2–3, above p. 164.
785 Cf. Rist 1967: 84. The translators offer us the following: AHA "Verbal expression", similarly MacK "verbal formula", both following Bréhier's "formule verbale"; and perhaps HBT's "Begriff (*Wort*)" and Brisson's "discours" should be seen in the same light.

other words, something is said, when the idea is being explicated, that is unpacked into its elements. This is surely an attractive, even an inevitable, thought. A verbal formula, not necessarily uttered, may express an idea, in some way presenting the content of the idea, for example in a definition.[786] So λόγος is a verbal formula for a thought, arrived at or retrieved by ἀνάμνησις. When this formula represents the thought, then we are able to remember it. Plotinus sums up the whole process by saying that when we have recalled the thought, then we have apperception (ἀντίληψις) of it, there is memory (μνήμη) and remaining (μονή).[787] Presumably the point is that we first have to be conscious of thinking, so that it remains, and then we can remember it. When we have done the recollection necessary to recollect our innate thinking, then we can remember it.

---

786 AHA (note 1 p. 130 to IV 3 30 16) glosses the "doctrine" in question as "the awareness of our own thinking which makes memory possible can only take place when pure thought is translated into images". The problem with this reading is that, while λόγος is many things in Plotinus it is certainly not an image. Cf. Atkinson 1983: 49–54 on the meaning of λόγος in V 1 3 7–8. At least three possible ways of taking λόγος in Plotinus: in νοῦς, in soul and uttered (see also I 2 3 27–31). Dillon (1986: n. 6 p. 64) interprets λόγος here following Blumenthal (1971: 88) as a 'discursive sequel' (so too McCumber 1978: 165): 'No straightforward translation of λόγος will quite do here, as what Plotinus seems to mean is a 'projection' of the original intuition (νόημα) onto the discursive level of thought, which involves mental images. Bréhier's 'formule verbale' is harmlessly uninformative, as is Harder's Begriff, and Armstrong's 'verbal expression'.' (Emilsson 1988: 134–5 follows the last suggestion) What Dillon does not say is quite what he means by "projection" (how pictorial is it? how conceptual?) nor how this is connected to Blumenthal's phrase. Several commentators are reminded here of a distinction that was apparently Stoic and is found elsewhere in Plotinus himself, namely that between λόγος ἐνδιάθετος and λόγος προφορικός (SVF II 135, Sextus Empiricus, Adv. math. VIII 275): for this distinction HBT adduce V 1 3 7–9, and Pophyrius abst. 187,20: humans differ from other animals not by uttered (προφορικός) speech, but by the mental (ἐνδιάθετος) kind. Philo distinguishes the sensible from the intelligible world using these two concepts (Rist 1967: 100); cf. V 1 6 9–10.

787 IV 3 30 10–11. Cf. IV 3 29 24: remaining, IV 3 26 52: retention. The question in both cases is what the relation between memory and these other phenomena is. See Dillon's rendering of these lines 9–11 (1986: 55–6) 'the λόγος, unfolding and proceeding from the thought into the imagination, displays the thought as it were in a mirror and thus results the apprehension of it, its continued presence, and consequently memory'. Emilsson (1988: 134–5) takes memory just to be the preservation of the representation.

Plotinus finishes the chapter[788] by using the second model, according to which the representative faculty presents a thought to the soul using a λόγος, to account for the fact that although the soul is always moving towards thinking the ideas, we do not always apperceive (ἀντίληψις) that it is. The reason lies in the Janus faced nature of the representative faculty, which we have already met, namely it receives both acts of thought and perceptions.[789] Plotinus apparently assumes it cannot do both at once, and since "we" i.e. embodied souls, do perceive sometimes, we quite naturally cannot be conscious of thinking all the time. Far from being the unity behind all mental acts, apperception depends on representation, and is therefore directed at either perception or thought, but not simultaneously at both.[790]

---

788 IV 3 30 11–16.

789 On φαντασία see above p. 110. Its two sides are well represented by IV 3 23 32: like something intellectual, and I 8 15 18: a blow from something irrational outside. Cf. Dillon 1986: 56 'the main thing is that the imagination is clearly recognised as receptive of images from above as well as sense-data', so φαντασία is situated at the 'border as it were of two levels of soul'.

790 On this difference from modern conceptions of consciousness, see Emilsson 1991: 164, and on consciousness more generally, see above p. 153. This passage poses especial problems for the relation of the representative faculty to perception, in that here representation is independent of perception, since it can be active, representing thoughts, apart from any perception. This is problematic, insofar as in other texts Plotinus says that consciousness of thought depends on reception of the cognition into the perceptive faculty (IV 8 8 6–9). AHA compares also I 4 9–10, HBT cite V 1 12 11; Atkinson (1983: 245 ad V 1 12 5–7) suggests that the representative faculty comes in the later writings (IV 3 and I 4) to replace the perceptive faculty of the early ones. For a close connection between representative faculty and perception he cites I 4 10 15, IV 4 17 12, III 6 4 45; he thinks the two are identified in V 1 12 5–7. φαντασία may also provide a representation of the intelligible world V 8 9 7, and of the good V 6 5 15 (Atkinson 1983: 225–6). This would suggest that the representation of ideas is a function of the perceptual φαντασία. (Another related topic is the role of ideas in perception VI 7 6 2–6, I 1 9 10, V 3 3 1–5, above p. 164. Cf. Blumenthal 1971: 106.) In some texts representation serves the understanding (see above p. 164), whereas representation, at least perceptual representation, here prevents thought. One response to this textual situation is to say that there is not really any hard and fast distinction between perception and representation. See above fn. 738. This is unsatisfactory, since Plotinus argues expressly that memory does not belong to the perceptive faculty (see esp. IV 3 29 1–7, above 3.2.5.1 Representation in perceptual memory) and that it does belong to the representative faculty. The two faculties cannot therefore be straightforwardly identical.

3.2.6 Shared memories and their loss

3.2.6.1 Shade and soul: shared memories, and an ethical separation

One of the problems mentioned in the *Introduction*[791] was the memory-self problem, concerning the relation between self and memory: what is the explanation for the fact that I can apparently only remember things that happened to me, things I have perceived, learned, experienced? One question that arises in this difficult area is whether this entails that only one person has a set of particular memories; or can different people have the same memories? This would be possible if the unity of the person were not a necessary condition for memory. This question is acute for Plotinus since he starts his treatment of memory from the problem of souls in the underworld, which in fact are shades of the souls which are with the gods. Now that he has identified φαντασία as the faculty responsible for memory both of perception (Chapter 29) and thought (Chapter 30), he returns in Chapter 31 to the shade and soul and their possession of two memories each. We have already discussed the division into shade and soul, and their various memories, and we have mentioned the example given, Homer's description of Heracles. Curiously, he sees no problem with the divided memory when shade and soul are apart,[792] but we now have to tackle the question of how the two are related when they are together in us. Plotinus assumes that shade and soul then form a unity, so the question is which one of them has memory. If both did, then the representations (φαντασίαι) would be double. What he has to do is to explain the fact that we apparently (in life) have a single memory faculty, although he thinks that there are potentially two (after death). I think that the way Plotinus divides shade and soul, generally speaking, is a matter of the way they lead their lives, the one practically and the other theoretically inclined. Although he uses spatial language for the separation of the two souls or soul and shade (*in* Hades, *in* heaven) after death, the basic nature of the separation is actually ethical. To repeat: in embodied life, one is theoretically, and the other practically inclined. After death, they may then be in different places in some sense, but the reason for their localities lies in their inclinations.[793]

---

791 Above p. 1–2.
792 IV 3 31 2–3: χωρὶς μὲν οὖν οὖσαι ἐχέτωσαν ἑκάτερα.
793 McCumber 1978: 162 asks why there is an account of the memories of the higher and lower souls in IV 3 and 4 which is obscure in itself and in apparent discord with Plotinus' other discussions. He thinks, rightly, that the problem can be re-

Their different inclinations provide the reason for their different memories.

One thing Plotinus excludes very clearly is that the soul should have exclusively intellectual memories and the shade perceptual ones, on the grounds, already mentioned above, that a complete difference in object of memory would then produce two living things with nothing in common.[794] Hence the shade has some intellectual memories, and the soul some perceptual ones. What these perceptual memories are in the case of the separate soul, is a question he pursues in Chapter 32, and will be discussed in the next section; the ethical slant of his enquiry there confirms our approach to the present chapter. Here, in Chapter 31, in dealing with the embodied soul, he describes the way the two faculties of memory are related in terms of harmony and control. So long as they harmonise, we do not notice that there are two of them. This harmony, he says, exists when the better of the souls is in charge:[795] then the representation is one, and the two representative faculties are not separate (χωρίς).[796] He compares unity of the representations to one shadow following another one, or like a smaller light placed under a larger one. In contrast, when the representations are not in harmony, then the inferior representative faculty becomes obvious, although it still escapes our notice that it is in something else, i. e. in the shade. The division between shade

---

solved by noting the question which introduces the division into higher and lower souls IV 3 25 35–8: which soul do such so called μνήμη and ἀνάμνησις belong to, or do they belong to the concrete living thing (he notes the reference to memory and recollection at IV 3 25 27–33)? No answer is given by Plotinus, but one is implied in IV 4 3.3 f: memory of the forms stops the higher soul from falling further. He criticises Blumenthal's view (1971: 91 f) that the lower soul is introduced to preserve the impassivity of the soul and to preserve the possibility of error and illusion. This does not answer the question why Plotinus assigns memory at all to the higher soul. Blumenthal's answer is to preserve character through memories between incarnations (1971: 95). This will not do, as McCumber sees: souls of heavenly bodies have no memories (IV 4 6 7–13) but preserve identity 'at least partially, it appears', through direct intuition of its orbit (IV 4 7 13- IV 4 8 4). In IV 3 and 4, the orientation of the soul is ascribed to memory. See below p. 213.

794 IV 3 31 5–8.
795 IV 3 31 9–13 Ἢ ὅταν μὲν συμφωνῇ ἡ ἑτέρα τῇ ἑτέρᾳ, οὐκ ὄντων οὐδὲ χωρὶς τῶν φανταστικῶν, κρατοῦντός τε τοῦ τῆς κρείττονος, ἓν τὸ φάντασμα γίνεται, οἷον παρακολουθούσης σκιᾶς τῷ ἑτέρῳ, καὶ ὑποτρέχοντος οἷον σμικροῦ φωτὸς μείζονι.
796 The same expression he has used for the shade in Hades and the soul in heaven (IV 3 31 2 and 10).

and soul is something we do not generally notice,[797] since the soul is in charge of the shade. It seems that what is meant by this domination of the inferior shade by the superior soul is a form of ethical control. It would seem to operate on two levels. There is a basic control, as it were, a normative level, which then may or may not be realised in what actually happens. The actual course of events is thus the second level at which the soul may control the shade.

John Dillon provides an example of how they conflict: one is meditating and one has bodily senses and organs under control, then the lower imagination (i.e. φαντασία) is not inoperative, although it is not apparently doing anything. It has merely subordinated its activity to that of the higher. In contrast, unsuccessful meditation is disturbed by conflicting images: 'Here the second spotlight is no longer focused on the same spot as the first; it begins to wander here and there, and distracting images impinge upon the central one.'[798] The point is of course that one meditates *on something*. Meditation requires an object, and so too with representation, in that it is the way objects are present to one. Hence if the lower, practical representation, concerned with perception, needs and passions, impinges, then the soul occupies itself with objects other than those to which the better soul is directed. Attention paid to practical matters detracts from philosophising and hence it is important that the soul have control of the shade so that we spend our time with intellectual memories.

Plotinus underlines the ethical direction of this whole discussion when he says that low company is soon forgotten when we move in better circles.[799] The superior soul, although it has access to all that happens to the compound has no real interest in remembering everything that hap-

---

797 Following HS's transposition of ὅτι from IV 3 31 15 to ὅ τι in line 14.

798 Dillon (1986: 56) refers to Blumenthal 1971: 94 ff for difficulties which the image involves Plotinus in. See also p. 90: Blumenthal thinks that the only possible interpretation of what harmony or disharmony could mean is that the lower imagination becomes evident when one devotes oneself to the memory of sensible objects. Blumenthal then attacks this theory on the grounds that sensible memory is no different from intellectual memory insofar as both are expressed in images, of which the only difference lies in their origin. So the superior memory could be conscious of all the inferior ones. Blumenthal's idea is that the disharmony lies in the fact some memories are in the one which are not in the other. But he misses the clear point that it is a matter of *control* and different interests in the shade and the soul; these two aspects are what have to be brought into harmony with one another.

799 IV 3 31 16–18, cf. also IV 3 27 15–20.

pens on a practical level. It is really, and properly, interested in thought. And the way it comes to concentrate on thought is by forgetting.

3.2.6.2 The good of forgetting: shared memories, their effects and their loss

The question, we should remember, that is guiding this discussion of memory is what can the soul remember when it is alone. We have reached a stage where we have seen that it can remember everything that shade and soul have experienced. And we have seen that memory is directed by inclinations. But not only is memory guided by the soul's interest, so is forgetting. What now follows is a justification of forgetting. For what is sometimes seen as a process of purification, the soul casting off impurities gathered in company with the body, is here a process of forgetting. Returning to the true self, to thought of ideas, is partly a process of recollection of the ideas, but also forgetting embodied existence.

But we begin modestly, with the ethically acceptable aspects of a citizen's life, before going on to treat the systematic function of forgetting. For surely the superior soul may remember its friends, children, wife and city,[800] in short everything which it would be proper for a civilised[801] person to remember.[802] Such objects belong to things that both shade and soul remember, but they do so differently. The shade remembers with passion (πάθος), and the soul without. Nonetheless, in some way *something* of the passion is passed on to the soul:

> For the passion, perhaps, was in the representative faculty even from the beginning, and those of the passions which had any good quality pass to the noble soul, in so far as it has any communication with the other one.[803]

---

800 For these memories, cf. IV 3 27 23–24.
801 This is the only chapter in which ἀστεῖος appears in Plotinus.
802 It will be worth bearing in mind that to have a memory of my country, there has to be some memory of the self the country is attached to. These are questions we approach again in IV 4 2, below p. 201.
803 IV 3 32 4–6 (AHA trans., altered) τὸ γὰρ πάθος ἴσως καὶ ἐξ ἀρχῆς ἐν ἐκείνῳ καὶ τὰ ἀστεῖα τῶν παθῶν τῇ σπουδαίᾳ, καθόσον τῇ ἑτέρᾳ τι ἐκοινώνησε. ἐν ἐκείνῳ refers back to τὸ μὲν in line three, which refers to the representative faculty, but without any division (as at IV 3 31 1; see HBT II b 505 ad loc, not to Bréhier's "l'homme"). For a perhaps parallel division of passion into an opinion and an unexamined representation, see III 6 4 13–23, esp. 19–21. The primary representation would then belong to the soul, the unexamined one merely to the shade. It is however, quite possible that the point here is another one, more concerned with those aspects of a passion that are harmonious with the soul.

In Plotinus' scheme of things the representative faculty is responsible for passion.[804] The soul is of course not itself capable of undergoing a passion, but it can be directed by the opinion that constitutes a passion. One might think of Socrates' patriotism as an example of a passion transposed into a higher key, into passionless opinion, by reason. Thus one side of shared memory is, again, a question of the good. The separation between soul and shade marks that between something affected and something which only attends to the good. The converse of this relation is that of course the shade, "the worse soul",[805] can learn from the soul. If it is a "civilised" shade, that is, one that lives harmoniously with the soul it is an image of, then it can strive for the active memories of the soul. Plotinus also envisages the possibility of violent restraint of the shade by the soul. The memories shared between shade and soul are thus not merely a static sharing of inventory, but make up a sharing that is aimed at the improvement of the shade. The ethical slant we noticed in the distinction of their memories is pursued here.

Perhaps surprisingly, the same is true of the soul's forgetting.[806] On the one hand, it certainly makes sense that the soul has to get rid of its past, if it is eventually to be completely absorbed in thinking, and on the other, it only needs to forget if its life here was not such as to produce memories of the better kind.[807] Plotinus even finds a Platonic quotation for this theory, namely that it is good here, in this life, "to stand outside human concerns",[808] and hence better, when "there", that is after death, also to be without memories of them. The further justification for this move is that the soul "both flees the many and brings together the

---

804 On πάθος, see Fleet 1996: 118–9, and I 1 5–7.
805 AHA translates "the whole soul", as a translation for τὴν μὲν χείρονα line 6 (cf. line 10), as opposed to the better one (κρείττων). Perhaps the idea behind this translation is that the soul anyway strives for its own active remembering, *and* the worse souls should do so too. *Ergo* the whole soul does.
806 HBT II b 505: line 17 ἐπιλήσμονα "die überraschende Eigenschaft der guten Seele"; cf. Plato's remark (*Republic* VI 486D1–2) that the soul should not be ἐπιλήσμων among those who love wisdom sufficiently, but rather being good at remembering (μνημονικός) (cf. also *Laws* IV 710C6); this may be a reason that Plotinus feels the need to defend the good of forgetting. Cf. the forgetfulness at *Phaedrus* 248C.
807 IV 3 32 13–15. Thus forgetting need not mean, at this stage, leaving all acquired memories behind (for these see IV 3 25 11).
808 The quotation is from Plato (*Phaedrus* 249C9–D1).

many into unity by eschewing the unbounded."[809] One way of understanding this gnomic saying is that the soul improves itself by philosophising. In other words, by doing dialectic, that is to say by determining
the relations between the ideas, it returns to itself. It would seem that at a
cognitive level this is what "eschewing the unbounded" means. If you determine what the ideas are, then you have nothing to do with the unbounded, since ideas are just what is definite and, as it were bounded.
But it is unclear if he does not also think that one thereby also avoids
the many. For Plotinus goes on to say that "in this way the soul is not
with the many, but is light and on its own". Thus it ceases to have com-
merce with individuals, i.e. the many that fall under an idea, and deals
only with ideas. In so doing it becomes light.[810] He draws a parallel between what the soul does *there* with what it does *here*. In both cases it
abandons all that is different,[811] that is to say, formed by the difference
which characterises the many. It is attractive to see abandoning the
many as the abandonment of perception, that is of individuals falling
under the ideas. In abandoning perception, the soul then turns to
thought. In so doing it turns away from the world of bodies, including
memories of bodily existence. Turning to thought brings forgetting embodied life in its train.

In concluding this discussion, Plotinus allows that Heracles will remember his virtue, but wishes to make room for a greater sort of hero,
namely one who has competed in the competitions of the wise, and
who is correspondingly in a higher place. In other words, he denies

---

809 It might be possible to see in IV 3 32 19–20 τὰ πολλὰ εἰς ἓν συνάγει a reference
to τὸ ἕν (cf. SP s.v. 322.54). It is reasonable that ideas, insofar as they gather
things together, simply are not comprehensible without unity; and perhaps
this unity also displays the way in which they serve the good. The unbounded
has marked connotations of a lack of value for Plotinus. The phrase refers to matter (I 8 3 13), body (IV 7 8²20), badness (I 8 9 6); and finally things can be numerically unbounded. HBT refer to *Epinomis* 992B, and to the principle for dialectic, also in the *Epinomis* 991E. In view of the quotation from the *Phaedrus* in
line 16, and the connection with the placement of souls in the cosmos, one might
also think of the difficult description of dialectic there (249B-C, 265D); in the
first passage ἀνάμνησις also plays a role. Plotinus also refers to the *Phaedrus* in his
own brief account of dialectic I 3 esp. 4 9–18.
810 This unique use of the word ἐλαφρά (LSJ translate "relieved") may be another
reminiscence of the *Phaedrus*, this time of the winged soul (246C).
811 IV 3 32 22: ἔτι οὖσα ἐνταῦθα ἀφίησι πάντα ὅσα ἄλλα. AHA adds "[from that
world]".

that Heracles, the model of the practical man, reaches the heights of a philosopher.[812] The heroism of the latter consists in contemplation.

3.3 "The soul is and becomes what it remembers."

3.3.1 Thinking without memory

The short answer to the question of what the soul will remember when it is separated from body,[813] that is, when actually contemplating ideas, is: nothing. This section presents a rather longer answer to this question, and we can summarise it as follows. Like Aristotle, Plotinus thinks that thinking, and being able to think, in this particular sense, require no memory, in that thought is an exercise of intellect and not memory. There is, therefore, much that the contemplating soul can forget, as we have seen in the last chapter. However, it does not need to forget all that it can remember.[814] For the soul faces reincarnation, or at least continued existence in the heavens, and so still preserves the capacity to remember. When the soul turns away from contemplation, actual memory starts[815] and then plays a central role in determining what kind of existence the soul inclines to.

---

812 Porphyry, in his need to get nine treatises for his fourth Ennead, breaks off the treatment in mid-sentence; an outrageous procedure which editors and translators have been curiously reticent about (Bréhier ends IV 3 with a comma, and without commentary; HS remark dryly 'continuatur sententia in IV 4 1 1'; AHA says that the break is odd, but less odd if one considers that the sentence is anakoluthic, and that the divide marks the transition from Heracles to the sage, hence putting great emphasis on the question at the start of IV 1; he compares it with the start of III 2, as do HBT, who punctuate with a -; strictly they should not have given IV 4 another chronological number at all; the same might apply to Brisson, who says this (2005: 14): "Si Porphyre a distingué les trois traités, il leur a toutefois réservé le même titre et les a publiés de façon à ce qu' ils se suivent et que leur cohérence ne fasse pas le moindre doute : il s'agit bien là d' une même enquête plotinienne, d' un même enseignement". And then at the end of IV 3 32, p. 245, n. 542: "La phrase se poursuit dans le traité suivant, ce qui indique bien la coupure faite par Porphyre est aléatoire". The division is, however, textually indefensible, although a new stage in this part of the enquiry does occur at this point.

813 The question is raised in IV 3 27 15–16, 23–24.

814 Despite IV 3 32 12–18.

815 In IV 4 3, below p. 207.

The discussion of the relation between memory and actual contemplation in IV 4 1 is very difficult. The core of the difficulty can be described as follows. The problem that Plotinus faces is that contemplation is not a temporal process, and so can allow, apparently, no memory. So he has to describe contemplation in such a way that time is not involved. How can there be an activity, where nothing changes from an earlier state to a later one?[816]

Plotinus, confronted with the problem of describing something of which we have no accessible experience appeals to consistency, that is he tries to present a view that is both in itself consistent, but also consistent with the rest of his views about the soul.[817] In this way, he wants to show what the soul will do when "in the intelligible and in the presence of that essence".[818] As he goes on to say, it is consistent to say that the soul contemplates the ideas, i. e. is active in relation to them, and that is what it means for the soul to be there.[819] He draws a conclusion from his conception of what "he thinks" means, namely that it does not include "he has thought".[820] That is to say, being active about the ideas means only being active about the ideas now, that is, in an eternal present which excludes any past. Hence when the separated soul actually contemplates ideas, it is outside time, and so does not actually remember anything of its embodied existence. In other words it excludes any memory of what we did, when in our bodies, e. g. that we philosophised here, or that we contemplated the ideas when embodied. However, as we shall see, the soul still possesses the capacity for memory.

Two Aristotelian associations may occur to the reader at this point, one suggesting that Plotinus is here following Aristotle and the other that he is correcting him. First, the correction. The first text that

---

816 On this problem see Sorabji 1983: Chapter 8.

817 ἀκόλουθον IV 4 1 2. This could of course mean that the view he goes on to sketch follows from something that precedes, but there do not seem to be suitable premises in what has already been said for this to be an attractive reading. Another way he arrives at conclusions about the way we exist after death is analogy with the embodied soul (IV 3 32 21–24).

818 IV 4 1 1–2 ἐν τῷ νοητῷ καὶ ἐπὶ τῆς οὐσίας ἐκείνης. I take this as a hendiadys for contemplating the ideas.

819 IV 4 1 3–4.

820 IV 4 1 8. HBT refer to IV 4 7 3: the heavenly bodies always see god and it is hence not possible to say that they have seen him.

comes to mind is the well-known description of actions as opposed to changes.[821] Actions are said to have a temporal structure of the form:

If a F-s at t1 and F is an action, then it is also true that a has F-ed at t1.

So Plotinus would be trying to exclude thinking from being an action in Aristotle's sense, in that according to the former, when a soul thinks at t1, it has not thereby thought at t1. According to Aristotle's theory of actions, thought, along with other actions, requires no time for completion. It is not a change towards an end, since the end has already been attained. Aristotle thinks that the possibility of saying that if one thinks at t1, then one has thought at t1 is grounded in the instantaneous completion of thought. This temporal structure is not acceptable to Plotinus, since in his theory thinking is complete in the eternal present, without any need for it to have reached its end just when it is being performed. One has to add that Aristotle himself would not draw the conclusion from the structure of actions that memory must be involved in them. In his view, if I am thinking at t1 it may be true that that at t1 I have also thought, but not true that at t1 I remember having thought. It is at least clear that he does not think that memory is a necessary concomitant of thought, which is an action in his sense.

So much for Plotinus' correction of Aristotle. Now for the point where he follows him. The relation between thinking and memory that Aristotle himself posits is what we find Plotinus describing.[822] Aristotle thinks that it is only possible to have a thought accidentally in one's memory. Thus thought does not include the memory of what one is thinking. It is above all not an exercise of a capacity to remember, but of a capacity to think. The cornerstone of Aristotle's view here is what I called "the argument from activity".[823] If you ask someone who is thinking what they are doing, they will say, I am thinking, and not, I am remembering. Indeed, an impartial observer would say the same.

Let us look at the way Plotinus excludes time, and hence all forms of active memory, from the disembodied soul's thinking:

---

821 Met. IX 6 1048b18–35; of thought (νοεῖν) line 25. See Jaeger's (1957) apparatus ad. loc. for the slim textual support for printing these lines here; see Burnyeat 2008b.

822 See above p. 42.

823 See p. 30; we return to it below p. 215.

If, as is thought, all thinking is timeless, and things there are in eternity and not in time, it is impossible to have memory there, not merely of things here, but of anything whatever: rather each thing is present, since there is neither discursive thought nor any transition.[824]

There are three concepts of change or motion that are relevant here. Two are here excluded from thought. The first is διέξοδος,[825] translated "discursive thought"; it might mean any form of change,[826] and the second is "transition" (μετάβασις). The third is "change" (κίνησις) and Plotinus sees thought as change in this sense.[827] So what he is going to do is to show how thought[828] as a change does not require before and after,[829] succession of a certain kind, and that it is therefore timeless.[830]

That it is a question of excluding a certain kind of succession is confirmed by the next section:[831] νοῦς does not perform division[832] either of kinds into their species, nor conversely the collection of species into universals. Because νοῦς is "all together"[833] it does not have such actual division and collection (of course, species and kinds can be divided and collected, but that is the work of διάνοια and not νοῦς)[834], and neither does

---

824 IV 4 1 11–16.
825 IV 4 1 15.
826 διέξοδος line 15. SP give three meanings a) passage, process, progression, discursion b) detailed survey c) detailed exposition, and rank the present use with a). HBT, Bréhier, AHA, MacK all favour discursive thought – i.e. either SPs b or c (and perhaps these two meanings are not really to be distinguished). Cf. *Theaetetus* 207C.
827 Change is of course one of the greatest kinds in the *Sophist*, and so applicable to the intelligible world, see VI 2 esp. 7–8, also: III 7 3; cf. for the connection between life, thought and change, see *Sophist* 249A.
828 This is said explicitly at IV 4 1 26–28.
829 For priority and posteriority in change see III 7 12, III 7 9 55, 57, 60, 62, 64.
830 Cf. IV 4 10 6 for the atemporality of life, and VI 1 16 16 for that of activity: the whole of the latter chapter is relevant to the question. For Plotinus there comes to the conclusion that change (κίνησις) can happen all at once, and hence in timelessness, quoting Phys. I 3 186a15–16 for Aristotle's view that this is true of μεταβολή e.g. freezing. See 253b23, 236a27. Ross (1936: 471) cites also illumination as an instantaneous change from De an. 418b20–26. HBT compare IV 3 25 13 on the atemporality of god, being and νοῦς; and VI 5 11 14 ff. McGuire and Strange (1988: 252) suggest that Aristotle's conception of activity is the model for eternal activity of νοῦς.
831 IV 4 1 16–25.
832 On διαίρεσις see the texts quoted above p. 192.
833 Following Kleist's emendation in line 18 of ἄνα to νῷ. Anaxagoras' slogan also occurs at I 1 8 8, III 6 6 23, V 3 15 21.
834 In dialectic: see I 3 4.

the soul, when it is just contemplating things, as here. It moves neither up nor down between universal and species.

Plotinus moves from νοῦς to soul, with a purely negative argument: he does not think that anything prevents the soul from having the same kind of cognition as νοῦς, presumably because the one thing that might disperse its attention, perception, is not active, because it cannot be activated in the absence of sense organs. So the soul's "collected attention is directed towards the collected".[835] Thought is not the apprehension of something entirely simple, but rather all acts of thought are of many things together. Thought is unified thought of an articulated whole. Plotinus illustrates what he means using an example, namely the perception of a face. Thus he uses the perception of a single thing and its parts to illustrate thought of the relations of ideas to one another. There are many perceptions – of the eyes, nose etc. – which all happen simultaneously (ἅμα).[836] When these different perceptions are distinguished ("divided and unfolded"), *then* there is something like a concentration of attention.[837] They have to be put together again, by our concentrating on them, and, it seems that this requires the retention of the separate elements that are reunited. Thus we have a simultaneous apprehension of an articulate whole. This is his account of the order among ideas:

> And, as the before and after in the forms is not temporal so too [the soul] will not make its act of intellection of earlier and later in time. For it is in an order, just as the order of a plant for the observer, which begins from the roots and goes right up towards the top is no different from the before and after in the order for the onlooker who sees the whole.[838]

---

835 IV 4 1 19–20.

836 One may well ask if simultaneity is not just as much a temporal relation as before and after; Plotinus obviously thinks that there is an eternal present (cf. line 14–5: ἔστιν ἕκαστον παρόν·), which is not temporal. Simultaneity is thus merely the negation of succession, as it were happening within the eternal present.

837 ἐναπέρεισις. AHA's translation (for this sense, see IV 3 17 23); HBT offer "Festhalten", presumably as a contrast to the unified glance which grasps the face in one, some kind of retention is needed to run through the elements; a satisfactory sense, if one could extract it from the Greek. The idea of concentration may be that of bringing the distinct elements together. Alternatively, he might be describing just what happens when νοῦς runs through an articulated whole: it does it just by moving along them with its attention. The weakness of this reading lies is that it makes ἐναπέρεισις a close relation of ἐπιβολή, and that is said to be gathered together (line 20).

838 IV 4 1 26–31 Τὸ δὲ πρότερον καὶ τὸ ὕστερον ἐν τοῖς εἴδεσιν οὐ χρόνῳ ὂν οὐδὲ τὴν νόησιν τοῦ προτέρου καὶ ὑστέρου χρόνῳ ποιήσει· ἔστι γὰρ καὶ τάξει, οἱονεὶ

These lines are difficult. The lesson they are trying to convey is that there is a kind of order among the objects of thought which is not temporal, although it is parallel to temporal order. We seem to begin with a typically Plotinian argument from the nature of the objects of thought to the nature of thought.[839] This conclusion is based, although not explicitly here, on the view that intellect, intelligible and intellection are identical.[840] If they are indiscernible, and one is not temporal then neither are the other two. Ideas, what thought is about, are not temporal, hence neither is thinking about them.[841] Nonetheless, Plotinus wants to assert that there is order among ideas, and that this order is firstly a kind of succession. An example might be: *animal* is prior to *human*. The temporal order of the plant might be here the way it grows,[842] from the root upwards, in temporal succession. But for someone who sees the whole at a glance, there is exactly the same order or arrangement of the parts as in their succession.

Read in this way there are two major weaknesses to the argument. Firstly, it seems to confuse the order of generation with logical order. Furthermore, logical order does not usually have consequences for the order of thinking: the fact that ideas possess a certain order does not entail that thinking of them will have the same order, unless the thinking is entirely regulated by the order of the ideas. This latter assumption is of course not an unreasonable one to make for Plotinus' view of νοῦς. Presumably he thinks that intellectual order determines the order of intellection. And secondly we are left asking about the succession in thought. For if thought is a form of κίνησις then we still have, as it were, one thing after another. And why should this order not be temporal?[843] The answer to this is that in thought the idea is grasped as a unity in which all of the

---

φυτοῦ ἡ τάξις ἐκ ῥιζῶν ἀρξαμένη ἕως εἰς τὸ ἄνω τῷ θεωμένῳ οὐκ ἔχει ἄλλως ἢ τάξει τὸ πρότερον καὶ τὸ ὕστερον ἅμα τὸ πᾶν θεωμένῳ. Translations of these very obscure lines vary greatly. Points of unclarity include the following: (1) what is the subject of ποιήσει? (2) Does "the before and after" carry on from the clause before (Bréhier, HBT, apparently; MacK) or does it refer to the soul (AHA)? (3) Is there one or two observers, one who looks it up and down and one who takes it in at a glance?

839 Cf. IV 7 10 esp. 30–37.
840 Above all V 3 5; cf. Menn 2001, Slezák 1979: 126–134.
841 This is the basis of the proof of the immortality of the soul in IV 7 10.
842 IV 4 1 26–31. See Smith 1996: 211 on this passage.
843 Cf. De an. I 3 407a8–10 where Aristotle argues that the fact that thought is successive does not mean that νοῦς is a magnitude.

elements are grasped at once. There is no change in the sense that νοῦς moves from one idea to another, and leaves one behind.

Up to now we have been considering the soul contemplating one thing, for example a face or a plant, as a model for the order in which the contents of its thoughts are arranged. The final question asked about the order of thinking concerns a succession of objects of thought.[844] When the soul first considers one thing, and then a multitude, indeed a totality (of ideas), how does it then have one in mind, and then the other? Thus it is a question of how the articulated whole of the realm of ideas can be thought of, in succession, but without time, and hence without memory. Plotinus' answer starts from the relation between the capacity of thought and its activities. The capacity of thought is one in such a way that it is differentiated by the different things it thinks about, that is, actually thinks about. Activity divides it.[845] But inversely, the capacity for thought is not exhausted, that is, used up, by each act of thought: it continues to exist as a unity unifying all the activities.

In other words, the soul has one power of thought which produces different acts when different things are thought of.[846] The power stays the same even when the acts are different. What remains unclear, however, is how the unity of the capacity is meant to avoid the succession of acts being temporally divided. For even if it is one capacity that is being actualised in different acts, the succession of acts would seem to form a temporal series.

It is perhaps a help to remember a way in which Plotinus thinks that some capacities can be realised without that change which involves matter. We have already met the distinction originating with Aristotle be-

---

844 IV 4 1 31–38, esp. 31–33.

845 HBT cite Aristotle, Met. VII 13 1039a7; see also VI 9 5 17, IV 9 5 13.

846 The text of IV 4 1 35–36 is corrupt and has not been satisfactorily emended. I follow HS' reconstruction of line 35, with Theiler's deletion of οὐ, following the Arabic *Theologia* II 20, and his σχιζομένη in line 36 instead of γινομένων, as does AHA, tentatively. The one power is one in such a way that the many are in another (either a) in what thinks or b) the many ideas are related to one another by being in another one) and all do not exist in virtue of a single act of thought. For the activities are not in virtue of a unity, but are in each case through a resting power, divided (<σχιζομένη>) in the different objects. HS' text of lines 33–38 reads: Ἦ ἡ δύναμις ἡ μία οὕτως ἦν μία, ὡς πολλὰ ἐν ἄλλῳ, καὶ οὐ κατὰ μίαν νόησιν πάντα. Αἱ γὰρ ἐνέργειαι οὐ καθ' ἕνα, ἀλλ' ἀεὶ πᾶσαι δυνάμει ἐστώσῃ· ἐν δὲ τοῖς ἄλλοις γινομένων. Ἤδη γὰρ ἐκεῖνο ὡς μὴ ἓν ὂν δυνηθῆναι τὴν τῶν πολλῶν ἐν αὐτῷ φύσιν δέξασθαι πρότερον οὐκ ὄντων.

tween capacities for changes that run between contraries, and capacities for change that are simply the actualisation of the nature of the thing concerned.[847] Thus the realisation of the soul's capacity to think is not a change in the first sense. The soul is able to receive the nature of the many, that is the many ideas, in itself, and so realise them in its acts of thinking. There is a relationship of before and after here, namely that between capacity and act; but none that Plotinus considers to be temporal. The point may be put as follows. The act does not do away with the capacity, so there is not a sense in which something perishes in the change. All that happens is the realisation of the soul's capacity to think.

Thus we have apparently moved here from an argument about the different acts of thought being held together by the capacity to think, to an argument about a single intelligible (ἐκεῖνο), that is, the soul, actually containing all the many ideas, which are only divided by the acts of thought.[848] What Plotinus apparently wishes to deny is that one can think about intelligibles in isolation; when you think of one, you are thinking of them all, without there being memory necessary when you move from one to another preserving the last form thought of. Although each act of thought is distinct, and one thing after another is thought of, and there is hence an order of thought, with before and after, it is the unity of the capacity (to think and be thought of) that holds the actual thinking together.[849]

3.3.2 No memory of self

Plotinus dismisses the question of memory of the objects of thought to pass onto the question of memory of the self in IV 4 2. The move is an obvious one, for as we have seen the relation between memory and thought is connected to the fact that the soul is always thinking. Part of the enquiry concerns ideas which the soul always thinks.[850] These

---

847 See above p. 125.
848 IV 4 1 34–38; line 36 is a crux, and I have tried to make sense of the passage without depending on it.
849 Because of the unclarity of lines 34–36, we cannot expect to understand 36–38 with any great certainty. I translate, tentatively: "For since that ("the intelligible object" AHA) is not one, it is able (what does the infinitive depend on?) to take up the nature of the many in itself, which before (the act of thought) did not exist."
850 IV 3 25 25 see above p. 144.

are the thoughts of the soul which it may have recollection of, but without involving time. The relation between IV 4 1 and 2 is that between thinking the various ideas, on the one hand, and, on the other, thinking of the soul, which has all these ideas in itself. Thus the next step is to ask if the soul, in thinking, has memory of itself. In other words, he asks if the soul is among its own objects of thought. He comes to the conclusion in IV 4 2 that there is no memory of the self, that is, of the soul, when the soul contemplates; but that it does have self-awareness.[851]

The first problem that one meets is that there are various candidates for the self.[852] For the soul has been through a variety of phases, any of which may count as a self which it remembers, to wit, its corporeal existence, as intellect, and as soul. Chapter IV 4 2 is basically divided in two. After an introduction of the problem two possibilities are considered and rejected, firstly that the contemplator remembers that he is intellect,[853] and secondly that he is soul.

Before turning to the soul and the intellect, memory of what one might call the person is excluded as the contemplator has no memory that he is Socrates. At this stage, all that seems to be excluded is an active memory that would intrude on, and hence disturb, contemplation, that is, thought of ideas. Any thought that the thinker is Socrates has no place in such an activity. Plotinus does not discuss it any further.[854] Thus the wise – the example is Socrates for good reason – have no memory of themselves, unlike Heracles, who remembers his own virtue, and therefore, presumably, who he is. Heracles cannot serve as the model for the sage, because he is a practical man and does not contemplate.[855]

---

851 The question asked is *how* the contemplator remembers himself (Ἑαυτοῦ δὲ πῶς;); this might be thought it to imply that he does, after all remember himself, whereas all that Plotinus concedes at the end of the chapter is self-awareness (lines 30–32). Note the masculine of the reflexive pronoun; AHA and HBT take this to be neuter, but it is more plausible that it is masculine, either of the contemplator or of Heracles, or rather, Socrates.

852 Cf. Sorabji's remark (2006: 118) that Plotinus holds there to be multiple selves, two or three or an indefinite number.

853 IV 4 2 3–15.

854 The syntax of the sentence in lines 2–3 is convoluted: Ἦ οὐδὲ ἑαυτοῦ ἕξει τὴν μνήμην, οὐδ' ὅτι αὐτὸς ὁ θεωρῶν, οἷον Σωκράτης, ἢ ὅτι νοῦς ἢ ψυχή. I follow MacK's translation which takes the subject to be the contemplator, which is then said not to be Socrates, intellect or soul.

855 Socrates: IV 4 2 3. For the role of Heracles as a practical man see IV 3 32 24–28, I 1 12 35–39. Of course, it is not an accident that Heracles is a Stoic hero.

Heracles does not attain that theoretical form of existence where actual memory of self has been cast off.

Now to the first option: does the contemplator remember that he is intellect? Plotinus starts by presenting two arguments for the structure of thought of νοῦς based on the way we think here, that is, when in a body: in contemplation one is not directed towards oneself. These possibilities are then considered as to the role of the self in the actual contemplation of the disembodied soul. Neither of them is apparently a form of memory, that is, explicitly connected to the past; both touch the question of how thinking can be directed towards itself. Firstly, one possesses oneself, but the activity of thought is directed at an object of thought;[856] and the self provides itself, as it were, as matter, and becomes informed in a way that corresponds to what it sees, and is still, potentially, itself.[857] That is to say, the self becomes determinate as itself, when thinking of something, since it has taken on the form of the thing thought of, in turning towards that principle which it issues from.[858]

Plotinus passes to the second possibility without saying if he accepts or rejects this first one. The second possibility[859] is based on the idea that the soul contains ("is") all ideas.[860] Thus, when thinking itself, it will think all things and hence also the idea of itself. There are two conclusions that Plotinus wishes to draw from this view of actual thinking. The two are the converse of one another. On the one hand, someone actually and attentively seeing himself will possess all that is in himself, and on the other, considering all things will include considering himself. Plotinus then asks: Is the thinker something thought or is it something beyond things thought? The first option, that the thinker is one of the things thought of, is then disposed of as requiring that there is a change (μεταβάλλειν) between acts of thinking, which was declared impossible.[861]

---

856 IV 4 2 6 ἐκεῖνο as at IV 4 1 36.

857 IV 4 2 9; HBT refer to V 3 6 5.

858 Brisson (2005: 246, n. 24), referring to III 9 5, V 9 4 11, V 1 3 23, II 5 3 14, remarks: "l'âme reçoit de l'Intellect sa forme comme la réalité qui lui est propre, et ainsi elle devient ce qu'elle est en se retournant vers ce dont elle procède. C'est du reste ainsi, en se retournant vers le principe dont elle est issue, qu'une réalité quelconque se détermine: avant ce retour, cette "conversion" la réalité est indéterminée, elle est une matière dépourvue de forme."

859 IV 4 2 10.

860 The exact relation between soul and νοῦς is not clear when soul is reduced to thinking. See Blumenthal 1974.

861 IV 4 1 15–16.

The problem lies in a change of attention, and this is excluded in the case of νοῦς.[862] The second option is not discussed explicitly, but obviously if the self is not among the things thought ("is beyond thought"), then there is no possibility of νοῦς relating to itself. Thus both options of νοῦς remembering itself are excluded.

So if the contemplating soul cannot remember itself as νοῦς, then can it remember itself as soul? The soul surely can change the objects of its attention. After all, it can move from the sensible to the intelligible; this is what distinguishes soul from νοῦς. The soul is still soul when it thinks; at least, it still exists.[863] The treatment goes into the soul's transition from the contemplation of ideas to the thought of the contemplator. In other words, the problem is how the soul is present to thought when it itself thinks. There is a movement that the soul goes through, namely from the consideration of ideas to the consideration of itself. The change in question is thus between the soul's thinking of ideas to the soul's thinking of the soul thinking. This is parallel to the treatment of νοῦς in the first part of the chapter, and the distinction lies in the soul's capacity to turn to intellect.

The problem of the relation to our life here has been abandoned in favour of the problem of the contemplating soul's self-awareness in disembodied life. Presumably the contemplating soul's freedom from memory is just what has been gained by the beneficial forgetfulness described earlier.[864] Contemplating ideas presupposes that one has forgotten one's embodied existence. The soul is able, being on the edge of νοῦς, to enter it;[865] in less flowery language, the soul can turn to thought. Then the soul will possess a distinction (παραλλαγή), that is, relative to the thing that stays the same, namely νοῦς. The soul comes to think, and when it does so, it comes to think itself. Where exactly are we meant to see memory here? One possibility is between the phases where the

---

862 Of course, Plotinus does think that νοῦς has self-awareness (not memory of self); see esp. V 3 10. Another possibility of understanding the change here is the move from potential to actual self. But that is mentioned several lines back (IV 4 2 8–10).

863 IV 4 2 29.

864 IV 3 32 esp. 13–15, above p. 190; see above p. 153 for forms of self-awareness.

865 IV 4 2 16–18; cf. the passages where soul is the last of the intelligibles, IV 8 7 5–6, IV 6 3 5 (HBT). This presumably concerns what the soul is, and so what it can, but need not do, viz. think. Further it is necessary that the soul here is individual; in other words, there are forms of individuals. On this question see the literature listed above in fn. 458.

soul actually contemplates, and before it does so. Thus there would be no call for νοῦς to have memory since νοῦς does not undergo this movement, only soul when it turns to contemplation. But this is not apparently the movement that Plotinus considers as a candidate for the one that might be necessary for the contemplating soul to remember itself, should it turn out to be able to do this. Instead, he considers one which was excluded from νοῦς in the first part of the discussion of memory of self, a movement between νοῦς contemplating itself, and contemplating all the ideas it encompasses.[866] For he continues:

> Or one should not say that a movement (μεταβολή) takes place when [νοῦς moves] to himself from the things belonging to himself nor when [he moves] from himself to the others. For he is everything and both are one.[867] But does the soul, when it is in the intelligible, experience this one thing after another, in relation to itself and to the things in itself?[868]

Plotinus answers this question in the negative, and, in this way excluding movement (μεταβολή) from the soul as well, excludes from it all memory. Phenomenologically speaking, if it makes sense to judge these things by our experience of thinking,[869] this conclusion seems right. When we move from thinking of the things we can think of to thinking of soul (roughly: what I am), then this movement is not one marked by memory, not, that is, marked by a change of time.

This passage is of interest because it seemingly marks the development or progression of the soul to thought.[870] The soul is unified with νοῦς but without being destroyed. The question then naturally arises, in which form the soul continues to exist when it is unified with νοῦς. This question is of importance for, as we shall see, it is possible for the soul to part company with νοῦς. So obviously, it continues to exist

---

866 IV 4 2 10–14.

867 Note the masculine reflexives, as at line 1. Obviously not νοῦς, in a straightforward sense, nor, for grammatical reasons soul (as AHA translate, as against HBT's neuter). The soul occurs as subject in line 22. So the "he" with which we began the chapter, would be one alternative, or else it would be soul insofar as it thinks; since one premise in the argument is that he is everything, and this would be true of some him only in virtue of νοῦς.

868 Ἢ οὐδὲ μεταβολὴν λεκτέον γίνεσθαι, ὅταν ἀπὸ τῶν ἑαυτοῦ ἐφ' ἑαυτόν, καὶ ὅταν ἀφ' ἑαυτοῦ ἐπὶ τὰ ἄλλα· πάντα γὰρ αὐτός ἐστι καὶ ἄμφω ἕν. Ἀλλ' ἡ ψυχὴ ἐν τῷ νοητῷ οὖσα τοῦτο πάσχει τὸ ἄλλο καὶ ἄλλο πρὸς αὐτὴν καὶ τὰ ἐν αὐτῇ; IV 4 2 lines 20–24. In the last part of the sentence I follow AHA.

869 See above p. 194 for this method of Plotinus' in investigating disembodied thinking.

870 Cf., above all, IV 7 10.

while thinking, and to have the capacity to exist while not contemplating ideas.

For the moment, however, the point is clear that when the soul contemplates the ideas, then the same holds of it as of νοῦς, namely, that it admits of no movement (μεταβολή). The change of the soul to thinking, the progression into νοῦς (προσχωρεῖν εἴσω)[871] is not the relevant point, but rather the lack of any movement when it is thinking. Then, it is unable to register any movement at all, including the one it has undergone in starting to think.[872] So the soul and νοῦς are both one and two,[873] the soul continues to exist, although what it is doing is thinking, and as such it is intellect. Rather surprisingly, Plotinus allows it self-awareness when in this state:

> When therefore in this state it could not move (μεταβάλλοι) but would be unalterably (ἀτρέπτως) disposed to thinking, while having awareness (συναίσθησις) of itself, as (ὡς) having become one and the same with the intelligible object, at the same time (ἅμα).[874]

Two important questions arise from this passage: what is the modality of ἀτρέπτως? And what function does the "as" (ὡς) clause have? The way in which the soul is "unalterably"[875]disposed to νοῦς is of course relevant to what will happen next. The soul still has to possess the capacity to turn away from νοῦς, so the phrase must mean something like "unalterably as long as it is inclined to think". So ἀτρέπτως means little more than "fixedly".

The problem with the ὡς at the end is partly one of tense, and partly one of function. Let us take the point about tense first: if γενομένη means "having become", then the question arises as to why the soul's grasp of its previous state is not a matter of memory, rather than self-awareness. For once the soul has become the same as the object of thought, it might conceivably remember what it was before this change. Obviously, in Plotinus' view, however, the self-awareness is not of the past becoming, but is merely of the awareness of the soul, i. e. as an intelligible object, which the soul

---

871 IV 4 2 18.
872 Cf. IV 4 1 7–11.
873 IV 4 2 29.
874 Οὕτως οὖν ἔχουσα οὐκ ἂν μεταβάλλοι ἀλλὰ ἔχοι ἂν ἀτρέπτως πρὸς νόησιν ὁμοῦ ἔχουσα τὴν συναίσθησιν αὐτῆς, ὡς ἐν ἅμα τῷ νοητῷ ταὐτὸν γενομένη. IV 4 2 30–32 trans. AHA altered. Bob Sharples' comments on this passage have been invaluable.
875 AHA's translation.

becomes when it thinks; for νοῦς and intelligible object are the same, as in thinking the soul is also identical with thought. The soul is aware of itself when thinking because it is thinking *inter alia* of itself. Thus there is no memory in the soul spanning its change from not-thinking to thinking the ideas.

As to the function of the ὡς clause, it may give the content the soul is aware of (taking ὡς as meaning "that"), or the reason why it has this awareness (taking ὡς as meaning "because"). A reason for adopting the latter reading is that it seems to be Plotinus' view that soul only has knowledge of itself when it thinks, and so this clause provides the reason for the possibility of self-awareness. The soul in thinking, thinks itself, and is identical with the object of its thoughts. But then the question arises as to how this awareness escapes the strictures on changing attention from objects of thinking to the thinker.[876] When the soul thinks of ideas, that is one act, and when it thinks of itself as a soul, that is another. How is it to move from the one to the other? Again, the idea may be in the background that since thought and its object are the same no movement is involved.[877] When turned to intellect, the soul thinks all ideas so no movement between ideas is necessary.

Thus when the soul contemplates, it does not remember. Plotinus now turns to the genesis of actual memory for the soul: it acquires memory when it leaves[878] thinking. It must, for this to be possible, have kept the capacity to perceive, and presumably, the capacity to want perception. Parting company with thinking entails perceiving. In fact in some way, when the soul thinks, it must have a potential desire for perception and individuality that goes with it to explain why it cannot stand the unity with thought. For what else could disturb thought, that is the unity of thinker and what he thinks, if not perception? Plotinus describes

---

876 See above p. 204.

877 IV 4 2 8–14 on νοῦς.

878 προκύψασα cf. IV 3 15 1, (for the contrary movement into thought see IV 4 2 18) and *Phaedrus* 249C3. HBT refer to IV 8 1 for the topos of the soul's descent; there at least, it seems to be something which Plotinus had done often. The present passage is much closer to IV 3 15 5–6 where the soul is said to be weighed down by its forgetfulness (λήθη). The genesis of memory here should be compared with the genesis of time, when soul leaves intellect (III 7 11 14–19); see Beierwaltes 1967: 249–252. On the question of the explanation of the soul's descent, see O'Brien 1977, 1993; 5–18, in II 9 8. O'Brien comes to the conclusion that it is caused by necessity which is not the expression of constraint, since it is natural (see esp. IV 3 13 17–20).

the factor responsible for moving the soul away from thought as the desire to be different. It is this desire that distinguishes soul from νοῦς, and which the soul must have even when thinking, even if it cannot be realised while the soul thinks.

When the soul acquires its individuality by turning away from thought, it acquires actual memory, and it might seem obvious that this memory is constitutive of the soul's identity, particularly because memory preserves at least one kind of continuity with earlier phases of existence. But things are not so straightforward, for the following reason. After contemplating the soul remembers embodied life as it was before contemplating. But when it is actually contemplating it has no actual memory, as we have seen. In the *Introduction* we mentioned the relation between self and memory:[879] identity of the subject is a necessary condition for memory. If this is so, then the soul's identity has to be preserved, when it contemplates. So identity cannot be constituted by actual memory.

What does the soul remember when it turns away from thought?[880] It has memory of both thought and of perceptibles.[881] This is what we would expect. The division into the two kinds of memory is maintained.[882] But there are difficulties. Above all, we have to square the concept of memory that is being used here with everything that went before. The problems are evident in the following lines:

---

879 See *Introduction* p. 1–2.
880 The spatial language used to describe this event is Plotinus' own. On the places of the soul when it leaves the intellect, see IV 3 15 and 17, and cf. IV 3 9 21–26.
881 IV 4 3 3 Ms. w reads ἑαυτῆς, which HBT read instead of ἐφεξῆς (MaK and Bréhier translate so too), citing IV 4 2 1: the idea is perhaps that the memory which the soul does not have of itself in IV 4 2, it then acquires on leaving thought, as part of its individuation (see above on individuals in thinking p. 204). It wants itself, and presumably therefore also has a memory of who it is. The problem with this reading is that the self is nowhere else a proper object of memory for Plotinus; the argument in the present chapter has to do with kinds of memory, intellectual and sensible, which determine the place of the individual soul. (One might object to this line of thought that in IV 4 2 Plotinus at least considers the possibility of a memory of oneself, and does not argue against it that the self is not something one can remember.)
882 See above p. 144 on IV 3 25 25.

in general [the soul] is and becomes what it remembers. For remembering is either thinking (νοεῖν) or representing (φαντάζεσθαι); and the representation is in the soul not by possession (ἔχειν) but just as it sees, so is it disposed.[883]

Hardly modest claims on behalf of memory! Evidently, when the soul is actually contemplating, unalterably turned towards the ideas, then it is not actually remembering anything. This fact makes it necessary for there to be memory which is not conscious. The point is that memory is not just something the soul has, rather it determines the fate of the soul. Determining what the soul is does not mean determining the identity of the individual soul, not what soul is in general; rather memory determines what the individual soul is at each stage (intellectual, heavenly or earthly), or what it will become.[884] Perhaps the idea is that you can only become what you have a memory of, since becoming something requires inclination, and one must have in mind that to which one is inclined, and that is not present, but must form part of one's past.[885] Of course, this memory is not actual, but potential, in that while contemplating there is no actual memory. Three cases may be distinguished among these memories, depending on where they lead the soul. You have a memory of having thought, it pleases you, and you rise, elevated by the memo-

---

883 IV 4 3 6–8. On this passage see esp. Warren 1965. He treats IV 4 4 as offering the fundamental tenets of Plotinus' theory. In sum he thinks of habitual behaviour and behaviour according to dispositions as types of unconscious memory. Conscious μνήμη 'properly so called (re-cognition of the past)': divided into memory of sensibles and intelligibles. On possession versus disposition, cf. having versus not having cognition in III 6 2 39–41, above p. 124.

884 Following Blumenthal (1971: 94): memory makes the soul what it is and controls its descent IV 4 3 7. Blumenthal quotes Trouillard 1955: 38: 'Dis-moi ce dont tu te souviens, et je te dirai qui tu es'; and refers to the unconscious memories mentioned at IV 4 7–13. This, of course, does not mean that memory constitutes the individual (pace Inge 1968: 227, Gerson 1994: 180–3, with n. 48, Wilberding 2006: 45–48, with n. 326), merely the inclinations of the soul at any given stage in its peregrinations. Clearly, in general, i.e. in all the stages of its existence, memory does not constitute the self: the soul does that, memory gives direction to the soul's striving. The dependence of memory on the soul, is part of memory's modesty for Plotinus (above p. 114). Brisson (2005: 246 n. 31) suggests that there is a system of rewards and punishments in the background here, past existence determining future ones, and this implies memory. Just how he takes this implication, he does not say.

885 Cf. the *Philebus* 35A-D. The point about desire is that it requires that we have a memory of the state which we desire, because this state cannot be the actual present state of the body.

ry.[886] Memory of earthy pleasures appeal to you and you sink correspond-ingly. And the third possibility is that the soul stays in the heavens, held by its memories.[887]

Now, however, to the detail. Here Plotinus says that "remembering was thinking or representing", but where have we already met this claim? We might think to begin with of the ascription of memory to the representative faculty.[888] And that is surely part of the answer. What about thinking? Memory of thoughts was *also* ascribed to the rep-resentative faculty, albeit in a rather hesitant fashion.[889] There is no way that memory was, strictly speaking, thinking; neither when thinking, nor when perceiving but also having memory of thinking, was remembering thinking.

Plotinus is obviously talking loosely here. Let us try to work out what he means by this claim. It is meant to buttress his view that the soul is or becomes that which it has in its memory. Consider the following scenario. At some stage the soul thinks the ideas, and if it is later to turn back to-wards thought then it must have a memory of thought. This was the sec-ond kind of memory from the start of the enquiry: the soul has memory of its own innate thoughts only in a different sense of memory from that directed at its experience.[890] But there this kind of memory was said to be without time. If the soul always thinks of ideas, and thoughts are not temporal, then there is no reason why my memory of ideas should be fixed to a particular time. Perhaps the following is a way of understanding the claim that memory was thinking. The role of the representative fac-

---

886 McCumber 1978: 164 on IV 4 3 refers to IV 6 3 10–17 for soul as being on the boundary of the intelligible, or between the sensible and the intelligible. McCumber understands becoming the intelligible in IV 4 3 10 as the progression inwards of IV 4 2, on the grounds that a "movement into memory" must be the type of memory referred to at IV 3 25 27–34 as the actualisation of the soul's "symphyta".' It would be happier to speak of recollection being a movement to the forms, and not speak of memory because that gives the impression that one did remember – "retain" – the forms. McCumber offers a picture of the soul moving from a position on the boundaries of the intellect to one purely within it, only then is "it" (presumably: the soul) identical with its objects, for-getting itself, and without any memory at all (IV 4 1 6–11). But we should note that the soul still of course has memory potentially insofar as it may not stand the unity with νοῦς; this is the point of IV 4 3.

887 IV 4 3 4–5, 8–10, Alt 1993: 232.

888 HBT refer us to IV 3 29 31, as does Brisson 2005: 246, n. 32.

889 IV 3 30.

890 IV 3 25 25 above p. 144.

ulty in recollecting thoughts was to present thoughts in a definition. And perhaps this product of recollection is what is here being called thinking. So we may understand the claim that "memory was thinking" to mean that memory was also directed at thinking, thus an act of memory might be recollecting thought.

A striking side to the description of remembering here is that it is not merely the possession of an image or representation. Remembering is in[891] the soul not by the possession of a representation, but through the way the soul sees: its state or disposition corresponds to the things it cognises.[892] The orientation of the soul lies in its memory. This seems to go against the separation between desire and memory in IV 3 28; but we suggested in our discussion of that chapter[893] that this separation is a question of the formation of character within a phase of the soul's journey, embodiment, whereas what is at stake here and in the next chapter[894] is the movement between phases. But actually this view of memory is compatible with the way Plotinus has determined memory before. For the *quasi* definition[895] had it that memory is a strengthening of the soul towards something that appeared to it, such that the soul is disposed towards it as if to something present. And one can understand the conception of memory here in the same way. Remembering thinking means that the soul is strengthened towards thinking, and is disposed towards thinking as though it were present, and so too with perception.

The soul has this freedom of movement between perception and thought just because it does not possess thought, that is the actual thinking of forms "perfectly", as does νοῦς[896] but only in a secondary way. The new function that memory acquires is of guiding the soul through its different phases. To do this, memory is not merely a representation, but rather a developed way of looking at things. Memory is not just guided

---

891 AHA translates "comes to the soul", presumably to avoid saying that something is in the soul without the soul possessing it (which is just how HBT translate). It might be possible to read possession here as dispositional: having the representation as a disposition is contrasted with the actual view; and it is the latter which gives the soul its marching orders. On possession cf. IV 6 3 12–16.
892 With HS following Beutler in the deletion of the second οἷα in IV 4 4 8.
893 Above p. 169.
894 IV 4 4 9–10.
895 Above p. 120.
896 Cf. IV 4 2 11. HBT follow the *Theologia* in connecting οὐχ οὕτω τελείως πάντα γίνεται, and Kirchhoff in deleting καὶ beforehand: soul is – in general – both perceptibles and intelligibles and so not perfectly either. For the soul as both intelligibles and perceptibles, cf. De an. III 8 431b22–3.

by what we want; it also directs our desires in the longer term. Plotinus is here stretching his conception of memory to its limits. The next two chapters, the final ones discussing human memory, continue this treatment of the relation between memory and what we want, and the course we take in the world.

3.3.3 Memory and the good

What can memory do in relation to the good? The crucial point is that the good is something we have cognition of,[897] but do not primarily remember. Even here, when embodied, we do not need memory in order to think of the good, in that we then have just the same cognitive capacities as when we are not embodied. Although that sounds optimistic, we must remember the conditions of embodiment play a central role in Plotinus' view of the constitution of our desires. For he says that when the soul has turned towards perception, then it has what it wants "according to its memory and representation".[898] This is a hard saying which needs interpretation. A first approach to its meaning lies in the fact that, put negatively, in a way we do have memory of the good, but not of the good itself. We remember good things, in which the good is not isolated as such. Put positively, the soul can remember previous phases of its existence in such a way that it strives back to them, in other words they serve, in memory, as things the soul represents to itself as good.

Why do representation *and* memory need to be both mentioned in connection with the good? One might think that representation and memory are mentioned here together because representation is being identified with memory. Plotinus would then be saying that one has what one wants corresponding to one's memory i.e. representation of the thing. This is a problem we have met in another guise already, namely whether memory is simply the remaining of a representation for Plotinus. We came to the conclusion that it was not, that in fact representation is just one condition for memory.[899] Here too, Plotinus does not force us to conclude that memory and representation are the same. For representation has other functions than serving memories, above all guiding de-

---

897 For the cognition of the good see VI 9 4, Hadot 1994: 148–156.
898 IV 4 4 5–6. Warren 1965: 253 has this saying as epigraph. He translates, 'If the soul should devote itself to the things below, then it has proportionately to memory and imagination, what it longed for.'
899 See above p. 175.

sires.[900] One's desires might be motivated by the concrete memory of something occurring in the past, or by a representation which is not attached to a concrete situation. Either one is a conceivable way in which desires can depend on memory or representation. They are distinct ways in which something can be seen as good when we are not thinking of the good itself.

Up to now in the discussion of memory, we have apparently been concerned with soul and intellect, among the three hypostases. The good has not directly been the subject of discussion. However, we now have an allusion to what may be the three hypostases: soul (here: "the third things"), intellect, and the good (here: "the first things").[901] The point of introducing them here is that body is not a decisive impediment to getting from the third to the first. It is Plotinus' view that both when thinking ideas and when actually perceiving, i.e. when in the body, the soul is capable of thinking of the good. Thus memory and indeed representation do not provide access to the good itself, they provide only a memory or a representation of it. Neither of these is identical with the good, so while they provide orientation for the soul, the kind of orientation they provide depends on the way the soul remembers or represents the good. This is obviously a continuation of the view of memory from the last chapter. There,[902] memory determined the position in the cycle the soul then inhabits: "in general it becomes and is that which it remembers". Now Plotinus describes the way in which the soul is guided by memory.[903]

Here, Plotinus actually retracts much of the importance which the last chapter appears to bestow on memory, when he says that memory even of the best things is not itself the best. But this view seems reasonable enough in itself. Memory of the good is not the same as thinking of the good. For the identity of thinking with what is thought,[904] makes contemplation of the good identical with the good. The reason for the role memory plays in relation to the good is that when one is inclined to sensation, committed to the sensible world, then one has what one

---

900 See IV 4 17.
901 IV 4 4 3–5: εἰς τὰ τρίτα ἀπὸ τῶν πρώτων ἡ ἄφιξις, reading τρίτα with Creuzer. HBT compare I 8 2.25, VI 8.7.1. Why the first things are in the plural is a mystery. There seems also to be a problem with Plotinus' expression here, since he says that the soul, "the third things", can get at ("arrive at") the first ones.
902 See above p. 208.
903 IV 4 4–5.
904 See Menn 2001.

wants, that is one has desires directed to what appears good, in a way that corresponds to one's representative faculty and memory. This is then the way the hard saying we started this section from is to be understood.[905] What one wants, in other words, is not the good, it just corresponds to what appears good, or what one has in one's memory as good. Both, however, are different from the good. The development of the idea from the last chapter is clear. There we were told that memory is not merely the possession of a representation, rather it is a question of a disposition depending on what the soul sees.

Now, the question of awareness is discussed:[906]

> But one must understand memory not only in the sense of a kind of perception that one is remembering, but as existing when the soul is disposed according to what it has previously experienced or contemplated. For it could happen that, even when one is not conscious that one has something, one holds it to oneself more strongly than if one knew.[907]

As we shall see, the point of awareness here is that Plotinus wishes to explain the relation between memory and thinking ideas. Thus he is discussing the memory universal-problem.[908] Plotinus actually thinks that awareness makes any activity of which one is aware more feeble.[909] Being aware that one is reading makes the reading less intense or concentrated, for example. So too here with memory as a power of the soul, which is weakened by reflexion on what one is doing. This fits with the way Plotinus understands the concept of memory as the strengthening of the soul with respect to something which appears to it.[910] Now this strengthening of the soul has a decisive effect on the way our striving is

---

905 IV 4 5–7.
906 IV 4 4 8–12 ἐν τῷ οἷον αἰσθάνεσθαι ὅτι μνημονεύει, ἀλλὰ καὶ ὅταν διακέηται κατὰ τὰ πρόσθεν παθήματα ἢ θεάματα. Γένοιτο γὰρ ἄν, καὶ μὴ παρακολουθοῦντα ὅτι ἔχει. This passage is a reminiscence of Heraclitus DK 22B56.
907 IV 4 4 7–11. Trans. AHA: Δεῖ δὲ τὴν μνήμην λαμβάνειν οὐ μόνον ἐν τῷ οἷον αἰσθάνεσθαι ὅτι μνημονεύει, ἀλλὰ καὶ ὅταν διακέηται κατὰ τὰ πρόσθεν παθήματα ἢ θεάματα. Γένοιτο γὰρ ἄν, καὶ μὴ παρακολουθοῦντα ὅτι ἔχει, ἔχειν παρ' αὐτῷ ἰσχυροτέρως ἢ εἰ εἰδείη. Cf. the treatment of virtue in I 2 4 19–25: Virtue is 'a sight and impression of what is seen, implanted and active, like sight with regard to what is seen. Did it not have and recollect them? It has them, but inactive, laid aside without light. So that they be illuminated and it is to know that they are in it, it must push [them?] to that which gives light. He had, not them, but impressions.'
908 Above, p. 3.
909 See above p. 153.
910 See above p. 120.

orientated. But there is something new here in that memory does not necessarily involve a conscious act of remembering ("perception that one is remembering"). Recall our example:

Example (E) Socrates remembers (at t2) that he saw Theaetetus two days ago (at t1).

The present model of memory involves Socrates in doing nothing at t2; whereas up to now,[911] Plotinus seemed to be saying that Socrates has to say (either aloud or to himself) or perceive that something is the case at t2. The difference is not merely that between actual and potential memory. Nothing in the present passage suggests that at t2 Socrates could say or perceive in the way the previous concept of memory requires. The decisive thing here seems to be representation on account of the way it affects desire, that is the general direction of our striving. We have seen in our discussion of the question of which part of the soul is responsible for memory that there is a degree of communication between the various faculties,[912] hence representations, better: representations serving memory, may in Plotinus' model of the soul communicate themselves to desire, thus modifying it.

Thus experiences (perceptions, perhaps also passions) and things thought of scientifically, even if they cannot actually be ascribed by the soul to itself, and so are unconscious, can be said to be remembered.[913] The point is that such experiences can have a greater effect on the soul's motivation than others which it is able to attribute to itself. This conception allows Plotinus to explain the fact that the soul, while actually thinking of ideas cannot perform a conscious act of memory; but nonetheless memory causes thinking ideas to come to a halt.

Now let us turn to the implications of remembering being an activity. If the soul has memory of what it has contemplated when it leaves the (immediate) presence of the ideas, then, Plotinus concludes,[914] it must have (the capacity of) memory while it is thinking too. We have here

---

911 See above p. 163 for a discussion of Plotinus saying that remembering is saying that.
912 See above p. 167 on IV 3 28.
913 On consciousness see above p. 153. One might take the present passage either to be saying one does not as a matter of fact ascribe the experiences to oneself or one cannot. The latter would be very strong, but gives the passage more point.
914 IV 4 4 14–20.

also a variant of the argument from activity:[915] remembering and thinking are not the same activity, and thinking is not the actualisation of the
capacity to remember. Thinking ideas makes memory disappear, but in
such a way that we have it again when thinking ceases. Active thinking
is not active remembering but does not preclude implicit remembering.

Whereas Aristotle used a mundane conception of thought (doing
maths is not the same as remembering doing maths), for Plotinus it
has an altogether grander significance. For it describes a whole phase of
existence of the soul. But I think that the core of the argument, i.e.
that memory and thinking are different activities, remains the same. Plotinus uses it to offer a last argument against impressions: the impressions
would still be there, if memory were impressions. Instead, it is a capacity
that can be rested and reactivated.[916]

The final discussion of memory and the disembodied human soul, in
IV 4 5, makes it clear that memory in heaven is the same as it is here, and
also requires a body, at least in its objects. Plotinus discusses above all our
present capacities and those we have when either thinking ideas or de-
scending from the ideas.[917] When souls move from contemplation to
heaven, they are in bodies, as it were, heavenly bodies,[918] and are able
to remember the souls they knew before, either because the latter have
a similar shape, or because their character is the same. Plotinus is further
concerned to show that memory is not the means by which we know
ideas, rather we know them by the very same capacity that we used to
contemplate them when we turned towards thinking.

We are dealing here again with the relation between the capacity for
memory and the capacity to think. Thus it is concerned with the universal-memory problem. So what is its relation to other cognitive capacities,
above all the intellect? We have memory on the one hand of the intelligibles, that is, ideas , and the question arises whether thinking of the intelligibles arose through this same capacity. This is a conclusion that Plotinus resists strenuously. It is only when the intelligibles are not known
("seen")[919] that we have memory of them. That is to say, present knowl-

---

915 See above pp. 30, 195.
916 IV 4 5 16–17.
917 HBT II b 509 cite IV 3 15 1 on the three places for the soul.
918 On astral bodies in Plotinus, see above fn. 663.
919 IV 4 5 2–3 Ἢ εἰ μὲν μὴ αὐτὰ ἑωρῶμεν, μνήμῃ, εἰ δ' αὐτά, ᾧ κἀκεῖ ἑωρῶμεν.
    ἑωρῶμεν: the tense is odd in the protasis. Harder, Bréhier, MacK translate as
    though it were present; AHA translates, 'If we did not see them themselves…',
    whereas for memory we must have seen them, but not be seeing them now. Per-

edge of ideas is actualised by the ideas themselves and not by some past experience of them. Thinking is not mediated, for example by representation. There is here perhaps an implicit criticism of speaking of the present thought of ideas as an act of memory. For doing so might be considered a simile, and Plotinus thinks that similes and syllogisms are not to be used in talking about the way we know ideas since we know them here, when embodied, just by the same power that we do there, when disembodied.[920]

Thus the power of memory is not concerned (directly) with ideas. This confirms the view of memory from which Plotinus started, namely that in the strict sense there is no memory of one's own, innate thoughts, since these are always occurring.[921] Plotinus allows this way of talking because of the way the "ancients" spoke; here he is critical of it, insofar as it presents a metaphor for the actual thinking of ideas. Memory of thinking is divided into memory of discursive thoughts on the one hand – thoughts I have had consciously in embodied existence; and recollection of the ideas the soul is always thinking. Recollection (ἀνάμνησις) is, however, only the means of getting to the ideas, and not the way that they are then present.[922] The present chapter confirms that Plotinus is very clear that the actual thinking of ideas is not simply a question of memory. For he says here that our memory is not of the ideas themselves. This can be understood to mean that we remember having thought them. Our grasp of the ideas themselves is through thinking, and we do that either *here*, or there. Thinking is the same, whether here in corporeal existence, i.e. competing with actual perception or there, when we only think.[923]

So memory begins, as we have already seen, only when we leave the uninterrupted presence of ideas, and are in heaven, perhaps on the way to earthly existence.[924] Plotinus' very tentative treatment of what we will remember in heaven, either coming from here, or from thinking, is very important because it makes clear what one important class of objects

haps the present in the protasis has been replaced by the scribe's eye rushing forwards to the apodosis.
920 IV 4 5 5–8 Οὐ γὰρ εἰκασίᾳ δεῖ χρώμενον ἀποφαίνεσθαι οὐδὲ συλλογισμῷ τὰς ἀρχὰς ἄλλοθεν εἰληφότι, ἀλλ' ἔστι περὶ τῶν νοητῶν, ὡς λέγεται, καὶ ἐνθάδε οὖσι τῷ αὐτῷ λέγειν, ὃ δύναμιν ἔχει τἀκεῖ θεωρεῖν.
921 IV 4 25, above p. 144.
922 See above p. 183.
923 Cf. IV 8 1 for the repeated acts of contemplation.
924 IV 4 3, above p. 206.

of memory are, namely souls.⁹²⁵ He refers to the souls whom we will recognise, and interestingly discusses how we will recognise (ἐπιγινώσκειν) them. Recognition requires recognisable characteristics, even if the souls in question have changed their shapes; they will still be recognisable from their conversation or character.⁹²⁶ Thus even in these elevated spheres memory remains modest, dependent not only on subjects, that is on souls, who may also be the objects of memory, but also on a grasp of their characteristics, previously perceived and enabling the soul to recognise earlier friends.

3.4 Conclusion: Plotinus on the six problems about memory

Let us conclude this chapter by summarising Plotinus' approach to the six problems about memory in the *Introduction*.

(P1) The derivation problem. For Plotinus memory is grounded on the more fundamental capacities of the soul to perceive and to think, and is divided according to which of these it has as its objects. The derivation is mediated by representation, as that which remains from a perception and as that which articulates a thought, when thought consciously by the embodied soul. Here, as with Aristotle, memory is modest, that is, dependent on existing subjects, and also on their capacity for perception. For memory is of things acquired, perceiving and learning. This acquisition is dated in the past of the remembering subject. The soul is purely active and cannot undergo anything such as taking on impressions in perception, so Plotinus has to find another way of explaining what the soul does in perception. Rather in perception it reads the affected body, and

---

925 IV 4 5 13–31. In line 15, he refers back to an earlier text, where he has said that soul there will remember many souls from here. HBT and HS refer to IV 3 27 15–18; where the question is asked what the soul, when alone will say. (See also IV 3 32 20–23.) There, however, it is the soul which has parted company from the soul from the world (IV 3 27 1–3), and which is therefore alone. Here, we are concerned with another part of the cycle, namely when the soul has come away from the ideas, and is in heaven; that is to say the point in the cycle is that described at IV 4 3 1–3. It is *between* the ideas and down here.

926 This latter point raises an interesting question of Plotinian psychology, since the souls are said to have lost their πάθη (IV 4 5 20, cf. IV 3 32 4), presumably their passions, and it seems that one needs passions to have character (IV 4 5 19 ἦθος, τρόπος). Cf. above fn. 663.

says: such and such is the case. Thus representations are not images, but provide part of the capacity to make propositional claims. When we actively remember, we do something, most characteristically, we say or perceive that something was the case. Representation is connected to all phenomena, in that the soul represents things to itself, and in so doing they appear to it.

(P2) The present-past problem. Plotinus' *quasi* definition of memory can be rendered as follows. The soul has the capacity to be disposed to something that appears to it, as though that thing were present when it no longer is. In the case of perception the capacity of the soul is strengthened, i. e. developed with respect to the object, so as to be able to represent it to the soul. This representation provides a crucial element of the capacity to make a memory claim. Representation forms a bridge between now (t2) and what is remembered (that which was perceived at t1). It is not the representation itself that is remembered, but that which is represented, what appears, the phenomenon, as it were: that which appeared in the perception at t1. The remaining of representation is one condition for memory, another is connected with the way the representation is present in the memory act. That is to say, the representation is present in such a way that the absent thing appears to the soul, as is required by Plotinus' *quasi* definition. Plotinus recognises a second form of memory, namely recollection of ideas. This second sense is not strictly a memory act, since the soul is always thinking, thus the act of recollection is not related to the past.

(P3) The memory-representation problem. One reading of φαντασία is that representations are in fact images, corresponding to a translation of φαντασία by "imagination". Plotinus' concept of φαντασία, however, is conceptual and propositional for two reasons. Firstly, because perception ends in φαντασία, a perception can be remembered by being preserved as a representation. This implies that representation is just as propositional and conceptual as perception is. The second reason points in the same direction, namely its function in thinking. Representations unfold, i. e. articulate, ideas as a kind of expression of them. Representation serves other purposes than memory for Plotinus, especially desire, and memory is picked out by its relation to the past. Thus it is restricted to those souls which experience alteration. But how time is grasped, and so how memory representations and claims are distinguished from others, is not something he discusses. He does have at least rudimentary answers to this question, in that actual remembering is doing something specific with representations. Even when such an act of memory does not occur (at t2), memories can have an effect on what we do and what we want. They, and representations, do this because they can modify what we want, what we strive for. This is above all relevant at that point in Plotinus' theory when the soul is thinking ideas and so is not able to remember actually, but nonetheless the soul may turn away from thought, and for this to be possible memory must be able to be effective, without any act of memory taking place.

(P4) The memory-recollection problem. Plotinus tends to think of recollection in terms of recollecting ideas. Recollection is thus connected with the ability to learn things, namely theoretical truths about the ideas, in a good Platonic style. Since this recollection relates not to what is acquired but to what souls always think, innate ideas, there is no time involved. But he also uses the phenomenon of recollecting to argue against memory impressions. Imperfect recall and the interrupted capacity to recall things are both used to show that the straightforward presence of material impressions does not explain memory.

(P5) The self-memory problem. The task pursued at greatest length by Plotinus is the investigation of what the subject of memory is; a question he answers firstly with regard to the faculty responsible for memory, namely an independent faculty of representation. He then also makes clear that the soul alone is the subject of memory. These are not moves that one need make: the subject might be, as for Aristotle, the concrete animal, and the faculty, perception. He then turns to the different, but related question of when, in its peregrinations, the soul remembers, and what it remembers. This assumes, of course, that souls migrate and change their state. His theory of the human soul posits a split between the practically orientated part, which includes vegetative faculties of the soul, and the contemplative part. After death the soul splits depending on whether it is orientated towards theory or practical life. Plotinus thinks that both soul and the shade in the underworld, which is the image of the soul, have memory. And their memories are not simply divided such that perceptions belong to the one, and thought to the other. For if that were the case, there would then be nothing joining them, they would be two living things, and not a single self, which is a general precondition for the existence of memory. Rather the practical shade must also have some innate learning, e.g. what justice is. And the soul itself, on the way to contemplating ideas, will remember as much of its life as is fitting for a civilised person. The point of the division between shade and soul is that it reflects different interests, and not in a metaphysical sense different entities: Heracles in Hades is the same soul as Heracles in heaven; merely the one is the shade of the other. It is an ethical distinction and not a metaphysical one. Thus there is no rupture in the self, such as would make it possible for someone to remember something someone else had experienced. Nonetheless, there do seem to be problems with the transitivity of memory, if we hold onto the identity of Heracles. One would usually think that if Tully and Cicero are the same person, then if Tully can remember Quintus, then so can Cicero. But this does not apparently hold with the relation between soul and shade. Heracles in heaven has different memories from Heracles in Hades. One way out of the problem is to say that they both could remember the same things if they had the motive to do so, if it were good for them and they were able to see that it were good for themselves. And if there is a moral distinction, then the two do not remember the same things because, although they are the same person, the two aspects are distinguished by the kind of motivation they have. The fact that these two remember different things after death, although the intellectual soul possesses the capacity to remember everything that the embodied soul has experienced, is to be explained by their different interests. Thus the split in the soul does not mean that there are two subjects of the same memory, rather there are two memories which belong to different aspects of the same soul.

(P6) The universal-memory problem. The soul is able to think without this activity being the realisation of memory. It is the realisation of the capacity to think. Thus memory is not the primary means of access to ideas, in a theory which holds that it is possible to think without representations. This is a major point of difference between Plotinus and Aristotle. But he does think that for discursive thoughts to be represented to an embodied soul, that is consciously, then there must be a representation. Conversely, for an embodied soul to reach the ideas, it must pass along a series of representations, when recollecting. This is a form of memory, at least Plotinus is prepared to allow it to be called that on the authority of the ancients, although no time is involved. The disembodied soul, even when thinking ideas, must preserve a capacity and is not purely actuality. For when thinking, it still has or may have the capacity for perceiving again, and so ceasing to think. When actually thinking, the soul has no memory either of its embodied existence, as Socrates

e. g. nor indeed of itself as having been a soul. Instead it is said to have consciousness of itself as a soul. The sovereignty of the good, which is also among the things contemplated, lies in the fact that it is always accessible to us not through memory but through intellect, even when we are embodied. But memory, although never of the good itself, in fact determines our interests since what we remember determines our representations, presumably because memory requires representations, and so determines *faute de mieux* what we want. In this way, the souls' peregrinations are determined by memory. It is crucial that memory here only plays the role of the second best way of guiding us, since we remember strictly neither ideas, nor the good. Memory guides us in the absence of the good or ideas.

4 General conclusion: Aristotle and Plotinus on memory[927]

En définitive, ce traité [IV 6] est
donc une conférence sur un
commentaire d'Aristote.[928]

Thus Emile Bréhier's conclusion on Plotinus' treatment of memory in IV 6. If this were true, it would be a resounding testament to the serious use of *De memoria* in later antiquity. For he thinks that Aristotle's theory of memory, both in IV 6 and in IV 3 chapters 25 ff, esp. 29–32 was behind much of what Plotinus had to say on the topic, either by being the subject of Plotinus' criticism, or by being adapted by him to his own theory. Of course, Bréhier's work has been superseded on many fronts – but the editors of Plotinus, Paul Henry and Hans-Rudolf Schwyzer[929], and his translators[930] still persist in the notion that there is a connection between

---

927 This chapter also appears as King 2009a.
928 Bréhier 1927: Vol. IV p. 171.
929 Henry/Schwyzer (cf. *Index Fontium* 1983: vol. III p. 332) refer the following passages to *De mem.*: 1.) IV 3 30 2–3: representation accompanies all acts of thought *De mem.* 1 449b30. Despite the closeness of the phrasing in both passages, this is hardly conclusive; see *De an.* III 7 431a14, 8 432a13–14. 2.) IV 6 3 64 to *De mem.* 1 449b7 (also Armstrong 1984 ad loc.): the same people do not generally have good memories and quick minds. See below on Bréhier. 3.) VI 6 3 4–5 to *De mem.* 1 450a25–7: the problem of the present-past, which I discuss below. 4.) IV 6 1 1 (also Armstrong 1984 ad loc.), where Plotinus denies that perception is an impression, and argues that memory cannot therefore be the remaining of these impressions in the soul, is to be compared with *De mem.* 1 450 a 30–32: the change in perception produces something like an imprint of the percept, like those using seals to make an impression. See below on Bréhier. 5.) The same passage is compared to IV 7 6 39–40.
930 The commentary on IV 6 in Harder, Beutler, Theiler (1962: IV b p. 410) is as follows: "Von Aristoteles ist die Schrift über das Gedächtnis erhalten 449b5 f; ihr folgt auch Alexander von Aphrodisias z. B. De an. 68, 4, 69 12, beide berücksichtigt Plotin." (It is possible he is referring to *De mem.* at 69.19–20, but also that he himself wrote a work with this title which we do not have.) In IV 3 25-IV 4 5 (1962: vol. IIb p. 500–510) they refer several passages to *De mem.*: 1.) IV 3 25 42, if the soul remembers, what is the capacity of the soul responsible, to *De mem.* 1 449b5, which part of the soul does the affection of memory and recol-

Aristotle's *De memoria* and Plotinus' work on memory. Perhaps it is not a *communis opinio*, but it is certainly a common opinion.[931] Bréhier alone of the commentators and translators of Plotinus has taken the trouble to give a detailed account of the way he regards this connection. Henry Blumenthal, writing on "Plotinus' Adaptation of Aristotle's psychology" accepts Bréhier's conclusion:

> Basically, in both Plotinus and Aristotle, the faculty [of memory] retains images presented to it either from sensations below or reasonings above. But

---

lection occur in? On the explanation of memory using φαντασία, see below. 2.) IV 3 26 52, body is an impediment to memory, to *De mem.* 2 453b3 dwarf-like people, i.e. those with disproportionately large upper parts, do not keep the motions (i.e. of the original perception), and thus cannot recollect successfully because of the weight bearing down on the central perceptive part (they also compare *De an.* 408b18). The conclusions Aristotle and Plotinus draw here diverge widely. See below. 3.) IV 3 29 23, the *phantasma* can be a percept to the person remembering, thus making the sight present to the representative faculty when the perception has ceased, since representative capacity and perception are distinct, is to be compared with *De mem.* 1 450b13: the present-past problem; see below. The following texts in IV 6 3 are referred to *De mem.*: 1.) IV 6 3 38: 451a12 practice preserves memory by repeatedly reminding one of the thing in question remembering can happen suddenly on account of hearing something or of practice. So too Bréhier (1927: IV 171), see below. 2.) IV 6 3 52, the old are similarly weak in perception and memory, to *De mem.* 1 450b6, the old are too hard to take on impressions, and so have bad memories (so too Blumenthal 1976: 54). 3.) IV 6 3 1, 74 to 450b16, 30 for the function of impressions in memory, see below. Armstrong (1984: ad loc.) refers the use of ἀνάληψις at IV 6 3 44 (see also line 29), practised messengers are good at performing so-called ἀνάληψις to 451a20: there Aristotle denies that recollection can be an ἀνάληψις of memory. As Plotinus draws the conclusion that memory is s strengthened capacity, and Aristotle that recollection and memory have the same objects, the connection is no more than verbal. Morel (2007: 378–380) sees 5 main similarities with Aristotle: memory derives from sensation, it concerns the past as such, thanks to φαντασία, memory is not passive, and finally that memory is distinct from thought and sensation. I agree entirely.

931 See also Blumenthal 1971: 81, Inge 1968[3]: I 226–8; Gerson 1994: 180–3 does *not* refer to *De mem.* Fleet (1996: at III 6 2 42) refers to *De mem.* 1 450a25. Armstrong (1967 ad loc.) refers to the Stoic controversy whether memory is like an impression – whether it is like a stamp made on wax by a seal, as Cleanthes had thought, or whether this would make memory impossible, as Chrysippus held: later impressions would obliterate earlier ones (SVF II 55–56, esp. 56 17–24 (Sextus adv. math. VII 372); cf., perhaps, Plotinus IV 6 3 25–27, IV 7 6 42–46). Instead, he thinks that the φαντασία which is involved in memory is an alteration of the soul. Either theory would be repugnant to Plotinus.

Plotinus whose discussion in the treatise *On Sensation and Memory* (IV 6) is clearly based on Aristotle's account in the *de Memoria*, as Bréhier showed, does not simply accept it as it stands. He makes several alterations of detail, mainly with a view to removing materialistic or at least apparently materialistic features of Aristotle's account. (Blumenthal 1976: 54)

The purpose of the present chapter is to examine the evidence. A principle behind my interpretation is that one can only compare such theories when one considers them in some depth; having considered both theories separately, we are in a good position to do this. If we restrict ourselves to verbal similarities, the pickings are very meagre; looking at the structure of both theories is both philosophically, and, I think, historically, much more rewarding.[932]

When considering his use of *De memoria*, there is a question of Plotinus' method: his project is not to say what some previous thinker has said, but in this case to say what the subject of memory is, and it need not surprise us if he runs together different positions. Plotinus is doing philosophy, not history of philosophy. Let us look at the end of IV 6. There, he says the following about his opponents:

> For they think about perception and memory as they do about letters written on tablets or pages, and neither do those who assume that the soul is a body see all the impossibilities which their hypothesis involves, nor do those who assume it to be bodiless. IV 6 3 75–79 (trans. AHA)

There are two groups here, both of whom talk about memory being like letters written on writing tablets or pages. They differ on the question whether the soul is bodily or not. They are thus Stoics and Peripatetics. Bréhier noted this, but did not draw the obvious conclusion, that the Stoics are among the opponents Plotinus has in mind. Clearly, Plotinus has a variety of ways of dealing with his opponents. There are texts where he argues closely with one opponent (II 7 against the Stoic notion of mixture), rather than a group of positions (IV 7 against a variety of conceptions of soul), and IV 6 belongs with the latter group. It is directed not merely at Aristotle, but at Peripatetics[933] and Stoics alike.

---

932 Of course, this is not the place to attempt a general assessment of Plotinus' use of Aristotle, or even of his psychology. For the latter, see e. g. Henry 1960, Blumenthal 1971: 12–13, 134–140, 1972, 1976, Corrigan 1981, Emilsson 1988: 31–5, 95–100, Armstrong 1991.

933 Porphyry cites among other Perpatetics Aspasius and Adrastus, along with Alexander of Aphrodisias, as having been consulted by Plotinus (Porphyry, *Vita Plotini* 14.13).

The text just quoted suggests that he has run together the two lines of thought, Peripatetic and Stoic, in his criticism of a wax block model of memory. And one obvious thought is that for the Peripatetic part he is criticising *De memoria*. But another thought is that Plotinus is clearly arguing against a materialist theory of memory such as one finds in the Stoics; and apparently he finds some of the resources for doing this in a Peripatetic theory. The most important similarity lies in the use of the representative faculty (φαντασία) as the capacity of the soul responsible for memory.[934] While this, of course, holds for the Stoics just as much for Peripatetics, one advantage of Aristotle from Plotinus' point of view is that he uses representations and images, but without treating them, or the soul they accrue to, as material. Of course, there are deep differences in the ways in which Plotinus and Aristotle consider the soul to be nonmaterial.

The evidence that Plotinus used *De memoria* is circumstantial: the verbal echoes are minimal, he does not use the Aristotelian text systematically, he does not work through the work refuting the arguments, and he does not quote directly from it, either using Aristotle's name or not. Nonetheless, there seem to be enough points of contact to justify the cautious judgement that he was indeed using *De memoria*. We have to ask, I think, just how someone who has such different metaphysical convictions from Aristotle might use the *Parva Naturalia*. Indeed, one could express one distinction between Plotinus' and Aristotle's views on the soul by saying that while for the latter, things common to body and soul[935] form the bulk, if not the acme, of psychic functions, the end of the soul for Plotinus, as a Platonist, is the separation of the soul from body. He regards this as the soul's return to its origin. Occasionally, this return is said to be a process of recollection (ἀνάμνησις).[936] But of course the conception of memory he works with is based on the

---

934 On the relation between these two theories of representation, see Emilsson 1988: 109–112. Blumenthal (1976: 54–55) sees a major innovation in Plotinus's account in the splitting of the imagination (φαντασία), to account for the possibility that shade and soul have different memories; he tries to find Aristotelian antecedents for this split; see Emilsson 1988: 167 n. 46 for a convincing critique. For the division between soul and shade, see above p. 157 ff. The eschatological side to Plotinus's theory of memory in IV 3 25 – IV 4 5 is obviously not based on Aristotle (cf. Blumenthal 1976: note 32).

935 *De sens.* 1 436a7–8.

936 I 8 15 28, II 9 12 7, II 9 16, 27, III 7 1 23, IV 7 12 9, V 1 1 27, IV 8 4 30, V 5 12 6–15.

way we, body-soul composites, remember. This is the way in which Aristotle approaches memory in *De memoria*:

> [**CF**[937]] For always whenever someone is active with respect to remembering, then he says in this way in the soul that he heard this or perceived it or thought it before. [**PD**[938]] Therefore memory is neither perception nor conception but the possession or modification of one of these, when time has passed.[939]

Aristotle draws attention to what someone is doing when we attribute memory to them, and draws as a conclusion a preliminary definition. Even to a Platonist, an analysis of the way in which we speak of memory, as it were the natural context of memory, is the necessary starting point for further reflections on memory in the peregrinations of the soul on leaving the body.[940] From a more systematic point of view the interest in such a comparison lies in what can be gleaned about the concept of memory; aspects which appear in such widely diverging theories have a chance of being central to the concept.

It is not easy to decide whether Plotinus read *De memoria*, let alone if he probably had the work "sous les yeux" when writing on the subject, as Bréhier puts it at one point, when talking about IV 3 29–32.[941] But in IV 3 25 ff. the reason for thinking that Aristotle is in the background is plausible, and of the utmost significance for a concept of memory: Plotinus is arguing that memory cannot be common to body and soul, in contrast to perception. Instead, he thinks that memory belongs to the soul itself, once it has received the perception (chapter 26), that is, the thing to be remembered. One reason for thinking that he is arguing against Aristotle at this point is that he gives weaving and boring as examples for the way a craftsman uses his tools, like the soul using the body in perception. And, as the commentators note[942] at least the example of weaving is used

---

937 **Canonical Formula**, above p. 32.
938 **Preliminary Definition**, above p. 34.
939 *De. mem.* 1 449b22–25.
940 See e.g. *Phaedo* 73C1–74A8 where Plato gives five conditions under which cognition (ἐπιστήμη) is recollection (above p. 15). Plotinus, however, notes at IV 6 3 71–74 how paradoxical his view of memory is to common sense.
941 "Il n'est pas moins vrai que les trois chapitres qui suivent (IV 3 29–32) présent le caractère d'une recherche scientifique, à la manière du petit traité d'Aristote Sur la mémoire, que Plotin a eu probablement sous les yeux en rédigeant ces chapitres." Bréhier 1927: IV 31.
942 Henry Schwyzer 1977 ad loc., Harder, Beutler, Theiler 1962: IIb, p. 500 ad IV 3 25 42, Armstrong (1984: vol. IV p. 114 ad IV 3 26 3) notes that Plotinus "char-

by Aristotle in *De anima* I 4 408b13: "saying the soul is angry is like saying it builds or weaves". Even if the reference is not to *De memoria*, Plotinus' argument can be seen as an attack on the Aristotelian idea that memory is common to body and soul, and so a topic for the *Parva Naturalia*. To sum up, the point at issue is: what is it that remembers, what is the subject of memory, the soul or body soul composite? A general assumption is at work here. Whether the answer given is the soul or the body and the soul, there is a conviction common to both authors at work here, namely that there must be a subject of memory. This is one aspect of the modesty of memory for both thinkers; it depends on a subject.[943]

My procedure is as follows. Before discussing Bréhier's arguments for thinking that Plotinus is using Aristotle's theory, I wish to consider one piece of external evidence that has as yet played no part in the literature on this topic. I will then run through some points of contact with Aristotle which Bréhier's interpretation of Plotinus covers up. Finally, I will make some more general points about the differences between the two theories.

Now for the external evidence. It suggests very strongly that a member of Plotinus' immediate circle had *De memoria* at his disposal. In a quotation given by Stobaeus, from Porphyry's *On the powers of the soul* we find a more or less exact quotation of Aristotle's final definition of memory in *De memoria*, embedded in a fairly elaborate account of the process of perceptual memory. I translate:

> Just as we grasp the other [capacities] of the soul from their activities so, if we look carefully also at memory of things grasped both by perception and by reason, when it occurs in virtue of a effective relation (συναναφορά) we posit this capacity of the soul which is called memory though the effective relation (συναναφορά), which [i.e. memory] Aristotle defines as the retention of a representation as an image of that of which the representation is an image (κατοχὴν φαντάσματος, ὡς εἰκόνος, οὗ φάντασμα εἰκών), such as is passed to the representative apparatus when the perception occurs. The affection which occurs in the representative faculty, whatever [this affection] may actually be, is called a representation; therefore when the perceptive faculty has been made to match by perception, [a process] which occurs in the image (εἰκών) of the object of perception, from which [object] the representation came about; the representation possesses the relation of an image (εἰκών) to the object represented. For something like an image (οἷον εἰκών) of the

---

acteristically" uses boring holes, instead of Aristotle's building a house as an example for the purposes of vividness.
943 See *Introduction*, p. 9, on Aristotle, p. 20, and on Plotinus p. 114.

thing comes about in the representative faculty, namely of the thing occurring to perception. Therefore when retention of the representation takes
place round about the representative faculty, this is called memory. This is
common, arising also in irrational animals. Articulate [memory], in virtue
of which we recollect, occurs in rational animals alone. For articulateness
is a property of reasoning. Hence the followers of Aristotle say that irrational
animals remember, but that they do not recollect, only humans both remember and recollect.[944]

Taken in its entirety, this is a fascinating interpretation of parts of *De memoria*. First a few remarks about the end of the fragment, which is relatively clear. With good reason the editor of Porphyry's fragments, Andrew
Smith, refers to the texts in *De memoria* where recollection is said to belong only to humans.[945] But note that Porphyry talks here about the followers of Aristotle; this weakens the link to *De memoria* even if what is
said here is quite consistent with Aristotle's own views. Furthermore, it
would appear that Porphyry allows memory, strictly speaking, of ideas,
also an un-Aristotelian notion. Here, he may also be following Ploti-

---

944 Smith 1993: Fr. 255F, from Stobaeus (III 25, 1): Ἐκ τοῦ Πορφυρίου Περὶ τῶν τῆς
ψυχῆς δυνάμεων. Ὥσπερ γὰρ ἐκ τῶν ἐνεργειῶν καὶ τὰς ἄλλας κατελαβόμεθα,
οὕτως ἀναθεωροῦντες κατὰ συναναφορὰν γιγνομένην καὶ μνήμην τῶν ἢ δι᾽ αἰσθή-
σεως καταληφθέντων ἢ διὰ λόγου, ἐθέμεθα καὶ ταύτην ψυχῆς δύναμιν, ἢ τῇ (5)
συναναφορᾷ καλεῖται μνήμη, ἣν ἀφορίζεται Ἀριστοτέλης κατοχὴν φαντάσματος,
ὡς εἰκόνος, οὗ φάντασμα εἰκών, οἷον ὅταν γένηται ἡ αἴσθησις, ἀνεδόθη ἐπὶ τὴν
φανταστικὴν κατασκευήν· τὸ γενόμενον ἐν τῇ φανταστικῇ τὸ πάθος, ὅ τι δή ποτε
ὄν, φάντασμα καλεῖται, ἔτι οὖν καὶ (10) ἀρθέντος τοῦ αἰσθητικοῦ ἐκ τῆς αἰσθή-
σεως, τὸ προσπῖπτον ἐν τῇ εἰκόνι τοῦ αἰσθητοῦ, ἀφ᾽ οὗ συνέστηκε τὸ φάντασμα,
εἰκόνος λόγον ἔχον πρὸς τὸ φανταστόν· οἷον γὰρ εἰκών τις ἐγένετο ἐν τῇ φανταστικῇ τοῦ ὑποπεσόντος ὑπὸ τὴν αἴσθησιν. ὅταν οὖν γένηται κατοχὴ περὶ τὴν
(15) φανταστικὴν τοῦ φαντάσματος, καλεῖται μνήμη. τοῦτο μὲν οὖν κοινὸν καὶ
ἐν τοῖς ἀλόγοις ζῴοις· ἡ δὲ διηρθρωμένη, καθ᾽ ἣν καὶ ἀναμιμνησκόμεθα, ἐν
μόνοις ἐστὶ τοῖς λογικοῖς· ἴδιον γὰρ λογισμοῦ τὸ διηρθρωμένον. διὸ καὶ φασὶν οἱ
περὶ τὸν Ἀριστοτέλην τὰ ἄλογα ζῷα μεμνῆσθαι (20) μέν, ἀναμιμνήσκεσθαι δὲ
μή, μόνον δὲ τὸν ἄνθρωπον καὶ μνημονεύειν καὶ ἀναμιμνήσκεσθαι.
My thanks to Andrew Smith and Denis O'Brien for discussion of the problems in the quotation of Aristotle's definition. One main difficulty lies in the
word συναναφορά – a rare word which may well bear the sense suggested in
the translation, gratefully borrowed by me from Andrew Smith. Understood
this way, this concept may indicate interest in the present-past problem; on
which, see below in the main text. On Porphyry's view of the connection between
body and soul as fundamentally in agreement with Plotinus, see Smith 1974:
ch. 1.
945 449b6–8; 453a4–14.

nus;[946] and in thinking that recollection is rational may be connected to a Platonic view of the recollection of ideas. But in our fragment he concentrates on the workings of memory of perceptual experience.

Now let us turn to this tricky account of memory itself. As noted by Smith, in this fragment there is a reference to the final definition (**FD**) of memory from *De memoria* 1. I translate again:[947]

> What memory is, and remembering, has been said, namely the possession of a representation as an image of that of which it is the representation. (451a15–16)

Now there are interesting divergences from Aristotle in Porphyry's use of the definition, to which we shall return, but the quotation is close enough for at least the availability of the definition to Porphyry to be certain. My translation reads:

> Aristotle defines [memory] as the retention of a representation as an image of that of which the representation is an image.

Of course, this need not mean that he had *De memoria* itself at hand. One might speculate that this had found its way into a handbook of definitions: definitions are useful and some readers, for example, teachers, may think they can be profitably divorced from the enquiry establishing them.

Apart from the minor matter of substituting retention (κατοχή)[948] for possession (ἕξις), Porphyry is being remarkably faithful to Aristotle, in retailing the definition. Furthermore, he offers a description of the process of memory which is in effect an interpretation of the passage (450a27–32, 450b11–451a2) in which Aristotle gives his solution of the present-past problem. This is the aporia of *De memoria* 1 450a25:

> One may well ask why one remembers the thing that is no longer there, when the affection (πάθος) is there, but the thing is not.

---

946 See IV 3 30, a comparison suggested to me by Andrew Smith, (cf. above p. 179); and cf. IV 3 25 27–30.

947 Cf. above, p. 82.

948 Stobaeus (III 25 3) also cites *De mem.* with the definition of memory in a very reduced form: Τὴν δὲ κατοχὴν τῶν φαντασμάτων μνήμην ἐπονομάζεσθαι. This suggests at least that it was common to interpret ἕξις as κατοχή, which might be a way of avoiding the ambiguity in ἕξις (state, possession). Plotinus also speaks of κατοχή IV 6 1 3, 3 57. See Taormina 2010.

The present-past problem is: how can something past be present, namely in memory?[949] Briefly, Aristotle's solution is to attend to the difference between a representation and using a repesentation as an image. Only the latter case counts as active memory.

It is worth pausing for a moment with Porphyry to see what gets changed, if not lost, in the process of interpretation. We will find that Porphyry is actually not being as faithful to Aristotle as the use of the final definition of memory from *De memoria* would suggest. The most important deviation from Aristotle concerns the way in which the memory relates to its object. For Porphyry does not think that the representation has to be taken as an image; rather some representations have the quality of an image in themselves. Memory is present only insofar as a representation which in fact is an image is retained. Thus the relation of the memory to that of which it is the memory is established by the kind of representation, not by the subject of the memory doing something with the representation.

How does Porphyry think perceptual memory works? As one would expect in a theory of perceptual memory based on Aristotle's account, the representation arises from the perception. Only when perception has been properly matched to, i.e. affected by, its object, does an image occur. Thus images are a subclass of representations. They are distinguished from other representations by their standing in an imaging relation to the object of perception. When this representation, in the narrow sense of an image, is retained, then there is memory. That is the capacity of memory, my capacity to remember the perception, consists in the retention of this image.

So what has Porphyry done with Aristotle? Well, he has decreased the importance of what we do when we actually remember, to favour the moment when we have the perception, and the resulting representation. Partly, this is because he is talking about the capacities of the soul. The important thing is the relation of the representation to the object of perception. For Aristotle's solution of the present-past problem hinges not on the resemblance of the representation to the thing perceived, but on the way in which we take a content of thought. Either we can take it as a representation of the experience, or else we let it float through our minds, for example, without relating it to an experience.[950] Only when we relate it to a perception, naturally to a *past* perception, do we have

---

949 See above, p. 1–2.
950 This is emphasised by Morel 2006b: 74–75.

memory. Representations that simply remain, even very life-like ones, do not constitute memory; representations remain which may occur in other contexts such as in dreams, as is made abundantly clear in *De Insomniis*. In memory itself, the question is whether we are capable of relating the representation to an experience.

So much for Porphyry; what about Plotinus himself? I know of no reason which would make more texts available to Porphyry that to Plotinus. So here too we can draw the cautious conclusion that *De memoria* was at least available to Plotinus. Even if it may be impossible to prove that Plotinus read *De memoria*, it would be surprising had he not done so given his interest in the topic: IV 3 25-IV 4 16 take up twenty five pages in Henry and Schwyzer's Oxford Classical Text, and IV 6 another five pages. After all, he is very interested in Aristotle's psychology.[951] His interest in memory is, furthermore rather different from Porphyry's in this fragment, and I think that he picks up on things that Aristotle had noticed. So in their reading of *De memoria* Porphyry and Plotinus are relatively independent of one another, as far as the evidence goes.

Let us turn to Bréhier. To begin with, he thinks that it is not doctrine but an *aporia* about memory which Plotinus has picked up from Aristotle.[952] Plotinus wishes to solve it without using *impressions*, at least of a material kind.[953] For he thinks that memory belongs to the soul alone, as a capacity (δύναμις) to do something. Thus he is opposed to a tenet fundamental to Aristotle's view of memory, namely that, as we have already seen, it is common to body and soul.[954]

The structure of Plotinus' argument in IV 6 3 is as follows. Having said what he thinks memory is, he then uses this account to explain various phenomena.[955] We will return to this account later; the arguments at this point can be understood if we just bear in mind that memory is an active capacity, that is, one to do things, not to undergo them. Bréhier considers this procedure as a way of refuting Aristotle. Of the eight arguments which Bréhier distinguishes in this passage of VI 6 3, he thinks that five refer to Aristotle's text. Plotinus wants to show that his explanation of these phenomena works, whereas Aristotle's does not.[956] Exami-

---

951 See above fn. 932 for references to some work on the topic.
952 Bréhier IV 169–170, see also Morel 2007: 378–380.
953 As seen by Blumenthal 1976: 54.
954 See above p. 24.
955 See above 3.1.4 What memory as a capacity can explain, p. 127.
956 Bréhier 1927: IV 170–171: "Le reste du chapitre est destiné a montrer que les faits indiqués par Aristote lui même prouvent que la mémoire est puissance ac-

nation of these five arguments will show partly more agreement between Aristotle and Plotinus than Bréhier allows, and partly more radical criticism.

The five arguments in Plotinus which Bréhier refers to Aristotle are the following:

1) Plotinus (ll. 29–40) argues that because exercise improves memory, memory must be a capacity. Aristotle remarks that repeated acts of memory improve memory (*De memoria* 1 451a12–14) by regarding the representation as an image. While Bréhier merely remarks on the analogous possibility of improving memory in both thinkers, I think that the analogy indicates that Plotinus cannot have thought that Aristotle thinks that memory can be explained merely by the preservation of representations. He must have understood that for Aristotle memory is something active and not merely passive, not merely the possession of an impression. For the person remembering has to regard the representation as an image of the perception, as is clear from Aristotle's Final Definition (**FD**, quoted above), which encapsulates his solution to the present-past problem.[957] So what can we conclude? If Plotinus read Aristotle, and understood that Aristotle thought memory can be improved by training, then he cannot have thought Aristotle to have considered memory to be simply the remaining of impressions. The person remembering has to do something with the representation, when actively remembering. As we will see, Plotinus too thinks remembering is doing something.

2) Aristotle uses the wax block model both for memory (450a32) and for perception (*De anima* II 12). Plotinus says that since perception is not an imprinting (τύπωσις),[958] memory cannot be the retention (κατοχαί) of impressions (IV 6 3 55–57). On the face of it this is a repetition of his main line of argument in IV 6 as a whole, as announced at the start of the first chapter. So why does Bréhier think that this is an *ad hominem* argument against Aristotle, revealing a contradiction between his theory of memory and his theory of perception? Presuma-

---

tive, et non impression passivement subie." He then cites Alexander (De an. 70, 3, Bruns) for the view that it is not merely the traces left by perception that enables one to remember, but the act relative to this trace. This is already to be found in Aristotle, however; see the preliminary definition quoted above, p. 226.

957 See also 449b22–23.

958 See also IV 3 26 7; τύπωσις is of course a Stoic term, used to define φαντασία (e.g. SVF II 53, 56, 59).

bly, the point is that once Plotinus has (to his mind) refuted the impression theory of perception, he has also refuted the impression theory of memory. Plotinus' does not agree that perception is comparable with imprinting a wax block (IV 6 3 55). Partly this is because he reads the model in such a way that it is incompatible with the presence of an *active* capacity in the subject of memory: imprinting requires that the soul is passive, whereas Plotinus thinks that the soul only has active capacities. So I think that we have here part of a radical criticism of Aristotelian psychology by Plotinus.

3) Both Aristotle (449b18–30) and Plotinus (IV 6 3 59) place great emphasis on the interval of time between the original perception and memory. Bréhier remarks that Aristotle mentions this (451a29–31), and that Plotinus takes it to be an argument for memory being a particular kind of active power, namely one that needs time to be established. Bréhier does not explicitly draw the conclusion that here again the two thinkers are thinking alike, even if the reasons they give for their views, and the conclusions they draw from them differ fundamentally. For example, the connection with time is one reason Aristotle has for attributing memory to the perceptive faculty.

4) They also agree that intelligence and memory often do not coincide (451a29–31, IV 6 3 63–67.) Henry and Schwyzer refer to *De memoria*. 1 449b7–8), a point of agreement which Bréhier overlooks. But he is quite right that the conclusions they draw from this phenomenon are different. Plotinus sees here an argument for memory as an active capacity, Aristotle a reason for distinguishing memory and recollection.

5) The final reference to Aristotle that Bréhier sees is simply a mistake, so I pass over it with a footnote.[959]

---

959 Bréhier finds the lines 67–70 only comprehensible by reference to Aristotle's theory that those who are too hard or too soft, namely the old and the young, are incapable of memory (450a32-b10). (This conception is in fact alluded to at IV 7 6 38–44.) Bréhier translates lines IV 6 3 67–70: "Et pourtant rien n' empêcherait, même s'il y a, dans l' âme un excès [de dureté], de lire des empreintes qui y seraient déposées, ni, si elle est peu consistante, d' être incapable de subir les impressions et de les retenir." In fact, Armstrong's view (to judge from his translation 1984 ad loc.) is right: this is a continuation of the preceding argument. I paraphrase as follows: any kind of superiority of soul (πλεονεξία ψυχῆς) would not prevent one from reading impressions in the soul. That is to say: since memory and intelligence preclude one another, and this would not be the case if memory consisted in impressions, memory cannot be impres-

One reason that these references cannot be taken as established beyond all doubt is that none of the verbal similarities is such as to be unmistakeable. Plotinus has ways of referring to well known texts by using catch words from them,[960] and he does not use them here. Obviously, *De memoria* does not have the status of one of the major texts for Plotinus. Even attending to the kind of theory in Aristotle and Plotinus will not provide indubitable proof. We also have to bear in mind that other theorists had impression theories of memory, notably the Stoics. This applies even to the *aporia* which Bréhier uses as his star witness for the Aristotelian background, as we have already seen. In one important fragment about Stoic theories of learning, we find the Present-Past problem:

> αἰσθόμενοι γάρ τινος οἷον λευκοῦ ἀπελθόντος αὐτοῦ μνήμην ἔχουσιν.

> by perceiving something e. g. white, they have a memory of it when it has departed. Aetius IV 11.1[961]

The point may be of course that any theory of memory will have to cope with this problem. Here is the Plotinian version again:

> But now that we have said this [about sense perception] we must next speak about memory; first we must say that it is not astonishing, or rather it is astonishing, but we should not disbelieve that the soul has a power of this kind, if it receives nothing itself and contrives an apprehension of what it does not have. For it is the expression (λόγος) of all things, and the nature of soul is the last and lowest expression (λόγος) of the intelligibles and the beings in the intelligible world, but first in the whole world perceived by the senses. Therefore it certainly stands in relation with both. IV 6 3 1–8 (AHA trans., revised)[962]

Here, Plotinus states the problem: how does the soul contrive apprehension of something it does not have? But he also expresses his resistance to the idea of (material) impressions at one and the same time. The soul takes in nothing of the thing, yet it has a memory of it: I understand this as a denial of impressions, along with the assertion of apprehension i. e. grasp of the thing experienced or thought. It is characteristic of Plotinus to link this capacity to what the soul is. Because the soul is both the expression of the intelligibles and of sensible things, it is able to grasp them even when they are not immediately present. This refers on the

---

sions; and someone's possession of a good memory does not force him to have an incapacity, namely of being affected and retaining the affection.

960 E.g. *Timaeus* 35A in IV 1.
961 Part of SVF II 83, cf. also II 55.
962 See above, p. 113.

one hand to memory of past experiences, but also to the memory of intelligibles, when the soul is in the sensible world, in other words, when fitted with a body and hence able to perceive.

When we compare central aspects of the two theories of memory, it emerges that Plotinus and Aristotle are much closer in their conceptions of memory than Bréhier thinks or one might expect. A very obvious similarity *was* noted by Bréhier[963], which we have already mentioned several times,[964] namely that Plotinus like Aristotle adopts an explanation of memory using φαντασία:

> If then the representation of the absent thing is present in this [sc. the representative faculty] it [sc. the representative faculty] already remembers, even if it is only present for a short time.[965]

How can we distinguish the two theories of memory? Whereas φαντασία is a change remaining from a perception in Aristotle's book,[966] and so bound to actual perception, Plotinus divorces φαντασία from perception: the soul can have φαντασία, and hence memory, when it does not perceive, that is when it has no body. This is a crucial difference: it enables Plotinus to understand memory as something that belongs to the soul alone, unlike perception. A major interest in IV 3 25 – IV 4 5 concerns the question just what the soul remembers in which stages of its journey. Obviously, the motivation for Plotinus' use of memory lies in the central importance of the soul rediscovering, recollecting where it comes from.[967]

A central feature of Plotinus' system is the Aristotelian notion that the soul is not subject to change.[968] For Plotinus this means that the soul quite simply undergoes no change. Aristotle can allow that the body of the concrete thing is modified (affected) which allows the soul to have a capacity like memory, which depends on the modification of the body. Thus Aristotle's explanation of memory is grounded on his view of the subject of memory, the concrete living thing. Plotinus' theory is also grounded on his view of the subject of memory, but the subject itself is quite different. Although Bréhier sees that the subject of memory is

---

963 Bréhier 1927: IV 32.
964 See above, p. 170.
965 IV 3 29 26–27.
966 *De an.* III 3 429a1–2.
967 See Morel (2007: 373–380) on IV 6. It seems to me that this is not true of all memory; in other words, memory may have the function of turning us towards thought. Not all memories need do this, however.
968 See III 6 1–6. For Aristotle, see King 2001: 58–64, Menn 2002: 97–101.

crucial to Plotinus' theory, he does not remark that there is here an important analogy with Aristotle.

How can Plotinus explain the fact that memory belongs to the soul alone? He requires that the soul, on its own, can remember, by being strengthened by a perception in such a way that the perception or the object of the perception is *quasi* present to the soul. Plotinus thinks that this requires a purely non-material account of memory, which makes use of φαντάσματα which remain present when the perception is over.[969] As to the question how he conceives of φαντάσματα: he does talk about τύποι, while denying the likeness to using a seal to make an impression – rather they are apprehended more like thought.[970] Unlike Aristotle, he thinks that φαντασία can be actually used without the body, but like Aristotle he thinks that it in some way derives from active perception. A perceptual judgement leaves a τύπος in the soul, an incorporeal, intelligible representation, of what is perceived. These representations are objects of φαντασία. Thus representation is perception that has been internalised by the soul.[971]

In reading Plotinus' theory of memory we should not restrict ourselves to simply noticing Aristotelian influence. The question is of course how Plotinus' theory is to be understood in the first place. Plotinus thinks that the solution of the *aporia* already mentioned, namely, the Present-Past problem of remembering something past in the present depends on what the soul is, namely the λόγος of everything. This enables Bréhier to view Plotinus' theory of memory in IV 6 3 (especially lines 5–19) as assimilating perceptions to innate ideas. For if the soul is the λόγος of everything, both intelligibles and sensibles, then both of these can be in the soul in the same way or in an analogous fashion. Like Leibniz' complete notions of a monad (to which Bréhier refers), each Plotinian soul (on this reading) contains not merely innate ideas but also all the perceptions that

---

969 IV 3 29 23.

970 IV 3 26 25–32. The longest treatment of φαντασία occurs in the texts on memory; there is no separate treatment of the concept. Other important texts are: I 8 15 18–19: 'Representation is brought about by the irrational part (sc. of the soul) being struck from outside. But (the soul) receives the blow on account of its divisible nature.' This clearly echoes the Aristotelian view; so too VI 8 3 10–12: 'But as for ourselves, we call imagination strictly speaking, what is awakened from the passive impression of the body;' but, in contrast: 'φαντασία in the primary sense, which we call opinion' (III 6 4 19–21).

971 Emilsson 1988: 110, citing III 6 1 7–11, IV 3 26 and 29; n. 49 p. 167: I 1 7 12–13, IV 4 23 32.

it ever has. These "innate" perceptions then just need to be made to shine out in order for an act of memory to take place. This misrepresents Plotinus. Bréhier thinks that being the λόγος of sensible things refers to every sensible experience. But there is no need to refer to every actual experience – it is enough if the soul has the capacity for possible sensible experiences. In this way, Plotinus does not exclude the possibility of having new experiences. This is necessary since Plotinus clearly thinks that we can acquire learning or experience.

Bréhier's interpretation masks the similarity with Aristotle. Recall our example:

Example (E): Socrates remembers (at t2) that he saw Theaetetus two days ago (at t1).

Because Bréhier assimilates perception to thought, there is no prior time t1 at which the perception of Theaetetus was laid down, as there is in Aristotle's theory. We have seen that this is also the case in Plotinus' theory, in considering the sophisticated reading of active memory.[972] This is apparent through his use of the metaphor of a woman in labour (IV 6 3 19): saying that when the soul actually remembers it is like a woman in labour; this presupposes impregnation, i.e. acquisition of experience and a period intervening between experience and memory. This is confirmed by Plotinus' talk of memory of acquired knowledge and experience.[973] In other words, a memory at t2 presupposes an experience at t1. Here, in the realm of sensible experience, Aristotle and Plotinus pursue the same line. The point of Aristotle introducing the imprinting through perception is that something has to happen to the living thing, if it is going to have a memory later (450a32, already mentioned above). Plotinus thinks that the soul acquires a capacity through the experience, namely the capacity to remember this experience. This is clear if we consider his fullest account of memory, which I call a *quasi*-definition:[974]

> Whenever therefore the soul is strengthened with respect to something that appears to it (πρὸς ὁτιοῦν τῶν φανέντων), the soul is disposed to it as if to something present (ὥσπερ πρὸς παρὸν διάκειται); the more the soul is

---

972 Above. p. 175.
973 IV 3 25 11. Cf. IV 4 6 3.
974 Above p. 120.

strengthened, the more the appearance is always present to it. IV 6 3 19–21[975]

The interpretation of this *quasi* definition is not easy: but it is clear enough that what happens to the soul at t1 is that it is strengthened, namely with regard to the experience, such that it is then able to recall the experience afterwards.

But Aristotle and Plotinus are clearly also in agreement in thinking that at t2 something has to be done. The importance of activity is missed by Bréhier.[976] At the start of the treatment of memory in IV 6 3,[977] Plotinus says that we should be prepared to believe in a power of the soul to grasp things which it does not possess. Bréhier thinks that these lines allude directly to Aristotle's statement of the present-past problem, which I have already mentioned several times: how can one remember something past by perceiving a present affection? And Bréhier sees in Aristotle's answer only the possession of an impression, and fails entirely to see that memory according to Aristotle is not merely the possession of something, that is, of a representation. The remember does something at t2 with the impression in order to remember the past experience, namely he regards the representation as an image of that of which it is a representation. This view is encapsulated in Aristotle's final definition of memory: Memory is not merely the possession of a φάντασμα, but of a φάντασμα taken in a certain way. This is an active achievement, not merely something given. What about the activity at t2 in Plotinus' theory? There is an analogue in the active presence of a representation, when the capacity of the soul is exercised. The φάντασμα has to be made to "shine out". We have seen that this characteristically involves saying something.

Bréhier thinks Plotinus attributes to Aristotle a passive impression theory of memory, that is to say, memory is the passive possession of an impression. The trouble with his reading is that it supposes that Plotinus simplified Aristotle drastically (supposing he knew *De memoria*), namely by only noticing the possession of an impression, and not that one does something with the representation, namely to regard it as a copy.

We have already noticed that Bréhier ignores the activity at t2 in Aristotle's account; this is tantamount to ignoring the distinction between activity and capacity. But Aristotle not only takes the activity of memory into account, he also takes the capacity to remember into account, name-

---

975 Above, p. 120.
976 Bréhier 1927 on IV 6, vol. 4 p. 169–170.
977 Quoted above, p. 234.

ly the presence in the rememberer of a moving cause, a principle of change (452a10). The point about the capacity to remember is that one can remember of one's own accord.

The question of the subject of memory is one that interests Plotinus deeply, taking it to mean, what is it that remembers: memory is of course not sufficient for the identity of the subject of memory.[978] This is the topic he pursues at great length in IV 3 and 4 – there he *assumes* a definition of memory, instead of looking for it, and asks rather which things are such by nature as to be able to remember.[979] It is tempting to think he is referring to Aristotle's definition, and I think his account would fit with an interpretation of that definition.

Aristotle also distinguishes the tasks of defining memory and of finding the part of the soul with which we remember.[980] For him, there is no doubt that the subject of memory is the concrete individual. This is the message of the famous passage in *De Anima* I, (4 408b13) already referred to more than once,[981] which is the basis of modern discussions of the homunculus fallacy: it is a mistake to use parts of living things, whether the soul or the brain, as the subjects of predicates which apply only to the whole living thing. The soul does not weave, a human being weaves, the brain does not think, a human being does.[982] A different, if closely related question concerns the explanation of memory. In *De memoria* he does argue that the perceptive faculty is responsible for, explains memory; this is part of what it means to say that memory is common to body and soul, a subject for the *Parva Naturalia:* for perception is the star case of a faculty common to body and soul.[983] Plotinus' different perspective is due to the fact that he wishes to examine memory in the different phases of the human soul, and allocate different memories to the different parts of the soul; but he also wishes to preclude certain souls, namely those of the world and the heavenly bodies, and indeed God and intellect, from memory in general (IV 3 25 13–24 and IV 4 6–17). Aristotle is more simply concerned to show that memory can also be present in animals other than ourselves.

---

978 Cf. Onsager 2004: 24–25, *pace* Inge 1968: 227, Gerson 1994: 180–3, with n. 48.
979 Plotinus himself only gives a *quasi*-definition, above p. 120.
980 449b4–5.
981 See above p. 24.
982 Also known as the mereological fallacy; see Bennett and Hacker 2003: 15.
983 436b1–7. On this passage, see Morel 2006a; and for Sens. in general see also Johansen 2006.

There are, Plotinus thinks, no organs of representation; the soul has this function even when it is not embodied. An important argument for this view concerns the disruptive nature of the body. Since the body is in flux, it causes forgetting, and prevents remembering, rather than being a condition of the latter's existence.[984] At this point, Aristotle and Plotinus part company most decisively. For Aristotle thinks that the soul can regulate changes in such a way that the living thing is preserved, namely by its vegetative functions.[985] And this regularity is the basis of his body based theory of memory. He thus explains the failure of memory in the young and the old by their bodies being too hard or too fluid to take or preserve the affection necessary for memory.[986] Aristotle can view memory as being common to body and soul, where Plotinus is quite clear that memories can be had without body. Thus although he too has a lot to say about things common to body and soul (much of it in I 1), systematic reasons prevent him from including memory among them (IV 3 26).

To conclude, some more general remarks. Aristotle and Plotinus are both advocates of a modest concept of memory, despite the fact that there are divergences in the way they understand the object of memory and hence the nature of memory. For Aristotle memory and recollection are properly speaking applied only to perceptions, and not to thoughts whereas Plotinus also allows recollection as a means of access to thinking forms. But in both cases memory is modest because it is determined, on the one hand, by a persisting subject of memory, and, on the other hand, by more basic cognitive capacities, such as thought and perception. Neither persisting subject nor the basic cognitive capacities require memory for their existence. Conversely, understanding memory does require us to understand its relation to its subject, the being that remembers. This is true for both Plotinus and Aristotle.

---

984 Cf. IV 7 5 22–24. The soul is not in flux, i.e. not amenable to change IV 3 26 39–44, 52–54. On flux in body, see II 1 1 2, 7–9, with Wilberding 2006: 100, 105 ad loc.
985 See King 2001: 49–58.
986 450a32–450b11. Blumenthal and HBT see in this a theory which Plotinus rejects; see above fn. 930.

Select Bibliography

Aristotle – editions, translations, commentaries

De memoria et reminiscentia

(Editions, translations and texts of De mem. are cited using only the name of the author; 'Ross' refers to W.D.Ross; 'G.Ross' to G.R.T. Ross.)

Beare, J. I. 1908. (trans. with notes). *De Memoria et Reminiscentia.* In: Beare, J.I., Ross, G.R.T. *The* Parva Naturalia. Oxford. (Oxford Translation Vol. III).

Bloch, D. 2007. *Aristotle on Memory and Recollection. Text, Translation, Interpretation and Reception in Western Scholasticism.* Leiden.

King, R.A. H. 2004. *Aristoteles. Werke in deutscher Übersetzung.* Begründet von Ernst Grumach. Herausgegeben von Hellmut Flashar. *Band 14 Teil II: de memoria.* Berlin.

Michael Ephesius. 1903. Commentaria in Aristotelis Parva Naturalia. In Wendland, P. (Ed.), *Commentaria in Aristotelem Graeca. Vol. XXII, 1.* Berlin.

Morel, P.-M. 2000. *Aristote. Petits traités d'histoire naturelle.* Paris.

Rolfes, E. 1924. *Aristoteles. Kleine naturwissenschaftliche Schriften.* Leipzig.

Ross, G.R.T. 1906. *Aristotle. De Sensu and De Memoria.* Cambridge.

Ross, W.D. 1955. *Aristotle's Parva Naturalia.* Oxford.

Siwek, P. 1963. *Aristotelis Parva Naturalia graece et latine.* Rome.

Sophonias (Pseudo-Themistius). 1903. In Aristotelis Parva Naturalia Paraphraseis. In Wendland, P. (Ed.), *Commentaria in Aristotelem Graeca. Vol. V, 6.* Berlin.

Sorabji, R. 1972, repr. with new foreword 2004. *Aristotle on Memory.* London.

Other works of Aristotle

Alexander Aphrodisiensis. 1901. In librum Aristotelis de Sensu commentarium. In Wendland, P. (Ed.), *Commentaria in Aristotelem Graeca. vol. III, 1.* Berlin.

Barnes, J. 1993². *Aristotle. Posterior Analytics. Translated with a Commentary.* Oxford.

————1984. (Ed.) *The complete works of Aristotle. Revised Oxford Translation.* Princeton.

Bekker, I. 1831 (sqq.). *Aristotelis Opera.* Berlin.

Detel, W. 1993. Aristoteles. Analytica Posteriora. *Aristoteles' Werke in deutscher Übersetzung.* Ed. H. Flashar. Vol. 3, Teil II. Berlin.

Eijk, P.J. van der. 1994. De Insomniis, De Divinatione per Somnium. *Aristoteles' Werke in deutscher Übersetzung.* Ed. H. Flashar. Vol. 14, Teil III. Berlin.

Hicks, R.D. 1907. *Aristotle. De Anima.* Cambridge.

Hussey, E. 1983. *Aristotle's Physics III – IV. Translated with Notes.* Oxford.

Jaeger, W. 1957. *Aristotelis Metaphysica.* Oxford.

Nussbaum, M.C. 1978. *Aristotle's De Motu Animalium.* Princeton.

Rapp, C. 2002. Rhetorik. *Aristoteles' Werke in deutscher Übersetzung.* Ed. H. Flashar. Vol. 4. Berlin.

Ross, W.D. 1924. *Aristotle's Metaphysics.* Oxford.

————1936. *Aristotle's Physics.* Oxford.

————1961. *Aristotle's De Anima.* Oxford.

————1949. *Aristotle's Prior and Posterior Analytics.* Oxford.

Sophonias (Pseudo-Themistius). 1903. In Aristotelis Parva Naturalia Paraphraseis. In Wendland, P. (Ed.), *Commentaria in Aristotelem Graeca. Vol. V, 6.* Berlin.

Plotinus – editions, translations, commentaries

Armstrong, A.H. 1966–1987. *Plotinus. Enneads.* VII vols. Cambridge, Mass/ London.

Atkinson, M.J. 1983. *Plotinus, Ennead V. 1. On the three principal hypostases; a comm. with transl.* Oxford.

Beierwaltes, W. 1967. *Plotin über Ewigkeit und Zeit.* Frankfurt/M.

————1991. *Selbsterkenntnis und Erfahrung der Einheit. Plotins Enneade V 3. Text Übersetzung, Interpretation, Erläuterungen.* Frankfurt a.M.

Bréhier, E. 1924–38. Plotin. Les Ennéades I-VI. Texte établi et traduit par E. Bréhier. Paris.

Brisson, Luc. 2005. *Plotin. Traités 27–29: sur les difficultés relatives a l'âme, trois livres.* Paris.

Fleet, B.1996. *Plotinus. Ennead III 6. On the Impassivity of the Bodiless. (Translation and Commentary).* Oxford.

Hadot, P. 1994. *Plotin Traité 9. C'est par l'un que tous les êtres sont des êtres.* Paris.

Harder, R. Beutler, R, Theiler, W. 1956–1971. *Plotins Schriften. Neubearbeitung mit griechischem Lesetext und Anmerkungen.* Hamburg. IV vols. Text (a), IV vols. Notes (b).

Henry, P. Schwyzer, H.-R. 1951, 1959, 1973. *Plotini Opera.* Paris – Brussels. (Editio maior).

Henry, P. Schwyzer, H.-R. 1964, 1977, 1983. *Plotini Opera.* Oxford. (Editio minor).

Kleist, H. von. 1883. *Plotinische Studien: Studien zur IV. Enneade.* Heidelberg.

MacKenna, S. 1956. *Plotinus. The Enneads. Second edition revised by B.S.Page.* London.

Morel, P-M. 2007. Traité 41. Sur la sensation et la mémoire. In : Plotin. *Traités 38–41* sous la direction de L. Brisson et J.-F. Pradeau 2007, Paris.

Wilberding, J. 2006. *Plotinus' cosmology. A study of Ennead II 1 (40).* Oxford.

Other ancient authors

Arnim, H. von. 1903–1905. *Stoicorum Veterum Fragmenta.* 4 Bde. Leipzig.

Bruns, I. Ed. 1887. Alexander Aphrodisiensis Praeter commentaria scripta minora. *Supplementum Aristotelicum vol. II, 1, 2.* Berlin.

Burnet, J. 1900–1907. *Platonis opera.* 5 vols. Oxford.

Burnyeat, M. 1990. *The Theaetetus of Plato. With a translation by M.J.Levett, revised by Myles Burnyeat.* Indianapolis.
Diels, H. und Kranz, W. 1951. *Die Fragmente der Vorsokratiker.* Berlin.
Dillon. J. 1993. *Alcinous. The Handbook of Platonism. Translated with an Introduction and Commentary.* Oxford.
Dodds, E.R. 1962². *Proclus. The Elements of Theology. A revised Text with Translation, Introduction and Commentary.* Oxford.
Duke, E.A., Hicken, W.F., Nicoll W. S. M., Robinson, D.B. Strachan J. C. G. 1995. *Platonis Opera. Tomus I.* Oxford.
Frede, D. 1997. *Platon, Philebos. Übersetzung und Kommentar.* Göttingen.
Gallop, D. 1975. *Plato's Phaedo. Translated with notes.* Oxford.
Gosling, J.C.B. 1975. *Plato, Philebus.* Oxford.
Hackforth, R. 1945. *Plato's Examination of Pleasure.* Cambridge.
Long, A. and Sedley, D. 1988. *The Hellenistic Philosophers.* Cambridge.
Rowe, C.1993. *Plato's Phaedo.* Cambridge.
Smith, A. 1993. *Porphyrii Fragmenta.* Stuttgart.
Sorabji, R. 2004. *The Philosophy of the Commentators 200–600 AD. A Sourcebook. Volume I Psychology.* London.
West, M.L. 1972. *Iambi et Elegi Graeci ante Alexandrum Cantati.* Oxford.
Whittaker, J. (Ed.), Louis, P. (Tr.) 1990. *Alcinous. Enseignement des Doctrines de Platon.* Paris.

Other works

Alt, K. 1993. *Weltflucht und Weltbejahung. Zur Frage des Leib-Seele Dualismus bei Plutarch, Numenios, Plotin.* Stuttgart (AAWM 8).
Althoff, J. 1991. Warm Kalt, Flüssig Fest bei Aristoteles. *Hermes Einzelschriften* 57. Stuttgart.
Annas. J. 1992. Aristotle on Memory and the Self. In: Nussbaum, Rorty 1992: 297–311.
Armstrong, A.H. 1977. Form individual and person in Plotinus. *Dionysius* 1: 49–68.
————-1991. Aristotle in Plotinus: The continuity and discontinuity of psyche and nous. *Oxford Studies in Ancient Philosophy* Suppl. 1991.
Ax, W. 1978. ψόφος, φωνή und διάλεκτος als Grundbegriffe aristotelischer Sprachreflexion. *Glotta* 56; 245–71.
Audi, R. 1998. *Epistemology.* London.
Baddeley A. 1982. *Your memory. A user's guide. A guided tour to one of the most complex and vital of human faculties.* Harmondsworth.
Barnes, J., Schofield, M., and Sorabji, R. (Ed.) 1975–79. *Articles on Aristotle.* 4 vols. London.
Bergson, H. 1897. *Matière et Mémoire.* Paris.
Bennett, M.R. and Hacker, P. M. S. 2003. *Philosophical Foundations of Neuroscience.* Oxford.
Bolton, R. 1987. Definition and Scientific Method in Aristotle's *Posterior Analytics* and *Generation of Animals.* In Gotthelf and Lennox (Ed.) 1987.

Block, I. 1961. Truth and error in Aristotle's theory of sense perception. In *Philosophical Quarterly* 11: 1–9.

Blum, H. 1969. *Die antike Mnemotechnik*. (Spudasmata 15). Hildesheim.

Blumenthal, H.J. 1971. *Plotinus' Psychology*. Den Haag.

————1972. Plotinus Psychology: Aristotle in the service of Platonism. In *International Philosophical Quarterly* 12, 1972) Repr. in Blumenthal 1993.

————1974. Nous and soul in Plotinus. Some Problems of Demarcation. In *Plotino e il Neoplatonismo in Oriente e Occidente. Atti del Convegno internazionale dell' Accademia Nazionale dei Lincei*. Rome. Repr. in Blumenthal 1993.

————1976. Plotinus' Adaptation of Aristotle's Psychology: sensation, imagination and memory. In The significance of Neoplatonism Ed. R.B. Harris, Albany, Repr. in Blumenthal 1993.

————1989. Plotinus and Proclus on the Criterion of truth. In P. Huby, G. Neal. (Ed.) *The Criertion of Truth*. Liverpool: 257–280.

————1993. *Soul and Intellect. Studies in Plotinus and Later Platonism*. Aldershot.

Bonitz, H. 1870. *Index Aristotelicus*. Berlin.

Boys-Stones, G. R. 2001. *Post-Hellenistic Philosophy*. Oxford.

Brague, R. 1990. Aristotle's Definition of Motion and its Ontological Implications. *Graduate Faculty Journal* 13: 1–22.

Brisson, Luc. 2006. La place de la mémoire dans la psychologie plotinienne, in *Études platoniciennes III. L'âme amphibie. Études sur l'âme selon Plotin*, Paris 2006, pp. 13–27.

Brown, L. 1991. Connaissance et réminiscence dans le Ménon. *Revue Philosophique* 181: 603–619.

Brunschwig, J. 1991. En quel sens le sens commun est-il commun? in G. Romeyer Dherbey & C. Viano Ed. Corps et âme. Sur le *De anima* d'Aristote., Paris 1996, 189–219.

Buchheim, T. 1997. Ähnlichkeit und ihre Bedeutung für die Identität der Person in Max Schelers Wertethik. *Phänomenologische Forschungen* (Neue Folge) 2: 245–258.

————2002. Was uns handeln macht. In Th. Buchheim, R. Schönberger, W. Schweidler, Ed. *Die Normativität des Wirklichen*, Stuttgart, 381–413.

————H. Flashar, R. King (Ed.). 2003. *Kann man heute noch etwas anfangen mit Aristoteles?* Hamburg.

Burnyeat, M.F. 1992. Is an Aristotelian Philosophy of Mind Still Credible? (A Draft). In: Nussbaum and Rorty (Ed.) 1992: 15–26.

————1994. Enthymeme: Aristotle on the Logic of Persuasion. In Furley, D.J. Nehamas, A. (Ed.). 1994. *Aristotle's Rhetoric. Philosophical Essays*. Proceedings of the 12th Symposium Aristotelicum, Princeton: 3–55.

————1995. How much happens when Aristotle sees red and hears middle C? Remarks on *De Anima* 2. 7–8. Additional Essay in the 1995 edition of Nussbaum and Rorty (Ed.) 1992: 421–434.

————2002. *De Anima* II 5. In: *Phronesis* 47: 28–90.

————2008a. *Aristotle's Divine Intellect*. Milwaukee.

————2008b. Kinesis vs. Engergeia. A much read passage in (but not of) Aristotle's Metaphysics *Oxford Studies in Ancient Philosophy* XXXIV 219–292.

Campbell, J. 1994. *Past, space and self.* Cambridge Mass.

————1997: The Structure of Time in Autobiographical Memory. In *The European Journal of Philosophy* 5: 105–118.

Canto-Sperber, M. 1996. L'imagination dans la philosophie de l'action. In Romeyer Dherbey, Viano Ed.: 441–462.

Cashdollar, S. 1973. Aristotle's account of incidental perception. In *Phronesis* 18: 156–175.

Caston, V. 1996. Why Aristotle needs imagination. In *Phronesis* 41: 20–55.

————1998. Aristotle and the problem of intentionality. In *Philosophy and Phenonomological Research* 58: 249–298.

————2005. The Spirit and the Letter. Aristotle on Perception. In Salles 2005 : 245–320.

Chaignet, A-E. 1862. *Histoire de la Psychologie des Grecs*, Paris.

Clark, G.H. 1942. Phantasia in Plotinus. In F.P.Clarke and M.C.Nahm (Ed.) *Essays in Honour of E.A.Singer.* Philadephia and London.

————1944 The theory of time in Plotinus. *Philosophical Review.* 53: 337–58.

Clark, Stephen R. L. 1996. Plotinus: body and soul. In Gerson: 1996.

Concise Oxford Dictionary. 1964 (5th Ed.) Oxford.

Coope, Ursula. 2005. *Time for Aristotle.* Oxford.

Corrigan, K. 1981. The internal Dimensions of the Sensible Object in the Thought of Plotinus and Aristotle. *Dionysius* V 98–126.

Dahl, N.O. 1984. Practical Reason, Aristotle and Weakness of Will. Minneapolis.

Delcomminette, S. 2006. *Le Philèbe de Platon.* Leiden.

Deuse, W. 1983. *Untersuchungen zur mittelplatonischen und neuplatonischen Seelenlehre. Akademie der Wissenschaften und der Literatur.* Mainz.

Dillon, J. 1986. Plotinus and the transcendental imagination. In: J.P. Mackey Ed. *Religious Imagination.* Edinburgh: 55–64.

————1996. *Middle Platonism (rev. ed.).* London.

Dörrie, H. 1955. Ὑπόστασις. Wort – und Bedeutungsgeschichte. *Nachrichten der Akademie der Wissenschaften in Göttingen. Philologisch-Historische Klasse.* Göttingen.

Düring, I., und Owen, G.E.L. (Ed.) 1960. *Plato and Aristotle in the Mid-Fourth Century.* Göteborg.

Emilsson, E.K. 1988. *Plotinus on sense perception.* Cambridge.

————1991. Plotinus and mind-body dualism. In Everson 1991: 148–165.

Everson, S. 1997. *Aristotle on Perception.* Oxford.

————(Ed.) 1990. Epistemology. *Companions to Ancient Thought 1.* Cambridge.

————(Ed.) 1991. Psychology. *Companions to Ancient Thought 2.* Cambridge.

————(Ed.) 1994. Language. *Companions to Ancient Thought 3.* Cambridge.

————(Ed.) 1998. Ethics. *Companions to Ancient Thought 4.* Cambridge.

Fondation Hardt. 1960. *Les Sources de Plotin. Entretiens sur l'Antiquité Classique. Tome V.* Vandoeuvres-Genf.

Foster, L. and Swanson, J.W. (Ed.). 1970. *Experience and Theory.* Cambridge, Mass.

Frede, D. 1992. The Cognitive Role of Phantasia in Aristotle. In Nussbaum and Rorty 1992: 279–295.

————2003. Aristoteles' Philosophie des Geistes. In T. Buchheim, H. Flashar, R. King (Ed.): 85–109.

Frede, M. 1990. An empiricist view of knowledge: memorism. In Everson 1990: 225–250.

————1996. La Théorie Aristotélicienne de l'intellect agent. In Viano, Romeyer, Dherbey, *Corps et Âme. Sur le de Anima d'Aristote.* Paris, 1996.

Freudenthal, J. 1863 *Über den Begriff des Wortes φαντασία bei Aristoteles.* Göttingen.

—1869. Zur Kritik und Exegese von Aristoteles' περὶ τῶν κοινῶν σώματος –χρκαὶ ψυχῆς ἔργων (Parva Naturalia). In *Rheinisches Museum* 24: 81–93, 392–419.

Gerson, Lloyd P. 1994. *Plotinus.* London.

—(Ed.) 1996. *Cambridge Companion to Plotinus.* Cambridge.

Goldschmidt V. 1982. *Temps physique et temps tragique chez Aristote.* Paris.

Graeser, A. 1972. *Plotinus and the Stoics.* Leiden.

Goodman, N. 1970. Seven strictures on similarity. In Foster and Swanson 1970: 19–29.

Goodwin, W. 1894. *A Greek Grammar.* (2nd ed.) London.

Gotthelf, A. and Lennox, J. 1987. *Philosophical Issues in Aristotle's Biology.* Cambridge.

Gregoríc, P. 2007. Aristotle on the common sense. Oxford.

Gregoríc, Pavel and Filip Grgíc 2006. Aristotle's Notion of Experience. *Archiv für Gesichte der Philosophie* 88: 1–30.

Guitton, J. 1959[3]. *Le Temps et l' éternité chez Plotin et Saint Augustin.* Paris.

Hadot, P. 1960. Etre, vie, pensée chez Plotin et avant Plotin. In: Fondation Hardt. 1960. *Les Sources de Plotin.* 105–41.

————1996. Plotin et le *de Anima* d'Aristote. In Viano, Romeyer Dherbey 1996: 367–376.

Halfwassen, J. 1994. *Geist und Selbstbewusstsein. Studien zu Plotin und Numenios.* Mainz.

Heinaman, R. 1990. Aristotle and the Mind-Body problem. *Phronesis* 35: 83–102.

————1995. Activity and change in Aristotle. *Oxford Studies in Ancient Philosophy* 13: 187–213.

Henry, P. 1960. Une comparaison chez Aristote, Alexandre et Plotin. In: *Les Sources de Plotin. Entretien sur l'Antiquité Classique Tome V.* Fondation Hardt. 429–444.

Hobbes, T. 1996. *Leviathan.* (ed. R. Tuck). Cambridge.

Holzhausen, J. (Ed.) 1998. *Ψυχή – Seele- anima. Festschrift für Karin Alt.* (Beiträge zu Altertumskunde Band 109) Stuttgart.

Hübner, J. 1999. Die aristotelische Konzeption der Seele als Aktivität. In *Archiv für Geschichte der Philosophie:* 1–32.

Hume, David. 1976. *A Treatise of Human Nature.* Ed. P.H. Nidditch. Oxford.

Inge, W.R. 1968[3]. *The Philosophy of Plotinus.* 2 Vols. London.

Irwin, T. 1988. *Aristotle's First Principles.* Oxford.

Johansen, T. K. 1997. *Aristotle on the sense organs.* Cambridge.
—2002. Imprinted on the Mind: active and passive in Aristotle's theory of sense-perception. In B.Saunders and J.van Brakel (Ed.), *Theories, Technologies, Instrumentalities of Colour,* University Press of America.
—2004. *Plato's Natural Philosophy.* Cambridge.
—2006. What's New in the De Sensu? The Place of the De Sensu in Aristotle's Psychology. In: King ed. 2006: 140–165.
Kahn, C. 1992, Aristotle on Thinking. In: Nussbaum and Rorty Ed. 1992: 359–380.
Kalligas, P. 1997. Forms of Individuals in Plotinus: A Re-Examination. *Phronesis* 42(2): 206–227.
Kosman, L. A. 1969. Aristotle's Definition of Motion. *Phronesis* 14: 40–62.
King, R.A.H. 2001. *Aristotle on life and death.* London.
—————————2006. *Common to body and soul. Philosophical approaches to explaining living behaviour in Greco-Roman antiquity.* Berlin.
————————2009a. Aristotle's *De memoria* and Plotinus on memory. In: Christophe Grellard, P-M. Morel, ed. *La fortune antique et médiévale des Parva Naturalia.* "Aristote. Traductions et Études", Leuven.
————————2009b. The concept of life and the life-cycle in *De Juventute.* In Sabine Föllinger ed. "Was ist ,Leben'? Aristoteles' Anschauungen zur Entstehung und Funktionsweise von ,Leben'. Stuttgart.
Kullmann, W. 1974. *Wissenschaft und Methode.* Berlin.
————, und Föllinger, S. (Ed.) 1997. *Aristotelische Biologie. Intentionen, Methoden, Ergebnisse.* Stuttgart.
————1998. *Aristoteles und die moderne Wissenschaft.* Stuttgart.
Labarrière, J.-L. 1984. Imagination humaine et imagination animale chez Aristote. *Phronesis* 29: 17–49.
————2000. Sentir le temps, regarder un tableau. Aristote et les images de la mémoire. In: C. Darbo-Peschanski (Ed.), *Constructions du temps dans le monde grec ancien.* Paris: 267–283.
Lang, H.S. 1980. On memory. Aristotle's corrections of Plato. *Journal of the History of Philosophy* 18: 379–393.
Lear, J. 1988. *Aristotle. The desire to understand.* Cambridge.
Lefebvre, R. 1997. Faut il traduire le vocable aristotélicien de Phantasia par "représentation"? *Revue philosophique de Louvain* 4: 587–616.
Lesher, J. 1973. The Meaning of Nous in the *Posterior Analytics. Phronesis* 18: 44–68.
Lloyd, A.C. 1964. Nosce te ipsum and conscientia. *Archiv für Geschichte der Philosophie* 46: 188–200.
Lloyd, G.E.R. 1978. The Empirical Basis of the Physiology of the Parva Naturalia. In Lloyd und Owen (Ed.) 1978: 215–239.
————and Owen, G.E.L. (Ed.) 1978. *Aristotle on Mind and the Senses: Proceedings of the Seventh Symposium Aristotelicum.* Cambridge.
————1990. The theories and practices of demonstration. *Boston Area Colloquium in Ancient Philosophy* VI, 371–401. Repr. in Lloyd 1996.
————1996. *Aristotelian Explorations.* Cambridge.

Locke, John. 1975. *An Essay Concerning Human Understanding.* (Ed. P. Nidditch). Oxford.

Lycos, K. 1964. Plato and Aristotle on appearing. *Mind* 73: 496–514.

Mackie, J.L. 1976. *Problems from Locke.* Oxford.

MacTaggart, J. M. E. 1927. *The nature of existence.* Cambridge.

Martin, C.B. and Deutscher, M. 1966. Remembering. In *Philosophical Review* 75: 161–196.

McCormack, T. 2001 Attributing Episodic Memory to Animals and Children. In: Christoph Hoerl and Teresa McCormack: *Time and Memory. Issues in Philosophy and Psychology.* Oxford, 285–314.

McCumber J. 1978. Anamnesis as memory of intelligibles in Plotinus. *Archiv für Geschichte der Philosophie* 60: 160–167.

McGuire, J.E. Strange, S. K. 1988. An annotated translation of Plotinus "Ennead" III 7: "on eternity and time". *Ancient-Philosophy.* 88: 251–271.

McDowell, J. 1994. *World and mind.* Cambridge Mass.

Menn, S. 2001. Plotinus on the Identity of Knowledge with its Object. *Apeiron* 34: 233–246.

————2002. Aristotle's Definition of the Soul and the Programme of the De Anima. *Oxford Studies in Ancient Philosophy* 24, 83–139.

Merlan, P. 1963. *Monopsychism, Mysticism, Metaconsciousness.* The Hague.

Modrak, D. 1987. Aristotle. The power of perception. Chicago.

Morel, P.-M. 1997. L'habitude: une *seconde nature?* In ib. Ed. *Aristote et la notion de la nature. Enjeux épistémologiques et pratiques.* Bordeaux.

————1999. Identité et individualité de l'âme humaine chez Plotin. *Cahiers Philosophiques de Strasbourg,* 8: 53–66.

————, Dixsaut, M., Tordo-Rombaut K. (Ed.). 2002. *La Connaissance de soi. Études sur le Traité 49 de Plotin.* Paris.

—2002 (1) La sensation, messagère de l'âme. Plotin, V, 3 [49], 3 in Morel, Dixsaut, M., K. Tordo-Rombaut Ed.: 209–227.

————2006a. "Common to body and soul" in the *Parva Naturalia.* In: King 2006: 121–139.

————2006b. Mémoire et Charactère. Aristote et l'histoire personelle. In: Aldo Brancacci et Gianna Gigliotti edd. 2006 *Mémoire et Souvenir. Six études sur Platon, Aristote, Hegel et Husserl.* Naples, 51–87.

Morton, J. 1994. Memory. In Guttenplan, S. (Ed.) *A companion to the philosophy of mind.* Oxford.

Müller, F.L. 1996. *Kritische Gedanken zur antiken Mnemotechnik und zum Auctor ad Herennium.* Stuttgart.

Nussbaum, M.C. and Putnam, H. 1992. Changing Aristotle's Mind. In Nussbaum and Rorty (Ed.) 1992: 27–56.

————and Rorty, A.O. (Ed.) 1992. *Essays on Aristotle's De Anima.* Oxford.

Neuhäuser, J. 1878. *Aristoteles' Lehre von dem sinnlichen Erkenntnisvermögen und seinen Organen.* Leipzig.

O'Brien, D. 1977. Le volontaire et la nécessité: réflexions sur la descente de l'âme dans la philosophie de Plotin. *Revue Philosophique de la France et de l'Etranger.* 167: 401–422.

O'Daly, J. P. 1973. *Plotinus' Philosophy of the self.* Shannon.

O'Meara, D. 1993. *Plotinus. An Introduction to the Enneads.* Oxford.

Onsager, A. 2004. *Plotinus on selfhood, freedom and politics.* Aarhus.

Owen, G. E.L. 1957 Zeno and the mathematicians. *Proceedings of the Aristotelian Society.*

Parfit, D. 1981. *Reasons and Persons.* Oxford.

Perler, D. (Ed.) 2001. *Intentionality in the Middle Ages and Antiquity.* Leiden.

Primavesi, O. 1998. Topos I. In *Historisches Wörterbuch der Philosophie.* vol. 10, Basel, col. 1263–1269.

Rapp, C. 2001. Aristoteles über φαντασία und Intentionalität. In Perler (Ed.) 2001: 63–96.

Rapp, C. 2006. Interaction of Body and Soul: What the Hellenistic Philosophers Saw and Aristotle Avoided. In King ed.: 187–209.

Rich, A.N.M. 1957. Reincarnation in Plotinus. *Mnemosyne* 10: 232–38.

Reid,T. 1785, 1849. *Essays on the intellectual Powers of Man.* In: Works of Thomas Reid, Ed. W. Hamilton. Edinburgh.

Rist, J.M. 1963. Forms of individuals in Plotinus. *Classical Quarterly* n.s. 13: 223–31.

————–1967. *Plotinus. The Road to Reality.* Cambridge.

Romeyer Dherbey, G., Viano C. (Ed.) 1996. *Corps et âme. Sur le De anima d' Aristote.* Paris.

Rorty, A.O. (Ed.). 1980. *Essays on Aristotle's Ethics.* Berkeley.

Russell, Bertrand. 1921. *The Analysis of Mind.* London.

Ryle, G. 1949. *The Concept of Mind.* London.

Salles, R. ed., 2005. *Metaphysics, Soul and Ethics: Festschrift for Richard Sorabji.* Oxford.

Scheler, M. 1980. Der Formalismus in der Ethik und die materiale Wertethik. Neuer Versuch einer Grundlegung eines ethischen Personalismus. In: *Gesammelte Werke.* Vol. II. Bern, Munich.

Shields, C. 1995. Intentionality and isomorphism in Aristotle. In: *Boston Area Colloquium in Ancient Philosophy* 11: 307–330.

Schofield, M. 1992. Aristotle on imagination. In: Nussbaum und Rorty (Ed.) 1992: 249–277.

Schroeder, F.M. 1987 Synousia, Synaesthesis, Synesis. Presence and Dependence in the Plotinian Philosophy of Consciousness. *Aufstieg und Niedergang der Römischen Welt* II Vol. 36,1, Berlin: 677–99.

Schwyzer, H.R. 1960. Bewußt und Unbewußt bei Plotin. In *Les Sources de Plotin. Entretien sur l'Antiquité Classique Tome V.* Fondation Hardt.

Scott, D. 1995. *Recollection and experience. Plato's Theory of learning and its successors.* Cambridge.

Shoemaker, S. 1963. *Self-Knowledge and Self-Identity.* Ithaca.

Sheppard, A. 1993. Phantasia and mental images: Neoplatonist Interpretations of *De anima*, 3.3. *Oxford Studies in Ancient Philosophy* Suppl. 1991: 165–73.

Sisko, J.E. 1997. Space, time and phantasms in Aristotle, *de Memoria 2*, 452B7–25. In *Classical Quarterly* 47: 167–175.

Sleeman, J.H., Pollet, G. 1980. *Lexicon Plotinianum.* Leiden.

Smith, A. 1974. *Porphyry's Place in the Neoplatonic Tradition. A Study in Post-Plotinian. Neoplatonism.* The Hague.

───1978. Unconsciousness and Quasiconsciousness in Plotinus. *Phronesis* 23: 292–301.

───1996. Eternity and Time. In Gerson Ed., 1996: 196–216.

───1998. Soul and Time in Plotinus. In Holzhausen Ed. 1998.

Solmsen, F. 1961. Greek Philosophy and the Discovery of the Nerves. *Museum Helveticum* 18: 150–197.

Sorabji, R. 1974. Body and soul in Aristotle. In *Philosophy* 49: 63–89. Repr. in Barnes, Schofield, Sorabji (Ed.) 1975–79, Vol. IV: 42–64.

───1979. Aristotle on the instant of change. Barnes, Schofield, Sorabji (Ed.) 1975–79, Vol. I: 159–177.

───1980. *Necessity, cause and blame.* London.

───1983. *Time, creation, and the continuum: theories in antiquity and the early middle ages.* London.

───1991. The problem of intentionality from Aristotle to Brentano. In H.J. Blumenthal, H. M. Robinson Ed., *Aristotle and the later tradition.* Oxford.

───1992. Intentionality and physiological processes; Aristotle's theory of sense perception. In Nussbaum und Rorty (Ed.) 1992: 195–226.

───1993. *Animal Minds and Human Morals.* London.

—2006.

—2006. *Self. Ancient and Modern Insights about Individuality, Life, and Death.* Chicago.

Stich, S. P. and T. A. Warfield. (Ed.) 1994. *Mental Representation.* Oxford.

Strawson, P.F. 1970. Imagination and Perception. In Foster, Swanson 1970; repr. in ibid. 1974. *Freedom and Resentment.* London.

Sutton, J. 1998. *Philosophy and memory traces.* Cambridge.

Szlezák, T. A. 1979. *Platon und Aristoteles in der Nuslehre Plotins,* Basel- Stuttgart.

Taormina, D. P. 2002. Perception du temps et mémoire chez Aristote. *De memoria et reminiscentia* 1. *Philosophie Antique* 2: 35–62.

───2010. Dalla potenzialità all'attualità. Un'introduzione al problema della memoria in Plotino. In: *Plato, Aristotle or both? Dialogues between Platonism and Aristotelianism in Antiquity.* Edited by Thomas Bénatouïl, Franco Trabattoni and Gerd Van Riel. Commentaria in Aristotelem Graeca et Byzantina. Berlin.

Toulouse, S. 2006. Le véhicule de l'âme chez Plotin. In: 'Etudes platoniciennes III. L'âme amphibie. Etudes sur l'âme selon Plotin', Paris: 103–128.

Trouillard, J. 1955. *La purification plotinienne.* Paris.

Tulving, E. 1983. *Elements of episodic memory.* Oxford.

Tsouni, G. 2005. Review of King 2004: In *Rhizai* 2005.2.

van Dorp, P. T. 1992. Aristoteles over twee werkingen van het geheugen: Platoonse reminiscenties. In *Tijdschrift voor Filosofie* 54, 1: 457–491.

Veloso-Rey, C. 2005. Note sur la bibliographie récente (2000–2005) du *De memoria* d'Aristote. *Methexis* XVIII.

Verbeke, G. 1985. La perception du temps chez Aristote. In: *Aristotelica. Mélanges offertes à Marcel De Corte,* Brussels-Liège (Cahiers de Philosophie Ancienne): 351–377.

Vogt, S. Aristoteles' Buchstabenmodell des Erinnerungsprozesses in De Mem. 452a17–26 – Freie Assoziation oder Mnemotechnik. (unpublished).

Wallis, R. T. 1972. *Neoplatonism.* London.

Warren, E.W. 1964. Consciousness in Plotinus. *Phronesis* 9: 83–97.

————-1965. Memory in Plotinus. *Classical Quarterly* NS 15: 252–260.

————-1966. Imagination in Plotinus. *Classical Quarterly* 16: 277–85.

Wedin, M.W. 1988. *Aristotle on mind and the imagination.* New Haven.

Weidemann, H. 1991. Grundzüge der aristotelischen Sprachtheorie. In P. Schmitter (Ed.) *Geschichte der Sprachtheorie.* Tübingen.

Welsch, W. 1987. *Aisthesis: Grundzüge und Perspektiven der Aristotelischen Sinneslehre.* Stuttgart.

Wiesner, J. 1985. Gedächtnis und Denkobjekte – Beobachtungen zu Mem. 1 449b30–450a14. In Wiesner, J. (Ed.) *Aristoteles. Werk und Wirkung.* Paul Moraux gewidmet. Vol. I. Berlin: 168–190.

————-1998. Aristoteles über das Wesen der Erinnerung. Eine Analyse von *de Memoria* 2, 451a18-b10. In: Holzhausen Ed. 1998: 120–131.

Wiggins, D. 1992. Remembering directly. In J. Hopkins and A. Saville Ed. *Psychoanalysis, Mind and Art.* Oxford.

————-2001. *Sameness and Substance Renewed.* Cambridge.

Index locorum

General Index